Corporate Accountability and
Sustainable Development

ECOLOGICAL ECONOMICS AND HUMAN WELL-BEING

Series Editors: JOAN MARTÍNEZ-ALIER AND PUSHPAM KUMAR
Technical Editor: VIRGINIA HOOPER

This Series offers the best and most recent work in the transdisciplinary field of Ecological Economics, whose focus is the study of the conflicts between economic growth and environmental sustainability.

Books in the Series:

Deliberative Ecological Economics
Edited by Christos Zografos and Richard B. Howrath

Payment for Ecosystem Services
Edited by Pushpam Kumar and Roldan Muradian

Science for Policy
Edited by Ângela Guimarães Pereira and Silvio Funtowicz

Water, Agriculture, and Sustainable Well-being
Edited by Amita Shah, Unai Pascual, and Jayanta Bandyopadhyay

Environmental History and Ecological Economics
Edited by John McNeill, Mahesh Rangarajan, and José Augusto Pádua

Indicators and Scenarios for Sustainable Development
Edited by Joachim Spangenberg and Nilanjan Ghosh

Corporate Accountability and Sustainable Development

Edited by
Peter Utting and Jennifer Clapp

OXFORD
UNIVERSITY PRESS

OXFORD
UNIVERSITY PRESS

YMCA Library Building, Jai Singh Road, New Delhi 110 001

Oxford University Press is a department of the University of Oxford.
It furthers the University's objective of excellence in research, scholarship,
and education by publishing worldwide in

Oxford New York
Auckland Cape Town Dar es Salaam Hong Kong Karachi
Kuala Lumpur Madrid Melbourne Mexico City Nairobi
New Delhi Shanghai Taipei Toronto

With offices in
Argentina Austria Brazil Chile Czech Republic France Greece
Guatemala Hungary Italy Japan Poland Portugal Singapore
South Korea Switzerland Thailand Turkey Ukraine Vietnam

Oxford is a registered trademark of Oxford University Press
in the UK and in certain other countries.

Published in India
by Oxford University Press, New Delhi

© Oxford University Press 2008

The moral rights of the author have been asserted
Database right Oxford University Press (maker)

First published 2008

ISBN-13: 978-0-19-569734-6
ISBN-10: 0-19-569734-0

Typeset in AGaramond 11/12.5
by Eleven Arts, Keshav Puram, Delhi 110 035
Printed in India by De-Unique, New Delhi 110 018
Published by Oxford University Press
YMCA Library Building, Jai Singh Road, New Delhi 110 001

Contents

Tables, Figures, and Boxes

TABLES

FIGURES

MAPS

BOXES

Abbreviations

AOX	Adsorbable organic halogens
APHIS/USDA	Animal and Plant Health Inspection Service/ United States Department of Agriculture
ATCA	Alien Tort Claims Act
BBBEE	Broad-Based Black Economic Empowerment
BEE	Black Economic Empowerment
BIO	Biotechnology Industry Organization
BIT	Bilateral investment treaty
CEB	Corporate environmental behaviour
CEC	Commission of the European Communities
CEDHA	Center for Human Rights and Environment
CEDRE	Centre de documentation de recherche et d'expérimentations sur les pollutions accidentelles des eaux
CETMAR	Centro Tecnológico del Mar
CFC	Chlorofluorocarbons
CLC	International Convention on Civil Liability for Oil Spill Damage
COD	Chemical oxygen demand
CORE	Corporate Responsibility Coalition
COSATU	Congress of South African Trade Unions
CPCB	Central Pollution Control Board
CPPRI	Central Pulp and Paper Research Institute
CREP	Corporate Responsibility for Environmental Protection
CSE	Centre for Science and Environment
CSP	Corporate Social Performance
CSR	Corporate social responsibility
DBCP	Dibromochloropropane
ECF	Elemental chlorine free
ECOSOC	United Nations Economic and Social Council
EIA	Environmental impact assessment

EMD	Environment Management Division
EPA	Environmental Protection Act
ETC	Environmental Technology Center
ETI	Ethical Trading Initiative
ETP	Effluent treatment plant
FAO	Food and Agricultural Organization
FCI	Final Compliance Index
FDI	Foreign Direct Investment
FOE	Friends of the Earth
FOEI	Friends of the Earth International
FSC	Forest Stewardship Council
GATT	General Agreement on Tariffs and Trade
GMO	Genetically modified organism
HNS	Hazardous and Noxious Substance
ICC	International Chamber of Commerce
ICT	Information and communication technology
ICFTU	International Confederation of Free Trade Unions
ICSID	International Center for Settlement of Investment Disputes
IFC	International Finance Corporation
IOE	International Organization of Employers
IOPC	Oil Pollution Compensation Fund
IOSC	International Oil Spills Conference
ISEE	International Society for Ecological Economics
ISO	International Organization for Standardization
MMSD	Mining, Minerals, and Sustainable Development
MNE	Multinational Enterprises
MoEF	Ministry of Environment and Forest
NAFTA	North American Free Trade Agreement
NIEO	New International Economic Order
NOAA	National Oceanic & Atmospheric Administration
ODI	Overseas Development Institute
ODS	Ozone depleting substance
OECD	Organisation for Economic Co-operation and Development
OHSAS	Occupational Health and Safety Management Systems assessment specification
ONE	Organization Natural Environment

OPA	Oil Pollution Act
OPCR	International Convention on Oil Pollution Preparedness, Response and Cooperation
OPRC	Protocol on Preparedness, Response and Co-operation to Pollution Incidents
PCB	Pollution Control Board
P&I	Principal and interest
PIL	Public interest litigation
PRI	Principles for Responsible Investment
PRTR	Pollutant Release and Transfer Register
PWYP	Publish What You Pay
R&D	Research and Development
RBV	Resource-based view
RDH	Rapid displacement heating
RFSTE	Research Foundation for Science Technology and Ecology
SAIL	Steel Authority of India
SD	Sustainable development
SD	Standard deviations
SPCB	State Pollution Control Board
TCF	Total chlorine free
TNC	Transnational corporation
TRIPS	Trade Related Aspects of Intellectual Property Rights
UNGC	United Nations Global Compact
UNRISD	United Nations Research Institute for Social Development
US EPA	Environmental Protection Agency of the United States
US FDA	Food and Drug Administration of the United States
UT	Union Territories
WBCSD	World Business Council for Sustainable Development
WCED	World Commission on Environment and Development
WIR	World Investment Report
WSSD	World Summit on Sustainable Development

Foreword

Until recently the field of Business Economics and Management, and Ecological Economics developed separately. The natural environment and ecosystems have not been the main issues in management studies or in business administration. When they do become issues, it is more to comply with norms and standards of government regulations that are seen as extra costs. Occasionally, business firms enhance their image by publishing reports that show their corporate social responsibility. To fill this gap this book comes as one of the most innovative and contemporary in the series Ecological Economics and Human Well-being.

Edited by acknowledged experts, Peter Utting and Jennifer Clapp, this volume takes a different approach—it is more analytical than prescriptive. In fact, the very notion of free gifts of nature and externality that date back to the 19th and early 20th centuries refer to the use of ecosystems services without payment, and to the impacts of business on the environment and society that are not included in the accounts. Later, one of the pioneers of ecological economics, K.W. Kapp, published a book in 1950, *The Social Costs of Business Enterprise* that was translated into many languages. This volume goes back to a forgotten strand in ecological economics.

Utting and Clapp, and the authors whose papers they have selected, look at different cases in India, South Africa, Europe, and the United States. There are analyses of regulations on how to apply the precautionary principle to new technologies. Case studies look at the variables that explain degrees of compliance with rules against pollution. The volume traces the movement from voluntary agreements to much stronger demands for corporate accountability, including cases in which liability is enforced through the Alien Tort Claims Act (ATCA). This book discusses how to put money values on uncertain environmental damages, how to design evolving institutions for environmental policy, and which instruments are more effective—regulations, taxes, or the class-action suits of Subaltern Legality.

There are attempts today by business to report on and be guided by a Triple Bottom Line—economic, social, and environmental—expressed in different units. The essays in this volume clearly convey that there are many opportunities to improve simultaneously on all fronts.

The studies collected here will be of interest not only to ecological economics but also to the many students and practitioners of management and business economics who by now have realized that the environment (exhaustible resources, enhanced greenhouse effect, water and soil pollution, loss of biodiversity and the loss of environmental services from nature) is not a specialized topic but is at the very centre of today's main decisions in global business and public policy.

July 2008

Joan Martínez-Alier
Pushpam Kumar

1

Corporate Responsibility, Accountability, and Law
An Introduction

JENNIFER CLAPP AND PETER UTTING

INTRODUCTION

Recent decades have witnessed profound transformations in regulatory regimes that aim to shape the social and environmental performance of business enterprises. In the 1970s, there was a ramping up of environmental and social regulations in many countries as a means by which to improve corporate performance on those fronts. Incidents of poor environmental practices in particular were revealed in a number of industrialized countries in the 1960s and 1970s, prompting more stringent regulations (Braithwaite and Drahos 2000). At the international level, various United Nations and OECD (Organization for Economic Co-operation and Development) conventions and guidelines came into effect, and there was serious discussion of a code of conduct for transnational corporations (TNCs) as a means by which to ensure that corporations did not relocate in order to take advantage of less stringent regulatory regimes in developing countries.

As neoliberal thinking and policies took effect in the 1980s, the enthusiasm for a more stringent regulatory approach was put to the side in favour of corporate self-regulation and voluntary initiatives as part of a broader agenda to promote corporate social responsibility (CSR). CSR generally refers to a range of initiatives adopted by companies, business associations, and so-called multi-stakeholder entities that aim to promote ethical corporate behaviour and minimize the negative impacts of business activity on society and the environment. CSR is often said to go beyond both government regulation that sets minimum standards, and philanthropy that generally assumes an ad hoc character and lacks mechanisms to ensure long-term sustainability.

It is also associated with the notion of 'continuous improvement'. In practice, CSR is driven by a complex array of factors, forces, and contexts related to market-based incentives and constraints; self-regulation by companies and business associations; 'civil regulation', involving civil society organizations and the so-called court of public opinion; and law and other elements of public policy.[1] CSR practices and instruments include, for example, codes of conduct; company 'triple-bottom-line' reporting on economic, social, and sustainability aspects; internal and external monitoring; certification of good practice by third parties; environmental management systems; stakeholder dialogues; corporate social investment in community development, and public-private partnerships.

The adoption of CSR-type initiatives has involved not only some of the world's largest TNCs whose environmental and labour practices have come under greater scrutiny, but also large national firms and small and medium-sized enterprises (SMEs) that form part of global value chains. The shift toward CSR as a primary means by which to ensure that firms act in a sustainable manner was heavily promoted at the 1992 Rio Earth Summit, where some of the world's leading corporations signalled their commitment to 'changing course' and to 'greening' their operations voluntarily (Schmidheiny 1992; Chatterjee and Finger 1994). The idea that firms were the best placed to know where they could improve their own environmental performance, and that adhering to environmental and social principles made 'good business sense' (Holme and Watts 2000), gained widespread adherence not just amongst business leaders, but also within many governments. These actors saw potential for firms to self-regulate to be more efficient not just for firms, but also for governments that could save on the costs of monitoring and enforcement of regulations. Voluntary initiatives were also supported by a growing number of non-governmental organizations (NGOs) that were themselves critical of state incapability, inefficiency and rent-seeking, and saw considerable scope for 'civil regulation' as a third way between government 'command and control' regulation and weaker forms of corporate self-regulation (Bendell and Murphy 2002).

While the CSR discourse and agenda gained widespread international attention, took on board an increasing number of issues, and innovated

---

[1] For an analysis of the interactions between these different dimensions, see McBarnet, Voiculescu, and Campbell 2007.

with new instruments and processes to gain effect, it also provoked an immediate response from critics who accused corporations of 'greenwash' and tokenism (Greer and Bruno 1997; Karliner 1997). Some fifteen years on from Rio, the limits of CSR and voluntarism are now better understood (Bruno and Karliner 2002; Eade and Sayer 2006; Frynas and Newell 2007; Utting 2002a). Despite a lack of a clear success with respect to improvements in the environmental and social performance of global firms, voluntary initiatives and 'partnerships' were again endorsed at the Johannesburg World Summit on Sustainable Development in 2002 as a key strategy for the pursuit of sustainable development (Rutherford 2003; Clapp 2005).

Frustrated with the limits of a corporate self-regulatory approach, a 'corporate accountability movement' gathered momentum in the 1990s (Broad and Cavanagh 1999). This movement has sought to expose corporate malpractice around the world and the weaknesses of corporate voluntarism. Further, it has proposed a variety of regulatory instruments and institutions to ensure corporate accountability, which implies obligations as opposed to simply responsibility. Such obligations include penalties for non-compliance as opposed to impunity or simply reputational costs for firms. In other words, the movement actively seeks to hold firms accountable when their behaviour results in poor environmental and social outcomes. It also aims to empower victims of abusive corporate practices to seek redress, and encourages states to adopt more stringent regulations that hold corporations, including their chief executive officers (CEOs), legally and financially liable for damages caused by their operations at home and abroad. In addition to the notion of 'foreign direct liability' (Ward 2001), proposals have emerged for an international corporate accountability treaty or organization, which would render firms liable regardless of the location of their operations (Friends of the Earth International 2001; Greenpeace International 2002). Further, attention has turned to old debates and institutions that were prominent in previous centuries when public opinion and authorities were concerned about the rapid rise and abuse of corporate power. These include, for example, corporate charters, prosecuting firms in their home countries for abuses committed in host countries (as with the United States' Alien Tort Claims Act of 1789), and the appropriateness of one of the foundations of modern capitalism—corporate limited liability.

This book explores a range of ideas, initiatives, and alternative approaches to the regulation of corporate activity that have emerged in recent years and which aim to go beyond standard notions of CSR that centre on corporate self-regulation and voluntary initiatives. Such approaches include: a) greater use of legalistic and binding regulation, b) greater reliance on public policy to deepen voluntarism, and c) forms of multi-dimensional, multi-stakeholder, and multi-scalar governance that aim to reassert social control over corporate activities and markets.

This introductory chapter outlines why the current emphasis on corporate voluntarism within big business circles and the international development establishment cannot meet the challenges of sustainable development, and why regulatory alternatives need to be promoted if we are to move forward with the goal of improving the environmental and social performance of large firms. We begin with an overview of CSR initiatives and their limitations, and identify key features of the corporate accountability agenda. Some of the main points that emerge in the chapters that follow are then summarized. These relate to three dimensions: the need to consider not only legalistic reforms but also 'radical' alternatives that involve more fundamental changes in some of the core institutions and power configurations that characterize contemporary capitalism; the need to fill regulatory gaps where both legal and CSR frameworks and instruments are weak; and third, 'multi-dimensional governance' where different regulatory approaches, actors, and scales of intervention come together in ways that are potentially complementary and synergistic.

I. FROM CORPORATE SOCIAL RESPONSIBILITY TO ACCOUNTABILITY

The CSR Agenda

The idea behind CSR is that firms should be responsible not just to their shareholders, but also to society more broadly—or to their different 'stakeholders' that may have particular environmental, social, and human rights concerns (Freeman 1984; Morgera 2004). Firms might adopt CSR initiatives because they improve efficiency (as in the case of reducing energy use or minimizing their contribution to the waste stream) and/or improve their reputation and competitive advantage (as in the case of 'ethical trading' and corporate social investment), or their access to new markets (as in the case of marketing 'green' products and public-private partnerships). Such benefits can ultimately translate into improvements in their economic bottom line.

So, there are good reasons why such measures can go some way to encouraging firms to act in environmentally and socially responsible ways (Holliday *et al.* 2002; Zadek 2001). There is a wide range of CSR initiatives, several of which are outlined below.

Codes of Conduct

Much of the early activity in relation to CSR centred on the adoption of company codes of conduct that established broad principles and guidelines governing the behaviour of firms in relation to a combination of corporate governance and economic, social, labour, environmental, and human rights aspects. Business and industry associations, such as the International Chamber of Commerce (ICC) and the International Council of Chemical Associations (ICCA) also developed codes and charters. Multi-stakeholder codes negotiated by various parties, such as the Ethical Trade Initiative Base Code, also emerged, as did 'model codes', such as the ICFTU's (International Confederation of Free Trade Unions) Basic Code of Conduct, designed to provide a benchmark (Jenkins, Pearson and Seyfang 2002). By the late 1990s, most large TNCs had adopted or adhered to some form of code of conduct.

Environmental Management Standards and Systems

Much of CSR activity in the 1980s and early 1990s centred on the establishment and improvements in company environmental management systems (EMS), through myriad technological, managerial, and institutional innovations. These included, for example, company environmental policy statements and training schemes, life-cycle assessment, pollution and waste control, recycling, environmental impact assessment, environmental disclosure and reporting, internal and external monitoring, and environmental certification. EMS standards were agreed internationally, most notably via the International Organization for Standardization's ISO 14000 series. Other international standards include the European Union's Eco-Management and Audit System (EMAS). In various countries and industries, these standards have become a *de facto* prerequisite for doing international business (Krut and Gleckman 1998; Clapp 1998). ISO is currently developing a voluntary 'Guidance Standard' to provide a set of international guidelines for social responsibility.[2]

---

[2]At the time of writing, this standard was expected to be published in 2010.

Sustainability Reporting

Given the limited credibility and ad hoc nature of early CSR interventions, attention soon focused on the need for companies to move on from a 'trust me' position to one where stakeholders demanded more systematic evidence of good practice. A key instrument in this regard was some degree of disclosure through environmental 'sustainability' or 'triple-bottom-line' reporting (Elkington 1998). Most large TNCs now report regularly on their economic, environmental, and social performance (Hopkins 2007). CSR has gained some legitimacy through this form of triple-bottom-line disclosure. Although quite costly, company reporting was one of the easiest of the voluntary CSR initiatives adopted by global firms, as it entailed simply reporting on activities, often with little attention to substance and measurement. The vague nature of many reports prompted the formation of the Global Reporting Initiative (GRI) to establish more rigorous reporting guidelines (KPMG and UNEP 2006; GRI 2006).[3] The GRI sets guidelines in an attempt to provide some degree of standardization and to ensure that company reports address multiple dimensions of corporate social, environmental, and human rights performance, and that they include meaningful indicators. Having formulated more comprehensive guidelines and having gained legitimacy, the GRI has fostered a degree of oversight and quality control in a field that was notorious for producing 'green glossies'. Furthermore, the financial services industry, in particular the growing field of 'ethical' or socially responsible investment, as well as the insurance industry, are demanding more of triple-bottom-line reporting in terms of both quantity and quality.

Private Market-driven Monitoring and Certification Schemes

The limitations of both 'trust me' codes and 'self-reporting' prompted calls for other instruments, which, it was hoped, would provide more substantial proof of good performance. A diverse range of private monitoring and/or certification schemes have emerged over the past decade with the aim of enhancing firms' social and environmental

[3]Initially a project of CERES and the United Nations Environment Programme (UNEP), the GRI is now an independent organization. CERES is a US-based coalition of companies, investors, foundations, and environmental and other public-interest organizations.

performance through third party monitoring and verification (Utting 2005). Several of these schemes are specific to a particular industry or product. With respect to the environment, they have emerged for organic and fair trade products, sustainable forest products (Forest Stewardship Council—FSC) and fisheries (Marine Stewardship Council—MSC), and chemicals (Cashore 2002). They also include others more focused on working conditions and labour rights in particular industries, notably apparel and footwear—for example, the Fair Labor Association (FLA) in the United States and the Fair Wear Foundation in Europe. Some schemes relate more generally to industry-wide labour or environmental standards, for example, SA8000 and ISO14001 certification, respectively. These schemes can be controlled entirely within a particular industry (such as, the chemical industry's Responsible Care programme) or are constituted as non-governmental organizations, or involve civil society actors as independent input and oversight providers (FLA and FSC). As a result, private market-driven initiatives have a wide ranging diversity in terms of the role of independent actors as standards setters, and in monitoring and enforcement mechanisms.

OECD Guidelines on Multinational Enterprises (MNEs)

Potentially one of the most important voluntary initiatives is the OECD Guidelines on MNEs. Adopted in 1976, these guidelines apply to firms in or from thirty-nine adhering countries. They cover a wide range of issues such as information disclosure, taxation, bribery, labour relations, human rights, and the environment. A chapter on environmental protection was added in 1991, and updated in 2000. These updates included a recommendation for extraterritorial application of the Guidelines for MNEs operating in non-OECD countries (FOE Netherlands 2002; FOE 1998). The Guidelines promote environmental management standards already in existence such as the ISO 14001. At the same time, however, they encourage performance standards rather than just management standards. They also recommend enhanced consultation with communities affected by corporate activities, as well as improved access to information on the environmental activities of MNEs (OECD 2000). While the guidelines are voluntary, a complaints procedure allows third parties to raise concerns and seek redress through a system of government offices known as National Contact Points (NCPs).

CSR in the Financial Services Sector

The CSR agenda has gradually expanded to involve not only primary sector and manufacturing companies but also financial services enterprises. The Equator Principles provide a set of social and environmental benchmarks for private financial institutions to assess project finance in developing countries. Formulated by private sector banks in consultation with non-governmental organizations and the World Bank's private lending arm, the International Finance Corporation (IFC), the principles are voluntary for those banks that adopt them. The idea is to ensure that private financial institutions do not fund projects in developing countries that may be unsustainable either socially or environmentally. In 2006, the principles were revised and strengthened.[4] The principles have been widely adopted, with some fifty private banks adhering to them by end-2006. A group of large institutional investors also signed up to the Principles for Responsible Investment (PRI) that were agreed upon in 2006. The PRI encourage banks, pensions' funds, insurance companies, and firms servicing institutional investors to be cognizant of environmental, social, and corporate governance issues in their investment decisions.

UN Global Compact

The largest international CSR initiative is the United Nations Global Compact, which involves a pact between the UN, business enterprises, and some civil society organizations. It calls on companies to adhere to a set of ten social, environmental, human rights goals, and anti-corruption goals. Launched in July 2000, the Global Compact requests firms to incorporate these goals into their mission statements as well as their operations (Therien and Pouliot 2006). In the area of the environment, corporations are specifically asked to support the precautionary approach (Principle 7), to undertake initiatives to promote environmental responsibility (Principle 8) and to develop and diffuse environmentally friendly technologies (Principle 9). By end-2007, some 3,600 companies, including 148 of the world's largest 500 corporations, had signed onto the Global Compact. However, there is no strict enforcement mechanism other than making a public pledge and submitting an annual 'Communication on Progress' (Utting and Zammit 2006). Indeed, the stated aim of the Compact is to promote dialogue on good practices and to constitute a 'learning

---

[4]See 'http://www.equator-principles.com'

forum'. For these reasons, the Global Compact is relatively easy to join, although new 'integrity measures' introduced in 2005 resulted in over 800 companies being publicly named as 'inactive' by end-2007 for failing to comply with even the minimal reporting requirements. Increasingly, the Global Compact has been co-operating with other international CSR initiatives such the GRI and ISO 26000, and is active in promoting public-private partnerships.

Public-Private Partnerships

The coming together of business and other interests and organizations in multi-stakeholder initiatives, is part of a broader trend that has seen the proliferation of 'public-private partnerships' (PPPs). Such arrangements serve multiple purposes but are generally defined as initiatives where public-interest entities, companies and, often, civil society organizations enter into an alliance to achieve a common purpose, pool core competencies, and share risks, responsibilities, resources, costs and benefits (Utting and Zammit 2006). They often aim to enhance policy dialogue, social learning, resource mobilization, and operational delivery. Some, such as the Extractive Industries Transparency Initiative (EITI), which encourages the publication of company payments and government revenues related to oil, gas and mining activities, also promote corporate accountability by attempting to strengthen verification and disclosure. The United Nations has played a key role in promoting PPPs, not only enshrining the goal of partnerships in declarations such as that agreed by world leaders at the World Summit on Sustainable Development, but also through the Global Compact and numerous programmes and projects of UN agencies, several of which are identified in Box 1.1.

Some two decades of active experimentation with the type of CSR measures outlined above has left a balance sheet that reveals a significant number of assets. These include increased awareness of environmental, social, and human rights issues within business circles and 'corporate culture'; a shift from 'denial' and defensive posturing to greater willingness on the part of senior management to dialogue with stakeholders and engage with standard-setting institutions; a readiness to adopt basic sets of principles and codes of conduct, as well as to report publicly on some aspects of social and environmental performance; and greater acceptance of the need for external monitoring and verification of working conditions and environmental management

Box 1.1: UN-Business Partnerships: Selected Initiatives

United Nations Commission on Sustainable Development

By mid-2006, the Commission's database listed 341 partnerships in the field of sustainable development. These are 'Type II' partnerships (that is, initiatives not negotiated between governments), established during and after the 2002 World Summit on Sustainable Development, that involve UN bodies, businesses, NGOs, and other institutions.

United Nations Children's Fund (UNICEF)

Approximately 1,000 partnerships or 'alliances' have been entered into in recent years, in many instances involving corporate funding to support various UNICEF activities. In 2005, UNICEF received contributions of US$ 100,000 or more from 250 corporations, with total proceeds from the corporate sector amounting to US$ 142 million.

United Nations Development Programme (UNDP)

Public-Private Partnerships for the Urban Environment (PPUE): In June 2006, 396 partnerships between business, local government, and local communities were listed. The aim is to increase the access of the urban poor to basic services such as water, sanitation, solid waste management, and energy.

Growing Sustainable Business (GSB): This partnership scheme plays a brokerage/facilitating role with a view to fostering the growth of small businesses in developing countries, and is currently active in five sectors—financial, energy, water and sanitation, telecommunications, and agriculture.

United Nations Environment Programme (UNEP)

The UNEP Finance Initiative, involving over 200 global financial institutions, aims to promote the linkage between environment and financial performance by developing and applying voluntary guidelines on key environmental concerns. It also aims to influence relevant international policies. UNEP also promotes local level public-private partnerships to improve public services and their provision to poor people while at the same time contributing to environmental objectives.

UNDP, UNEP and IUCN (World Conservation Union)

Together these organizations are involved in the Supporting Entrepreneurs for Environment and Development (SEED) partnership that fosters the Seed Associate Partners Network.

World Health Organization (WHO)

WHO has entered into approximately 90 partnerships in the field of health, including more than 20 global public-private health partnerships devoted to improving access of low-income groups and developing countries to currently available drugs, vaccines, and other health and nutrition products, and promoting research and development to create new health products related to certain diseases.

Source: Based on Utting and Zammit 2006.

systems. But the CSR balance sheet also reveals serious and ongoing liabilities, an issue to which we now turn.

Limits to CSR

From the perspective of sustainable and rights-based development, the major limitations of CSR relate to the limited universe of companies seriously engaged; weak instruments, implementation, and impact; as well as the range of issues that are still marginalized or 'off limits' in the CSR agenda (NGLS/UNRISD 2002).

While the rhetoric surrounding CSR gives the impression that much of big business has turned a new leaf with respect to corporate responsibility and that the supply chains for these firms are following suit, the reality is that only a small percentage of the world's approximately 78,000 TNCs, 780,000 affiliates, and several million suppliers have seriously embraced CSR principles.[5] The data in Table 1.1 demonstrate this fact, showing the number of business entities participating in some of the major CSR institutions and initiatives. It is also evident from various case studies of on the ground implementation of codes of conduct and other CSR initiatives (Prieto 2006; Sood and Arora 2006; Cappelin and Giuliani 2004; Fig 2007).

---

[5]UNCTAD 2007. For data on the number of TNCs and affiliates, see UNCTAD's annual World Investment Report (WIR).

Table 1.1 Participation in Selected Multi-Stakeholder Initiatives, December 2007

Multi-stakeholder Initiative	Entities
ISO 14001 Certification	129,199[a]
Global Reporting Initiative (GRI) [b]	2,667
United Nations Global Compact	3,639[c]
Forest Stewardship Council	913[d]
Marine Stewardship Council	52[e]
Partnerships for Sustainable Development	332[f]
SA 8000	1,373[g]
Ethical Trading Initiative	43[h]
Fair Labor Association	21[i]
Extractive Industries Transparency Initiative	37[j]

Notes: [a]Refers to entities certified by December 2006, some of which may not be companies. [b]Data accessed 3 December 2007. [c]Refers to participating companies, of which 148 are in Fortune's Global 500. [d]Forest management and chain of custody certificates. [e]Certified fisheries or fisheries 'in assessment'. [f]Partnerships registered on the database of the UN Commission for Sustainable Development. [g]Refers to certified facilities. [h]Also includes the Ethical Tea Partnership, an association that comprises 18 tea packers. [i]Refers to 'Participating Companies' that commit to implement FLA Standards in factories throughout their supply chains. Also participating in the FLA are 2,900 licensees selling goods to FLA affiliated colleges and universities. [j]Includes 28 companies and an additional nine that are members of the International Council on Mining and Metals.
Sources: Official website of each initiative.

The inherent weakness of CSR interventions and instruments is apparent in various respects. It is particularly evident in relation to company codes of conduct, which often have glaring gaps in terms of the issues they address, be it, for example, labour rights, the situation of women workers, sub-contracting, or lobbying practices (Barrientos *et al.* 2003, Jenkins *et al.* 2002, Kolk and van Tulder 2006, Prieto 2006). While the range of issues addressed under company codes of conduct have expanded, procedures related to implementation are often weak. This is also apparent in the case of international codes or sets of principles, such as the OECD Guidelines for Multinational Enterprises, the UN Global Compact Principles, and the Equator Principles. While they have all expanded, implementation and compliance mechanisms still lack rigour.

Despite some improvements, sustainability reports often fail to provide a good picture of the real state of a firm's social and environmental performance. They are often short on meaningful indicators to measure performance and impacts, and are not particularly useful for assessing how positive CSR initiatives are faring in relation to negative social and environmental performance. The world's largest environmental certification scheme, ISO 14001, for example, verifies whether aspects related to environmental management systems are in place; not whether these have had any concrete outcome in terms of the improved environmental performance of companies (Krut and Gleckman 1998; Clapp 1998). In relation to labour standards, far more attention is likely to be focused on improvements in occupational health and safety as opposed to industrial relations and labour rights. At least 2000 companies produce stand-alone social, citizenship, environmental, or sustainability reports (White 2005). By December 2005, some 750 companies were applying some of the reporting indicators suggested by the GRI, but only 120 companies claimed to be using them systematically.

Other concerns about social and environmental reporting, codes, and social auditing systems relate to their cost and complexity as well as the proliferation of different methods and institutions (Utting 2002a). Given the tremendous size of global corporations, their geographical reach, their value chains that may involve thousands of suppliers, and the increasing range of CSR issues, it seems improbable that a third party can keep a tab on all of this, and do so in a meaningful way. Commercial auditors often have neither sufficient time, autonomy nor skills to adequately assess the state of industrial relations and the situation of workers and host communities (O'Rourke 2000; CCC 2005).

The upshot of these limitations is that we still know relatively little about the impact of CSR on groups most affected by unsustainable development, social exclusion, and indecent work (Blowfield 2007). This is even true of the growing number of public-private partnerships that explicitly claim to support sustainable and social development. These have proliferated in recent years but little is known about their developmental, social, and environmental impacts (Utting and Zammit 2006; Witte and Reinicke 2005).

Another basic weakness of the CSR agenda from the perspective of social and sustainable development relates to issues that are marginalized or remain off-limits. CSR tends to ignore some of the big issues linked to environmental and social sustainability. Until recently, for example, there was relatively little discussion within CSR circles of negative trends associated with employers' contributions to social insurance and employee health schemes. While some firms are concerned with reducing the ratio of inputs to outputs—or eco-efficiency—the trend in terms of increasing overall amounts of energy consumption and use of non-renewable resources at the level of the firm or industry receives little, if any, attention in the CSR agenda. While the range of CSR concerns related to developing countries has broadened, priority issues are often those of particular concern to activists and others in the North, for example, child labour, 'sweatshops', and environmental degradation associated with mining and deforestation. Issues relevant to particular stakeholders, such as women workers, sometimes get short shrift (Kilgour 2007, Prieto 2006), as indeed, does the entire sphere of social reproduction (Pearson 2007). Also marginalized in the CSR agenda are certain developmental concerns of poorer countries related to such issues as the cost and impact of CSR initiatives and instruments on smaller enterprises, the situation of informal sector workers, and whether TNCs or large retailers cut and run when their suppliers come under the CSR spotlight (Zammit 2003).

Many companies that are proactive in the field of CSR have improved the working conditions of their core workforce but simultaneously have laid-off workers and relied increasingly on sub-contracting, which often implies a deterioration of labour standards. UNRISD studies in South Africa, India and Brazil, and the study by Oxfam on the national development impact of Unilever-Indonesia, have highlighted this situation.[6] The analysis of corporate social spending in Brazil, carried out by the Instituto Brasileiro de Análises Sociais e Econômicas (Ibase), reveals the apparently contradictory situation where companies are spending more per worker on health and safety in their core enterprises, yet the number of workplace accidents and injuries per thousand workers is also increasing. A possible explanation relates to the increasing reliance on sub-contracting (Sucupira 2004).

Similarly, some companies that are active on various CSR fronts are embroiled concurrently in socially controversial privatization schemes, notably in sectors such as water. Such schemes may facilitate access to piped water through the expansion of infrastructure, but the affordability of clean water for low-income groups often declines,

[6]See Fig 2007; Sood and Arora 2006; Cappellin and Guiliani 2004; and Clay 2005.

particularly in contexts where government support through social policy is weak. As a result such families often have to spend a greater share of their income on water.[7]

Some of the world's largest corporations and business associations actively promote CSR while simultaneously lobbying forcefully for macroeconomic, labour market and other social policies associated with forms of labour market flexibilization, de-regulation, and fiscal 'reform' that can result in the weakening of institutions and systems of social protection (Farnsworth 2005; Balanyá et al. 2000). In short, CSR generally attempts to curb specific types of malpractice and improve selected aspects of social and environmental performance without questioning various contradictory policies and practices that can have perverse consequences. Also off-limits are some of the basic features and institutions of corporate capitalism related, for example, to corporate size and power, limited liability, and growing inequalities linked to the distribution of profits and wages (International Forum on Globalization 2002).

The problem, however, is not just that structural conditions impose limits on CSR, or that perversity and do-good coexist; it is also that the scaling up of the CSR agenda or the process of 'embedding liberalism' via voluntary initiatives seem to be dwarfed by ongoing economic liberalization or 'disembedding' of the type exposed by Joseph Stiglitz in *The Roaring Nineties* (Stiglitz 2004) and theorized by Mark Blyth in *Great Transformations* (Blyth 2002). Yet the scale of this disembedding is often downplayed in CSR discourse, or it is assumed that the CSR snowball, as it gathers momentum, will eventually outstrip and overtake any disembedding process (Utting 2007).

These main weaknesses of the CSR agenda can be summed up ecological economic terms as failing to address two of the three key components of sustainability as defined by the field: scale, distribution, and efficiency (Daly and Farley 2004). Ecological economics is primarily concerned with issues of scale—it is about how big the size of the economy should be, in physical terms. It assumes that there is an optimal scale beyond which an economy is not sustainable. This is in large part because as the metabolism of society increases (in terms of energy and material flows, and in terms of human appropriation of

[7]In 2006, the United Nations Research Institute for Social Development (UNRISD) conducted field work in eight countries to assess the impacts of water privatization in terms of access and affordability for different income groups.

biomass), natural systems might lose their resilience. Once the associated threats to resilience are presumed to exist, questions of distribution within the economy and between present and future generations become extremely important for considerations of sustainability. In other words, if we accept a limited size of an economy, how the economic benefits are distributed amongst society gains increasing relevance, as the idea of a constantly growing pie in which everyone benefits (even if some benefit more than others) is not tenable. Environmental problems associated with excessive scale and maldistribution are exacerbated by the tendency of neoclassical economic analysis not only to focus almost exclusively on economic growth as an indicator of well-being, but also to undervalue natural resources and to ignore the way in which firms shift social costs to the broader public (see K.W. Kapp 1950). Efficient allocation of resources, the main concern for neoclassical economists, is also important for ecological economists, but it is of secondary importance to issues of scale and distribution. The CSR agenda, when looked at in these terms, focuses primarily, if not exclusively, on questions of efficient allocation, while largely ignoring scale and distribution issues. This is not surprising, as CSR emerged primarily as a business approach to demonstrate social and environmental responsibility by means which also were economically beneficial to the firm (either through efficiency gains, access to new markets, or enhancing reputation, as mentioned above). It did not emerge as a response to the problems of overconsumption or global inequity. It assumed that social cost-shifting by firms could be avoided even in a growing economy.

The Corporate Accountability Agenda

For reasons such as those outlined above, CSR has been increasingly criticized for being weak and ineffective as a stand-alone approach to promote sustainability (Frynas and Newell 2007). CSR on its own does not guarantee 'accountability' to citizens or communities. It does not address issues of economic scale, nor issues of social equity and distribution. These 'off limits' areas of responsibility have given impetus to a movement which calls for stronger mechanisms of accountability, rather than just responsibility, to ensure that corporate activity is indeed sustainable. Increasingly, activists, scholars and policy makers are considering a variety of measures that, potentially, oblige firms to improve their environmental and social performance, and which focus attention on aspects of corporate power, rights, and practice that are often marginalized or ignored in the CSR agenda. This corporate accountability movement gathered momentum around the time of the World Summit on Sustainable Development (WSSD) in 2002. In the run-up to the WSSD, various NGOs and networks called on the United Nations to adopt a corporate accountability treaty or organization (Clapp 2005). This movement is not just a reaction to the weaknesses of CSR. Campaigns targeting particular products, companies and sectors, have been around for much longer. But the contemporary reaction to CSR has certainly added fuel to the recent activism associated with corporate accountability.

Like CSR, the term corporate accountability can mean different things to different people. There is broad agreement on at least one element of accountability, namely, the notion of 'answerability': companies must answer to the concerns of their main stakeholders. But interpretations of how companies should be held to account vary considerably, and in some cases differ little from variants of CSR that emphasize reporting, monitoring, and verification. Many of the civil society organizations and networks, as well as academic political economy perspectives or critiques of CSR, are concerned with going beyond CSR, not only enhancing the environmental and social performance of firms, but also seeking penalties for non-compliance and redress for those affected. They therefore emphasize another aspect of corporate accountability, which does render it qualitatively different from CSR: corporate accountability is also about the need for companies to incur some sort of cost when they fail to comply with agreed standards (Bendell 2004; Newell 2002).

There is, of course, nothing new about the idea of imposing penalties on companies found to be in breach of certain standards. This, after all, is a basic feature of regulation. But the contemporary corporate accountability agenda is different in various respects. First, the term corporate accountability, like corporate responsibility, is partly an outcome of the discursive struggle that has occurred during the era of neoliberalism. The ideological dominance of neoliberal thinking has rendered the use of terms like regulation problematic for those who want to challenge the dominant model of macroeconomic policy associated with economic liberalization. In other words, calling for increased regulation is unlikely to garner much support outside of the activist movement, and it is outside of the movement that activists are trying to convince of the need for change. Such critics have, therefore, had to adjust their vocabulary. Employing terms like accountability potentially stands a better chance of gaining traction in the discursive terrain, than the use of others which, for some, conjure up negative images of 'command and control' and 'state failure' (Dryzek 1997; Fuchs 2005).

Second, unlike 'command and control' regulation, corporate accountability involves a broader set of standards and new modes of governance, such as certain multi-stakeholder processes and institutions associated with CSR norms (Utting 2002b). Within these governance arrangements, civil society or public-interest organizations have a major say—unlike other CSR initiatives that are controlled or heavily influenced by corporate interests, as in the case, for example, with Responsible Care and, some would argue, ISO certification. Corporate accountability is thus seen by some to include what has been termed 'private sector hard law' (Cashore 2002). Certain types of certification noted earlier, such as sustainable wood, organic food, or fair trade coffee, are seen by many to be within the frame of promoting accountability. But there are a range of such certification schemes, and the role of business in auditing them varies. Moreover, only a very small slice of business activity is captured by these schemes, and it is not clear whether it is suitable for more than a handful of sectors. The key issue that the corporate accountability movement seeks to address is how to ensure that the myriad standards being established through privatized systems of governance are not only implemented amongst a much larger universe of enterprises, but also that the issues of penalties and redress, mentioned above, are addressed.

Third, corporate accountability is associated with a wider range of regulatory mechanisms, and emphasizes certain instruments that remain off-limits or fairly marginal in the CSR agenda. The role of government as 'final authority' is also key to the concept (WRI 2003, pp. 135, 108). Accountability measures often involve legal liability where firms are required to pay fines or financial compensation to victims where malpractice occurs. What has been called 'foreign direct liability', under which firms in some countries can be prosecuted in their home country for abuses committed abroad, is also advocated by some (Ward 2001). Promoting greater transparency and public disclosure is an important element of corporate accountability, either through government-mandated disclosure, or tighter oversight by private standard-setting bodies. Pollutant Release and Transfer Registers

(PRTRs), for example, have been seen as important tools for promoting transparency with respect to corporate environmental practices, and for ultimately improving environmental performance (Kolominskas and Sullivan 2004). But this new body of regulation associated with corporate accountability goes well beyond mechanisms associated with national law. It also includes a growing body of international law that addresses issues of accountability amongst corporate actors (Muchlinsky 2007). Such legal instruments may assume very different characteristics in terms of their being 'hard' or 'soft'. Some, such as the Bamako Convention, related to controls on flows of hazardous waste to and within Africa, adopt a much stronger language (Clapham 2006); unlike others such as the ILO Tripartite Declaration of Principles on Multinational Enterprises and Social Policy (ICHRP 2002).

As mentioned above, some advocacy organizations have proposed the adoption of an international corporate accountability treaty. Detailed proposals for a corporate accountability agreement were put forward by Friends of the Earth and Greenpeace International just before the WSSD in 2002 in order to force the issue on to the agenda. Both proposals called for stricter international rules which would make corporations, and their CEOs, legally liable for any damages that result from their activities (FOEI 2001, Greenpeace International 2002). These proposals also called for the establishment of rights for communities and citizens to sue companies, including foreign corporations, that are implicated in damage, as well as minimum environmental, social, labour, and human rights standards. Those corporations that breach these new duties would be subject to sanctions.

Fourth, corporate accountability is associated with a broader range of penalties for non-compliant companies than is the case with CSR. Such arrangements may result in traditional penalties associated with law and government regulation, such as imprisonment, fines, and monetary or other compensation to victims. But the corporate accountability agenda also emphasizes and imposes other costs on companies. Different actors and institutions can impose different sorts of penalties (Utting 2002a). NGOs and trade unions, for example, expose certain practices or launch campaigns that 'name and shame' companies, thereby potentially threatening brand value and undermining company efforts associated with reputation and risk management. In certain circumstances, trade unions can, of course, also engage in strike action. Ethical investors can bring shareholder resolutions at annual general meetings. Global union federations are also entering into Framework Agreements with TNCs that establish both a core set of standards that the company agrees to uphold throughout its global structure and industrial relations procedures to deal with grievances.

The corporate accountability movement has played an important role in reasserting the role of states, through law and public policy, in efforts to minimize the contradictions between foreign direct investment and the expansion of corporate power on the one hand, and sustainable and social development on the other. This is potentially an important corrective to two of the dominant features of neoliberalism, namely the ideology and practice of self-regulation and 'de-regulation', and efforts to put in place a legal apparatus that secures corporate rights related to property, trade and investment, and pays far less attention to corporate obligations related to social, environmental, and human rights dimensions.[8]

But the debate about how to regulate big business is not only seeing some movement of the pendulum from self-regulation and voluntary initiatives to legalistic or binding regulation; it is also going beyond the voluntary versus mandatory dichotomy, and examining how quite different approaches to regulation and institutional arrangements interact—or might interact—in ways that are more complementary and synergistic (McBarnet *et al.*, 2007; Ward 2003). Various terms, such as institutional complementarity (Boyer and Hollingsworth 1997), hybrid regulation (Gunningham and Sinclair 2002) or articulated regulation (Utting 2006), can be used to describe this coming together of different regulatory approaches and institutions.

II. Multiple Pathways

The chapters in this book aim to explore some of the pathways and instruments to enhancing corporate accountability—that is, going beyond CSR and enhancing environmental and social performance of firms through public policy, legalistic approaches, and regulatory regimes characterized by institutional complementarity. Several such approaches are essentially reformist, in the sense that they do not challenge core features of the capitalist system and the role of transnational corporations as key agents and beneficiaries of globalization.

---

[8]This legal apparatus has been referred to as the 'New Constitutionalism' (Gill 1998).

Others are more 'radical', in that they pose a more fundamental challenge to corporate power and certain core institutions of capitalism.

Radical Restructuring

Several authors in this volume suggest that corporate accountability requires more than reforming regulatory regimes in order to promote a more sanitized and sustainable capitalist system, or what has been referred to as 'embedded liberalism' (Ruggie 2003). It is of the utmost importance, for example, to address issues of scale and distribution, which are key to ecological economics and social justice. After all, what is the point of reducing, say, the ratio of inputs to outputs, if the level of output growth is such as to deplete the planet's natural resource base and destroy its sinks? Should we really praise companies for increasing levels of philanthropic giving and CSR spending, when they simultaneously shed their core labour force and rely increasingly on sub-contracted labour that enjoys few, if any, social protections and labour rights? And should managers and companies be able to hide behind the shield of limited liability, that can potentially protect them from redressing wrongs?

It is these anomalies that suggest the need for more radical changes in the rules of the game that shape and structure the capitalist system. Such perspectives have, of course, been around for several centuries and often end up as no more than interesting topics for conversation that fail to generate any political momentum for institutional change. Be that as it may, it is nevertheless important to reflect on this dimension of institutional change for the basic reason that it serves to focus attention on the limits and contradictions of CSR, and the way in which dominant discourses mystify reality. Important here is the concept of 'framing', that is, the process by which only certain issues and institutions are deemed to be legitimate objects of discussion, debate, and reform (Bøås and McNeill 2004), while other issues constitute convenient 'blind spots' that remain off the agenda (Ocampo 2006).

As Stefano Pogutz points out in Chapter 2, management theory has interpreted the notion of sustainable development and defined CSR largely in terms of eco-efficiency and has ignored fundamental questions of the ecological boundaries to growth and the un-substitutability of different forms of capital. The chapter highlights these key differences between sustainability as defined by management theory and ecological economics, and calls for the former to take on more of the insights of the latter. In other words, management theory needs to accept that there are physical limits to growth, and that natural capital cannot be substituted with other forms of capital. Efficient and sustainable firms, as defined by managerial science and CSR, do not necessarily contribute to sustainable development at the macro level of the economy. The chapter highlights the missing link between macro and micro dimensions of sustainability and suggests that bridging the distance between these two fields is key to shaping production and consumption systems conducive to sustainable development.

Not only does the CSR agenda tend to ignore key macro issues, so too does government regulation. As Arild Vatn observes (Chapter 3), state-based environmental regulation is fundamentally ex-post: it arises to deal with externalities, with the state 'running after a moving target'. He suggests the need for greater reliance on ex-ante regulations, such as input regulations to reduce throughput (Daly 1997), but notes that introducing such an approach in the context of contemporary institutional structures would be fraught with difficulties and contradictions. As such, it is also important to promote different types of institutions that are guided by motivation structures other than the bottom line related to profit. This would require laws and government policies favouring non-profit institutions and institutionalizing the 'triple-bottom-line' as a basis for determining the value of shares. Radical restructuring would also involve changing the power and dynamics of large firms, for example, by breaking them down into smaller units, and converting them into genuinely publicly-controlled firms or cooperatives.[9]

Bringing Law and Public Policy Back In

As mentioned above, the corporate accountability agenda reasserts the regulatory role of the state. While economic globalization and liberalization have ushered in various forms of 'de-regulation', and 'embedded liberalism' has promoted voluntary initiatives associated with CSR, the corporate accountability movement has refocused attention on the roles of state institutions and instruments associated with law and public policy. In this sense, the corporate accountability agenda brings the state back into the process of progressive regulatory

---

[9]See also Korten 2001; International Forum on Globalization 2002.

reform in various ways. It emphasizes the need for new laws and government policies that, for example, oblige companies and institutional investors to adopt specific CSR instruments such as social or sustainability reporting and disclosure, or that extend directors' duties to the non-financial arena. Governments or regional bodies like the European Commission, may become far more proactive in promoting CSR, through promotional activities and fiscal incentives, in an attempt to rapidly scale up the universe of companies adopting CSR policies and practices. Or, laws and regulations may hold corporations legally and financially liable for malpractice, regardless of where this may occur. Through empowerment and the defense or realization of rights, certain aspects of law and public policy are also crucial for enabling social actors such as workers, trade unions, NGOs, and communities, as well as the media, to exert pressures on companies to improve their social and environmental performance (Gunningham 2007; Utting 2006).

The critical role of law in improving the social and environmental performance of companies is examined in several chapters. Of importance, however, is not only the need to put voluntarism in its place by reasserting the role of law and public policy, but the emphasis on new forms of legal liability operating at multiple scales.

Peter Utting (Chapter 4) examines the changes that have occurred in the legal context that affect the social and environmental performance of TNCs. He considers, in particular, three developments related to legal liability that have gained in prominence in recent years. These include the gradual hardening or ratcheting-up of voluntary initiatives, to a point where they merge with law; the expanding body of international law that relates more directly to the activities of corporations; and 'subaltern legality', where victims and activists use the legal process to seek social and environmental justice. Drawing on examples from around the world, he suggests that these developments augur well for social and sustainable development. But they also confront major challenges. Whereas the CSR movement that supports voluntary approaches is politically strong, being made up of a large and dynamic coalition of actors, the corporate accountability movement is still politically immature. Another challenge relates to what Utting refers to as 'hegemonic legality', namely the capacity of elite interests to undermine or roll back progressive reforms and shape the regulatory environment, precisely in ways that prevent the sort of restructuring suggested by Vatn in Chapter 1. Utting also identifies some of the weaknesses in the social movements and networks that try to exert pressures on regulatory institutions to apply laws and other regulations.

Jennifer Clapp (Chapter 5) posits the need for legal reforms to deal with growing corporate power in the agri-food sector. The chapter outlines the extent to which TNCs in this sector have sought to address the environmental side-effects of the global spread of the industrial agricultural model and associated threats to the livelihoods of small farmers in developing countries. Particular attention is paid to the spread of genetically modified organisms (GMOs), including those that were released illegally because they were never approved by any regulatory body anywhere but which were nonetheless transported around the world. Although the corporations responsible for these illegal releases all claimed to follow CSR initiatives of various sorts, in each case there was little accountability—either in the country of release or internationally. Given the relatively weak response via standards and practices associated with CSR, an international legally-binding agreement on corporate accountability is proposed as a potential means by which to compensate victims of unwanted transfers of GMOs.

Several of the chapters in this volume examine the role of government regulations and policies in strengthening CSR practices. This perspective is important in view of the tendency for CSR discourse to overstate the effectiveness of voluntary approaches. Of particular importance, however, is not only the need to strengthen certain regulatory or legal instruments. Rather, there is a need to examine the interface between different modes of regulation and governance, and to consider pursuing simultaneously different institutional paths.

Chapters referring to South Africa and India highlight this need for regulatory pluralism at the national level. Neil Eccles, Ralph Hamann, and Derick de Jongh (Chapter 6) identify the key drivers of corporate social accountability in South Africa. Examining the accountability standards and procedures of the country's largest firms in five sectors, these authors explain sectoral variations in terms of the different institutional frameworks that govern company performance, and variation in the relative strength of those frameworks. Some sectors, such as mining, confront a comprehensive legal framework, which is reinforced by a sector charter and clear penalties for non-participation. In other sectors, such as retail and information and communication technology (ICT), such frameworks are absent, while the financial sector occupies a middle-ground. The authors argue that the gradient of institutional framework strength correlates well with sector accountability scores, and argue that both legalistic and voluntary frameworks are needed to promote corporate accountability.

Runa Sarkar (Chapter 7) identifies the combination of regulatory approaches and incentive structures that promote corporate environmental responsibility in India. Examining the case of four public and private firms in the steel and paper industries, Sarkar finds that although all the firms are highly profitable, they have quite different approaches to environmental management. While regulatory pressures usually elicit a reactive response, social pressures tend to elicit innovative responses. In addition to legalistic frameworks, factors like judicial activism, competitive market conditions, and appropriate resource pricing can provide incentives conducive to improved environmental performance.

Limits to Legalistic Approaches

Any approach that emphasizes the role of law and public policy needs to be cognizant of the considerable limits, constraints, and contradictions associated with such approaches. Laws may be weak by design given the interests involved in their negotiation. And they can easily be 'hollowed out' by focusing on process and the letter of the law, as opposed to the spirit of the law and the recognition and protection of substantive and procedural rights (McBarnet 2007, p. 47). 'Creative compliance' and 'clever legal gamesmanship' may become the norm (Parker 2007, p. 209). The limits of legalistic approaches are particularly obvious in many developing countries where key aspects of state regulatory capacity have been weakened through the so-called rolling back of the state promoted by neoliberal policies, or simply through the failure of technocrats, concerned with cultivating a pro-business, pro-FDI, environment, to prioritize enforcement. The discussion of hegemonic legality in Chapter 4, referred to above, suggests that the limits of legalistic approaches have to do not only with regulatory or institutional design and capacity but also politics, ideology, and power relations. Such limits are the focus of two other chapters.

Referring to India, Prabha Panth and Rahul Shastri (Chapter 8) point out that despite the adoption of more stringent regulations on industrial pollution in that country, actual compliance with those regulations has been weak in a number of states. Examining data on compliance across different states, the authors show that states with a greater number of highly polluting industries did not necessarily have better rates of compliance with pollution regulations. Further, those states with higher rates of growth of highly polluting firms—those classified as 'red'—had higher reported compliance rates. The authors argue that this finding is counter-intuitive, which leads them to question whether compliance rates, as reported by the government and by industry, are in fact accurate. The correct yardstick to use to evaluate administrative performance with respect to pollution regulation in India, they argue, is the rate at which highly polluting firms are closed down by the government, rather than the reported compliance rates. Closure implies a real cost that can deter the growth of highly polluting units. They suggest that reported rates of compliance are largely fictitious and only serve as indicators of a positive industrial climate in states that want to encourage investment in red industries rather than discourage pollution.

At the international level, Maria L. Loureiro (Chapter 9) examines whether international conventions and liability rules to compensate the victims of oil spills have any deterrent effect on their occurrence and magnitude. Drawing on different international databases reporting oil spills, Loureiro shows that over several decades, international conventions were not successful in deterring large oil spills. Conventions have tended to be weak with the bar placed low in order to facilitate agreement by multiple countries with diverse interests. Furthermore, countries with shipping interests carry considerable weight in international negotiations and typically exert pressure to limit the amount of compensation. The analysis does find, however, that more stringent conventions do appear to have a deterrent effect. Increases in the financial responsibility of polluters does create incentives that reduce the probability of oil spills. In keeping with this finding, Loureiro suggests that recent changes approved unilaterally by the European Union (EU) may also have a positive effect on regulation stringency, consequently reducing the pollution caused by oil spills in European waters. It took, however, two major oil spills off France and Spain, forceful advocacy by these governments and civil society, and unilateral action by the EU, to get to this point. Nevertheless, considerable doubts remain about whether the levels of compensation agreed upon in such accords are adequate. Compensation in Europe has typically been a fraction of total claims and well below levels paid in the United States.

III. FUTURE PROSPECTS

With corporations as key actors in today's globalized economy, their practices and behaviour are of utmost importance to questions of environmental and social sustainability and justice. While in the 1970s the focus was on regulating these actors to ensure sustainability at the domestic and international levels, a major shift toward self-regulatory and voluntary approaches has characterized the approach to sustainability since that time. From more than two decades of worldwide experience with CSR, it is clear that a growing number of firms can point to specific improvements in environmental management and social performance. However, as this chapter has illustrated, CSR is not a reliable approach for the promotion of sustainability. Not only have too few firms adhered to the principles of CSR, but implementation and oversight have been weak, and few sanctions exist for non-compliance. Furthermore, the CSR agenda largely ignores the bigger issues of scale and distribution that are central to the concept of sustainability.

These weaknesses have given fuel to the movement pushing for corporate accountability. This movement, in attempting to gain widespread adoption of the concept of accountability as opposed to just responsibility, has worked in creative ways to operationalize the concept. The result has been a range of developments and proposals on the table, from an enhancement of government-based regulations with stronger monitoring and enforcement, to alternative forms of governance on multiple scales—involving not just state actors, but also NGOs and corporations working in a more cooperative manner to ratchet-up voluntary initiatives and reconnect with public policy. While not all agree on the best means by which to achieve accountability, there is growing awareness that the current emphasis on CSR alone is not sufficient. Moreover, it is important to bring this message beyond the activist movement and to other actors—the state, mainstream civil society organizations including business associations, and indeed corporations themselves.

While it is necessary to be somewhat practical about the ways in which accountability and improved corporate practices can be best approached within this movement, it is also important not to lose sight of the theoretical underpinnings that explain why it is necessary to move beyond the current CSR agenda (Utting 2007). The deeper structural changes in the global economy as well as the discursive power of corporate actors have had an important influence on the ways in which the debate has unfolded both in theory and in practice (Fuchs 2005). Without radical ideas and theoretical insights to expose these dimensions of the problem, as well as to envision how the world could be more sustainable, we would not have a vision to work toward. It is unlikely in today's complex and globalized world that change will occur overnight. But even if we aim for small steps, we still need to know in which direction we should be moving. This book aims to provide readers insights to each of these dimensions of the interface between corporate actors and the question of sustainability.

REFERENCES

Balanyá, Belén, A. Doherty, O. Hoedeman, A. Ma'anit, and E. Wesselius, *Europe Inc.:Regional and Global Restructuring and the Rise of Corporate Power*, London: Pluto Press, 2000.

Barrientos, Stephanie, C. Dolan, and A. Tallontire, 'A Gendered Value Chain Approach to Codes of Conduct in African Horticulture', *World Development* 31 (9), 2003, pp. 1511–26.

Bendell, Jem, *Barricades and Boardrooms: A Contemporary History of the Corporate Accountability Movement*, Programme on Technology, Business and Society, Programme Paper No. 13, Geneva: UNRISD, 2004.

Bendell, J. and D.F. Murphy, 'Towards Civil Regulation: NGOs and the Politics of Corporate Environmentalism' in *The Greeting of Business in Developing Countries: Rhetoric, Reality and Prospects*, Peter Utting (ed), London: Zed Books, 2002.

Blowfield, Michael, 'Reasons to be Cheerful? What we know about CSR's impact', *Third World Quarterly*, 28 (4) 2007, pp. 683–95.

Blyth, Mark, *Great Transformations: Economic Ideas and Institutional Change in the Twentieth Century*, Cambridge: Cambridge University Press, 2002.

Bøås, Morten and Desmond McNeill, *Global Institutions and Development: Framing the World?* London: Routledge, 2004.

Boyer, Robert and J. Rogers Hollingsworth, 'The Variety of Institutional Arrangements and their Complementarity in Modern Economies', in *Contemporary Capitalism: the Embeddedness of Institutions*, J. Rogers Hollingsworth and Robert Boyer (eds), Cambridge: Cambridge University Press, 1997.

Braithwaite, John and Peter Drahos, *Global Business Regulation*, Cambridge: Cambridge University Press, 2000.

Broad, Robin and John Cavanagh, 'The Corporate Accountability Movement: Lessons and Opportunities', The Fletcher Forum of World Affairs, 23 (2), 1999, pp. 151–69.

Bruno, Kenny (wish Joshua Karliner), 2002. *Greenwash + 10: The UN's Global Compact, Corporate Accountability and the Johannesburg Earth*

Summit, Corporate Watch, 2002, available online at: *www.corpwatch.org/ un*, accessed on May 22, 2008.

Cappellin, Paola and Gian Mario Giuliani, *The Political Economy of Corporate Responsibility in Brazil: Social and Environmental Dimensions*, Programme Paper on Technology, Business and Society, Paper No. 14, Geneva: UNRISD, 2004.

Cashore, Benjamin, 'Legitimacy and the Privatization of Environmental Governance: How Non–State Market–Driven (NSMD) Governance Systems Gain Rule–Making Authority', *Governance*, 15 (4), 2002, pp. 503–29.

CCC (Clean Clothes Campaign), *Looking for a Quick Fix: How Social Auditing is Keeping Workers' in Sweatshops*, 2005.

Chatterjee, Pratap, and Matthias Finger, *The Earth Brokers: Power, Politics and World Development*, London: Routledge, 1994.

Clapham, Andrew, *Human Rights Obligations of Non-State Actors*, Oxford: OxfordUniversity Press, 2006.

Clapp, Jennifer, 'Global Environmental Governance for Corporate Responsibility and Accountability', *Global Environmental Politics*, 5 (3), 2005, pp. 23–34.

Clapp, Jennifer, 'The Privatization of Global Environmental Governance: ISO 14000 and the Developing World, *Global Governance*, 4 (3), 1998, pp. 295–316.

Clay, Jason (principal author), *Exploring the Links between International Business and Poverty Reduction: A Case Study of Unilever in Indonesia*, Oxford: Oxfam GB, Novib, Unilever, and Unilever, Indonesia, 2005.

Daly, Herman, 'Reconciling Internal and External Policies for Sustainable Development', in *Sustainability and Global Environmental Policy*, O.K. Dragun and Kim Jacobson (eds), Edward Elgar, 1997, pp. 11–32.

Daly, Herman and Joshua Farley. *Ecological Economics: Principles and Applications*, Washington, D.C.: Island Press, 2004.

Dryzek, J., *The Politics of the Earth: Environmental Discourses*, New York: Oxford University Press, 1997.

Eade, Deborah and John Sayer (eds), *Development and the Private Sector: Consuming Interests*, Bloomfield CT: Kumarian Press, 2006.

Elkington, John, *Cannibals with Forks: The Triple Bottom Line of 21st Century Business*, Gabriola Island BC: New Society Publishers, 1998.

Farnsworth, Kevin, 'Promoting Business-centred Welfare: International and European Business Perspectives on Social Policy', *Journal of European Social Policy*, 15 (1), 2005, pp. 65–80.

Fig, David (ed), *Staking Their Claims: Corporate Social and Environmental Responsibility in South Africa*, Geneva: KwaZulu-Natal Press, 2007.

Freeman, R.E., *Strategic Management: A Stakeholder Approach*, Boston: Pitman, 1984.

Friends of the Earth International, *Towards Binding Corporate Accountability*, 2001, available at *http://www.foei.org/publications/corporates/accountability.html*

Friends of the Earth Netherlands, *Using the OECD Guidelines for Multinational Enterprises: A critical starterkit for NGOs*, Amsterdam: FOE Netherlands, 2002.

Friends of the Earth England, Wales and Northern Ireland, 'A History of Attempts to Regulate the Activities of Transnational Corporations: What Lessons Can be Learned?', 1998, available at *http://www.corporate-accountability.org/docs/FoE-US-paper-history_TNC-Regulation.doc*

Frynas, Jedrzej George, and Peter Newell, *Beyond CSR? Business, poverty and social justice: an introduction*, Third World Quaterly, Special Issue, 28 (4), 2007, pp. 669–81.

Fuchs, Doris, *Understanding Business Power in Global Governance* (Baden-Baden: Nomos, 2005).

Gill, Stephen, 'New Constitutionalism, Democratization and Global Political Economy', *Pacifica Review*, 10 (1). 1998.

Global Reporting Initiative, *G3 Reporting Framework*, 2006, available at: *http://www.globalreporting.org/ReportingFramework/G3Online/*

Greenpeace International, *Corporate Crimes: The Need for an International Instrument on Corporate Accountability and Liability*, Amsterdam: Greenpeace International, 2002.

Greer, Jed, and Kenny Bruno, *Greenwash: The Reality Behind Corporate Environmentalism*, New York: Apex Press, 1997.

Gunningham, Neil, 'Corporate Environmental Responsibility: law and the limits of voluntarism', in *The New Corporate Accountability: Corporate Social Responsibility and the Law*, Doreen McBarnet, Aurora Voiculescu and Tom Cambell (eds), Cambridge: Cambridge University Press, 2007.

Gunningham, Neil and Darren Sinclair, *Leaders and Laggards: Next Generation Environmental Regulation*, Sheffield: Greenleaf Publishing, 2002.

Holliday, Charles, Stephan Schmidheiny and Philip Watts, *Walking the Talk: The Business Case for Sustainable Development*, Sheffield: Greenfield Publishing, 2002.

Holme, Richard and Phil Watts, *Corporate Social Responsibility: Making Good Business Sense*, Geneva: World Business Council for Sustainable Development, 2000.

Hopkins, Michael, *Corporate Social Responsibility and International Development*, London: Earthscan, 2007.

International Council on Human Rights Policy (ICHRP), *Beyond Voluntarism: Human Rights and the Developing International Legal Obligations of Companies*, Versoix, Switzerland: ICHRP, 2002.

International Forum on Globalization, *Alternatives to Economic Globalization: A Better World is Possible*, San Francisco: Berrett-Koehler, 2002.

Jenkins, Rhys, R. Pearson, and G. Seyfang, *Corporate Responsibility and Labour Rights: Codes of Conduct in the Global Economy*, London: Earthscan, 2002.

Kapp, K. William, *The Social Costs of Private Enterprise*, Cambridge, Mass: Harvard University Press, 1950.

Karliner, Joshua, *The Corporate Planet: Ecology and Politics n the Age of Globalization*, San Francisco: Sierra Club Books, 1997.

Kilgour, Maureen A, 'The UN Global Compact and Substantive Equality for Women: Revealing a 'Well-hidden' Mandate', *Third World Quarterly*, 28 (4), 2007.

Kolk, Ans and Rob van Tulder, 'Poverty Alleviation as a Business Strategy: Evaluating Commitments of Frontrunner Multinational Corporations,' *World Development*, 34 (5), 2006, pp 789–801.

Kolominskas, Chaim and Rory Sullivan, 'Improving Cleaner Production through Pollutant Release and Transfer Register Reporting Processes', *Journal of Cleaner Production*. 12 (7), 2004, pp. 713–24.

Korten, D., *When Corporations Rule the World*, New York: Kumarian Press, 2001.

KPMG Global Sustainability Services and United Nations Environment Programme (UNEP), *Carrots and Sticks for Starters: Current Trends and Approaches in Voluntary and Mandatory Standards for Sustainability Reporting*, Paris: UNEP, 2006.

Krut, Riva and Harris Gleckman, *ISO 14001: A Missed Opportunity for Global Sustainable Industrial Development*, London: Earthscan, 1998.

McBarnet, Doreen, 'Corporate Social Responsibility beyond Law, through Law, for Law: the new corporate accountability', in *The New Corporate Accountability: Corporate Social Responsibility and the Law*, Doreen McBarnet, Aurora Voiculescu and Tom Campbell (eds), Cambridge: Cambridge University Press, 2007.

McBarnet, Doreen, Aurora Voiculescu and Tom Campbell (eds), *The New Corporate Accountability: Corporate Social Responsibility and the Law*. Cambridge: Cambridge University Press, 2007.

Morgera, Elisa, 'From Stockholm to Johannesburg: From Corporate Responsibility to Corporate Accountability for the Global Protection of the Environment?', *RECIEL* 13 (2), 2004.

Muchlinsky, Peter. *Multinational Enterprises and the Law*, Oxford: Oxford University Press, 2007.

Newell, Peter. 'From Responsibility to Citizenship: Corporate Accountability for Development', *IDS Bulletin*, 33 (2), 2002.

NGLS/UNRISD (eds), *Voluntary Approaches to Corporate Responsibility: Readings and a Resource Guide*, NGLS Development Dossier, Geneva: United Nations, 2002.

Ocampo, José Antonio, 'Foreword: Some reflections on the links between social knowledge and policy', in *Reclaiming Development Agendas: Knowledge, Power and International Policy Making*, Peter Utting (ed), Basingstoke: UNRISD and Palgrave Macmillan, 2006.

OECD (Organisation for Economic Co-operation and Development), *The OECD Guidelines for Multinational Enterprises*, 2000, available at *http://www.oecd.org/dataoecd/56/36/1922428.pdf*

O'Rourke, Dara, *Monitoring the Monitors: A Critique of PricewaterhouseCoopers (PwC) Labor Monitoring*, 2000, available at *http://Web.mit.edu/dorourke/www/index.html*, accessed on 25 February 2005.

Parker, Christine, ' Meta-regulation: legal accountability for corporate social responsibility', in *The New Corporate Accountability: Corporate Social Responsibility and the Law*, Doreen McBarnet, Aurora Voiculescu and Tom Campbell (eds), 2007.

Pearson, Ruth, 'Beyond Women Workers: Gendering CSR', *Third World Quarterly*, 28 (4), 2007, pp. 731–49, 2007.

Prieto, Marina, 'Corporate Social Responsibility in Latin America: Chiquita, Women Banana Workers and Structural Inequalities', *Journal of Corporate Citizenship*, 21, 2006, pp. 85–94.

Ruggie, John Gerard, 'Taking Embedded Liberalism Global: The Corporate Connection', in *Taming Globalization: Frontiers of Governance*, David Held and Mathias Koenig-Archibugi (eds), Cambridge: Polity Press, 2003.

Rutherford, Paul, '"Talking the Talk": Business Discourse at the World Summit on Sustainable Development', *Environmental Politics*, 12 (2), 2003, pp. 145–50.

Schmidheiny, Stephan, *Changing Course: A Global Business Perspective on Development and the Environment*, Cambridge, Ma: MIT Press, 1992.

Sood, Atul and Bimal Arora, *The Political Economy of Corporate Responsibility in India*, Programme Paper on Technology, Business and Society, Paper No. 18, Geneva: UNRISD, 2006.

Sucupira Joao, 'Balanço Social: diversidade, participacão, e segurança do trabalho', Democracia Viva, 20, June–July, 2004, pp. 58–64, available at *www.premiobalancosocial.org.br/artigos.asp*.

Stiglitz, Joseph E., *The Roaring Nineties: Why We're Paying the Price for the Greediest Decade in History*, London: Penguin Books, 2004.

Therien, Jean-Philippe and Vincent Pouliot, 'The Global Compact: Shifting the Politics of International Development?', *Global Governance*, 12, 2006, pp. 55–75.

UNCTAD (United Nations Conference on Trade and Development), *World Investment Report 2007: Transnational Corporations, Extractive Industries and Development*, Geneva: UNCTAD, 2007.

Utting, Peter, 'Regulating Business for Sustainable Development', in *Organizations and the Sustainability Mosaic: Crafting Long-Term Ecological and Societal Solutions*, Sanjay Sharma, Mark Starik and Bryan Husted (eds), Cheltenham: Edward Elgar, 2007.

Utting, Peter, 'CSR and Equality', *Third World Quarterly*, Vol. 28 (4), 2007, pp. 697–712.

Utting, Peter, 'Corporate Responsibility and the Movement of Business' in *Development and the Private Sector: Consuming Interests*, John Sayer and Deborah Eade (eds). Bloomfield CT: Kumarian Press, 2006.

Utting, Peter. *Rethinking Business Regulation: From Self-Regulation to Social Control*, UNRISD Paper, No. 15, 2005.

Utting, Peter, *The Greening of Business in Developing Countries: Rhetoric, Reality and Prospects*, London: Zed Books, 2002a.

Utting, Peter, 'Regulating Business via Multistakeholder Initiatives: A Preliminary Assessment', in *Voluntary Approaches to Corporate Responsibility: Readings and a Resource Guide*, NGLS Development Dossier, NGLS/UNRISD (eds), Geneva: United Nations, 2002b.

Utting, Peter and Ann Zammit, *Beyond Pragmatism: Appraising UN-Business Partnerships,* Programme Paper on Markets, Business and Regulations, Paper No. 1, Geneva: UNRISD, 2006.

Ward, Halina, *Legal Issues in Corporate Citizenship,* Stockholm/London: Swedish Partnership for Global Responsibility/IIED, 2003.

Ward, Halina, *Governing Multinationals: The Role of Foreign Direct Liability.* Briefing Paper No. 18, The Royal Institute of International Affairs, February , 2001.

White, Allen, *New Wine, New Bottles: The Rise of Non-Financial Reporting.* Business for Social Development (*www.bsr.org,* accessed 30 June, 2007), 2005.

Witte, Jan Martin and Wolfgang Reinicke, *Business UNusual: Facilitating United Nations Reform through Partnerships.* New York: UN Global Compact Office, 2005.

World Resources Institute (WRI), *World Resources: 2002–2004*, Washington, D.C.: WRI, 2003.

Zammit, Ann, *Development at Risk: Rethinking UN-Business Partnerships*, Geneva: South Centre/UNRISD, 2003.

Zadek, Simon, *The Civil Corporation: The New Economy of Corporate Citizenship*, London: Earthscan, 2001.

2

Sustainable Development, Corporate Sustainability, and Corporate Social Responsibility
The Missing Link

STEFANO POGUTZ

INTRODUCTION

Although the topics of economic growth, social equity, and environmental limits have been explored and debated for several decades, since the early 1990s there has been an increasing demand for sustainable development (SD) across institutions and governments, as well as the business world, civil society, and individuals. On the one hand, substantial advances in environmental research and in computer science have demonstrated to the broad public that global environmental threats—climate change, ozone depletion, resource scarcity, air pollution, and the loss of biodiversity—are urgent and critical problems that may compromise the well-being of future generations as well as the biodiversity, and climate stability of the planet (Sneddon *et al.* 2006). On the other hand, as a result of the Johannesburg Summit in 2002, the question of an equitable distribution of resources and benefits within society and the widening gap between industrialized and developing countries have raised new concerns. Even a large majority of those who were previously sceptical about sustainability, seriously doubting the necessity for an intense and costly U-turn across the world's economies in order to halt the decline in equity and the environmental crisis, have gradually aligned their views with the advocates of SD (Carey and Shapiro 2004; The Economist 2005 and 2006). A general consensus on the need for a decisive change in our model of production and consumption has gradually gained strength, and the call for a more humane society, based on respect for the so-called three pillars of sustainability—the environment, economy, and society—has united politicians, business leaders, NGOs, and scholars.

As a result, many governments and international agencies have implemented programmes to incorporate sustainability goals into their policies and regulations. The European Union, since 1992 when the Fifth Environmental Action Programme was launched, adopted several communications and policies (CEC 2001a; CEC 2001b).[1] Industrialized countries like the United States, Canada, European nations, Japan, South Korea, and others established agencies and implemented regulations concerning sustainability (for example, the Environmental Protection Agency in the US and the European Environment Agency). Moreover, an impressive number of conventions and protocols have been signed and enforced at the global and local levels (the Kyoto Protocol, the Convention on Biodiversity, the Basel Convention, Agenda 21, and so on).

Similarly, the role of companies has rapidly moved from a defensive approach—denying the existence of environmental threats like global warming—to a more mature and responsible attitude toward sustainability. First, a growing number of large corporations have organized themselves into associations and networks to communicate with institutions, develop and implement sustainability strategies, innovate products and processes, and circulate best practices. Probably the most important of these is the World Business Council for Sustainable Development (WBCSD), an alliance that to date brings together about 180 international companies—from more than thirty countries and twenty industries—in a shared commitment to SD through economic growth, ecological balance, and social progress. Second, at the individual level, companies have become active in incorporating sustainability issues into their mission and values by a

[1]The European Community produced The Fifth Environmental Action Programme (1992–2000) as a main response to the 1992 Rio Earth Summit with the goal to take society towards a sustainable pattern of development. A key feature of the programme was the recognition that environmental legislation in itself was not sufficient to improve the environment quality. Therefore, the programme introduced a broader range of instruments: incentives and other financial measures and voluntary agreeements. Moreover, this programme introduced new general principles in European Community such as the concept of shared responsibility, and encouraging changes in social behaviour by engaging all the actors concerned (public authorities, citizens, consumers, enterprises, and so on). Since 2001, the Sixth Environment Action Programme entitled 'Environment 2010: Our Future, Our Choice', covering the period 2001–2010 has been enforced.

variety of means. These include the adoption of innovation programmes focused on the development of environmentally friendly technologies (Hall and Vredenburg 2003; Hart and Milstein 1999; Porter and Van der Linde 1995; Rondinelli and Berry 2000; Shrivastava 1995b), adherence to environmental management standards such as the ISO 14000 (ISO 2005), the publication of sustainability reports, and the incorporation of environmental and social issues into their communication initiatives (KPMG 2005). Third, new concepts like eco-efficiency, cleaner production, product stewardship, and design for the environment, among others, have become guiding principles for business leaders and managers in the development of responsible strategies, incorporating environmental and social concerns into decision-making processes. Furthermore, in the last few years, the stories of corporations turned 'green'—like 3M, DuPont, BP, Chevron-Texaco, Toyota, GE, Starbucks, Unilever, and more recently Wal-Mart—show that business has become a major actor in the race to SD, broadly redefining its role in society (The Economist 2005 and 2006; Gunther *et al.* 2006; Freeman 2006).

Although these positive initiatives have been increasing over the years, spreading across countries and sectors and demonstrating an impressive effort on the part of government, policymakers and the business world, several studies show that these attempts have been ultimately ineffective and disappointing (Baumert *et al.* 2005; Sneddon *et al.* 2006; WWF *et al.* 2006). For example, according to the goals established by the Kyoto Protocol, few of the large industrialized countries who have ratified the treaty comply with the new guidelines— Canada, Japan, Germany, Britain, Italy, and Spain have all failed to comply, and these countries still greatly exceed the 1990 baseline emission levels.

Several reasons have been advanced to explain why, despite a strong international commitment, a serious enforcement of regulations at the national level, and a new trend in corporate behaviour, the global SD performance is still so inadequate and unsatisfactory.

In some recent articles, scholars like Sneddon (Sneddon *et al.* 2006) and Stiglitz (2006) have tried to simplify this question by exploring both the theoretical criticism of sustainability and its pragmatic fragility. Many authors strongly criticize the lack of determination at the government level and citizens' multiple scales (Sneddon *et al.* 2006). Others have criticized the effectiveness of tools like international agreements in guiding nations and firms toward change. For example, the Nobel prize winner Joseph Stiglitz, in a recent article discussing the Kyoto Protocol and global warming (Stiglitz 2006), highlighted that without effective enforcement mechanisms, these treaties are useless. A second problem is related both to the involvement of developing countries, like India and China, in the global framework of sustainability and the overcoming of a trade-off between enhanced economic growth and environmental protection.

In order to address the question of the disappointing results of attempts toward sustainability, this chapter contributes to the ongoing debate by taking the discussion from the macro level to the firm level— that is, corporate sustainability and corporate social responsibility— and explores how management scholars have incorporated the paradigm of SD into their discipline (Gladwin *et al.* 1995). I argue that one of the causes of the global 'sustainability gap' must be traced back to the theoretical level, and that the missing links between economics and managerial disciplines, or between the macro and micro levels, must be explored.

The focus on the key role of corporations in pursuing sustainable development has been broadly emphasized in recent reports, papers, and articles emanating from the managerial perspective.[2] Moreover, the organizational and managerial literature has developed a consistent theoretical framework to support the integration of these issues into strategic management practices.[3] Also, the notion of corporate social responsibility (CSR) has gained respect among academics in the business management field as a positive contribution to global problems like poverty, social exclusion, improvement in labour conditions, and environmental degradation.[4]

This chapter tries to show that in spite of the increasing interest in sustainable development in its various dimensions, management science has somehow failed to transpose the bio-economic definition of sustainability to the corporate level, mainly because it interprets the concept of limits differently. More precisely, even though the economic and managerial disciplines are interdependent, much of the research on corporate sustainability (CS) and CSR seems incapable of incorporating the idea of 'carrying capacity' into its conceptual

[2]Fussler and James 1996; Schmidheiny 1992; Schmidheiny and Zorraquin 1996.

[3]Aragon-Correa 1998; Bansal 2005; Hart 1995; Hoffman 1999; Porter and van der Linde 1995; Russo and Fouts 1997; Sharma and Vredenburg 1998; Sharma and Henriques 2005; Shrivastava 1995a; Starik and Marcus 2000; Walley and Whitehead 1994.

[4]Carrol and Bucholtz 2002; CEC 2001c; van Marrewijk 2003.

framework. As a result, what the managerial paradigm defines as a 'corporate win-win strategy,' which successfully leads to an efficient firm oriented toward CS or to CSR, does not guarantee that the corporation is contributing to sustainable development on a macro scale.

Following a broad overview of the debates on the definition of sustainable development, corporate sustainability, and corporate social responsibility, the chapter turns to discuss the concept of 'resource' and the different meanings assigned to it by the bio-economic and managerial perspectives. The argument is that this difference derives from basic principles and the lack of integration at the base of managerial theory. The chapter then explores the questions of limits and different types of capital and their implications at the corporate level. Again, it is posited that management research and theories dealing with sustainability differ in their interpretations of boundaries and capital substitutability over time. In conclusion, suggestions for further research on the missing link between these macro and micro dimensions are provided.

I.   DEFINING SUSTAINABLE DEVELOPMENT, CORPORATE SUSTAINABILITY, AND CORPORATE SOCIAL RESPONSIBILITY

Sustainable Development: From the WCED to the Bio-economic View

The idea of sustainable development has developed over the last forty years mainly with a macro perspective. Since its early years, a proliferation of interpretations has been advanced in terms of vision, values, and principles, cutting across different disciplines including economics,[5] social sciences,[6] and the natural sciences.[7] To date, probably the most popular definition of sustainable development is the one provided by the World Commission on Environment and Development (WCED) in their 1987 report, *Our Common Future*: 'development that meets the needs of the present without compromising the ability of future generations to meet their own needs'. The WCED defined this concept intentionally very broadly so that no specific category of needs would prevail (UN *et al.* 2003). At the same time, this broad

[5]Barbier 1987; Daly 1992; Daly and Cobb 1989; Perrings 1997; Pearce *et al.* 1989; Passet 1996; Norgaard and Howarth 1991, Sen 1987 and 1999.
[6]Bateson 1972; Capra 1996 and 2002; Jonas 1985; Morin 1980; Naess and Rothenberg 1990.
[7]Carson 1962; Commoner 1990; Lovelock 1988; Odum 1993; Shiva 1992.

approach has been widely accepted and endorsed by governments, corporations, and other organizations around the world (Gladwin *et al.* 1995). Within this framework, since the Rio conference in 1992, the approach based on the 'three pillars' of sustainability, which integrates economic, social, and environmental considerations into the model, has been further consolidated, influencing both the institutional and corporate path to SD (Elkington 1994 and 1997). According to this approach, each of the pillars is independently crucial and urgent in the short run, but in order to reach the goal of sustainability in the long run, the three pillars must be satisfied simultaneously. Moreover, these three dimensions are deeply interconnected and may influence and support each other.

There are several critiques of this view of sustainability, both at the theoretical and practical levels (see Atkinson, Hett, and Newcombe 1999; Lehtonen 2004, Sneddon *et al.* 2006). First, a conceptual opposition denies that the three dimensions are qualitatively and hierarchically equivalent. The ecological economics school (Costanza 1991; Daly 1992; Martinez-Alier 1987), along with several other scientific disciplines (Capra 1996; Odum 1993; Shiva 1992), approach sustainable development based on a bio-economic model, representing the three dimensions with three circles inscribed one inside the other. In this model, the bio-sphere identifies the external limit of the system and contains the social sphere, which in turn includes the economic sphere, representing the last and more internal dimension. This approach reflects the idea that economy and society owe their hierarchical dependence to ecological systems and organize themselves within the environmental constraints (Daly and Cobb 1989; Daly 1992). In other words, the bio-economic model proposes a view of sustainable development in which the idea of limits and the carrying capacity of the ecosystem guide the growth of the other two systems (Köhn 1998; Small and Jollands 2006).

Second, the 'institutional' definition of sustainable development does not address one of the critical questions in the discussion on sustainability: the dispute over different types of capital. The capital approach has been developed based on an economic perspective, but has been extended by economists to other domains, including the natural and social sciences. Three main kinds of capital, mirroring the main pillars of SD, have been identified: economic, natural, and social.[8]

[8]Costanza 1991; Dasgupta 2002; Dyllick and Hockerts 2002; Hicks 1948; Köhn 1998; Pearce *et al.* 1990; Putnam 1993 and 2000.

According to this capital-based approach, the question of sustainable development is seen to depend on the maintenance of different forms of capital stocks over time (El Serafy 1991; Dyllick and Hockerts 2002). This perspective has opened a broad and intense debate over the possibility of substitution between the different kinds of capital. Different interpretations of this concept can be grouped into two main schools of weak and strong sustainability.[9]

The first approach, weak sustainability, assumes that all forms of capital are equivalent and any loss within one kind can be compensated with other forms (Solow 1986). An example is the production of chemical fertilizers to compensate the loss of natural fertility in soil, that is, the substitution of man-made technology for natural capital (UN *et al.* 2003). In other words, weak sustainability permits the degradation of natural resources as far as they are covered with an increase in stocks of other forms of capital. The second approach, strong sustainability, posits that some types of capital, in particular several forms of natural capital, have no substitute. The assumption is that different forms of capital are complementary but not perfect substitutes (Costanza 1991). Therefore, these forms of capital must be preserved independently of one another. An example often proposed to support this view is nature: a forest plays several vital roles—as a habitat for living species, preserving biodiversity, absorbing CO_2, contributing to the water cycle—all of which to date cannot be replaced by other forms of capital (Dyllick and Hockerts 2002; Lovins *et al.* 1999). In this sense, a useful definition of sustainability is provided by Costanza *et al.*: 'the amount of consumption that can be continued indefinitely without degrading capital stocks— including natural capital stocks' (Costanza *et al.* 1991).

Another problem, often added to the debate, is the uncertainty of the consequences of our actions on natural and social capital. Several scholars suggest applying a precautionary principle in order to reduce the risk of unexpected effects (Norgaard and Howarth 1991). Costanza (1991), for example, considers that keeping the amount of natural capital constant can assure sustainability. This strict approach has been embraced by international institutions such as the UN, whose recent reports (UN *et al.* 2003) specify that the still-limited scientific understanding of the environment requires the adoption of a 'precautionary principle' in dealing with the natural capital.

[9]Costanza 1991; Pearce and Turner 1989; Pearce *et al.* 1991.

For the reasons outlined above, many have come to the conclusion that a strong perspective on sustainability is probably a more appropriate basis for a model of true sustainable development for governments, society, and the business community. As a consequence, academics have provided several more prescriptive definitions of SD over the years, in an effort to incorporate sustainability into the bio-economic model while accepting no substitution among different types of capital. The following definition (Costanza *et al.* 1991) is probably one of the most popular (Gladwin *et al.* 1995), because it focuses on the concept of limits and considers the relation between the economic, social, and environmental dimensions: 'Sustainability is a relationship between dynamic human economic systems and larger dynamic, but normally slower-changing ecological systems, in which a) human life can continue indefinitely, b) human individuals can flourish, and c) human culture can develop; but in which the effect of human activities remains within bounds, so as not to destroy the diversity, complexity, and function of the ecological support system.'

Corporate Sustainability and Corporate Social Responsiblity: The Firm's Perspective

If the concept of SD originated at the macro level, CS and CSR can be considered the theoretical counterpart in dealing with firms and business (CEC 2002). Although scholars and practitioners often interpret CS and CSR as being nearly synonymous, pointing to similarities and the common domain (van Marrewijk 2003), the two concepts have different backgrounds and different theoretical paths. According to management science, the notion of CS can be defined first as the capacity of a firm to create value through the product and services it produces and to continue operating over the years. *Sustainability*, in this context, entails the creation of a sustainable competitive advantage.

After the United Nations Conference on Environment and Development in 1992, when a large debate developed over how businesses and firms should contribute to the objective of SD, a different view of CS emerged among academics and the business community. In general, according to this new approach, CS can be considered as the attempt to adapt the concept of SD to the corporate setting, matching the goal of value creation with environmental and social considerations. According to the Dow Jones Sustainability Index, 'Corporate Sustainability is a business approach that creates long-term shareholder value by embracing opportunities and managing risks deriving from economic, environmental, and social developments'.[10] The *Journal of Environmental Strategy* defines corporate sustainability as 'the capacity of an enterprise to maintain economic prosperity in the context of environmental responsibility and social stewardship.' Another important definition of CS that includes the integration of different forms of capital is provided by AccountAbility (1999, p. 94): 'the capability of an organization to continue its activities indefinitely, having taken due account of the impact on natural, social, and human capitals.' Finally, Hart and Milstein (1999, p. 56) define a sustainable enterprise as 'one that contributes to sustainable development by delivering simultaneously economic, social and environmental benefits—the so-called triple-bottom-line'.

Three main considerations emerge from these definitions. First, corporate sustainability concerns preserving the competitiveness of a firm in the long term, which is the maintenance of the firm entity itself. Second, it focuses on the capacity of the firm to balance what the scholars of organization and management theory have called the 'business case'—economic sustainability—with environmental and social sustainability. This definition embodies the 'triple-bottom-line' concept that Elkington theorized in 1994, referring to a situation in which firms focus not only on the economic value they add, but also on the environmental and social value they add or destroy, trying to harmonize their efforts as they pursue these different goals (Elkington 1994 and 1997). Finally, CS includes an attempt to assimilate the environmental and social dimensions into business operations: processes, products, and procedures.

From a theoretical perspective, the idea of CS has sparked a growing interest among the managerial disciplines, oriented toward the goal of exploring both why companies commit themselves to sustainable development and how they implement it (see for example, Schmidheiny 1992; Shrivastava and Hart 1995; Bansal 2005). In practical terms, the CS approach leads to a very concrete and pragmatic problem: how to measure performance based on the three dimensions outlined and how natural and social values can be incorporated into corporate accounting (Figge and Hahn 2004; Dyllick and Hockerts

---

[10]See *http://www.sustainability-index.com/06_htmle/sustainability/corpsustainability.html*

2002). One of the key issues in sustainability involves understanding the relationship between a 'sustainable business' in terms of the corporate entity itself and the contribution of the company to SD in a broader sense.

The evolutionary path of the concept of CSR is different from that of CS. The first recognized contribution in the literature dates back to Bowen (1953, p. 6), who stressed the responsibilities of businesses and wrote that social responsibility refers to 'the obligations of businessmen to pursue those policies, to make those decisions, or to follow those lines of action which are desirable in terms of the objectives and values of our society.' Since this seminal study, CSR has evolved through a number of theoretical and empirical contributions and a growing interest among practitioners and academics, which has in turn fostered the proliferation of different approaches, definitions, and terminologies. In this sense, Carroll (1994, p. 14) pointed out that CSR is 'an eclectic field with loose boundaries, multiple membership, and differing training/perspectives; broadly rather than focused, multidisciplinary; wide breadth; brings in a wider range of literature; and interdisciplinary.'

Despite the scepticism of prestigious scholars like Friedman (1962 and 1970), who criticized both the vagueness of the notion and the possibility of introducing CSR into business operations, an important attempt to formalize the concept was proposed by Carroll in the late 1970s (1979 and 1991; Carroll and Buchholtz 2003). He argued that 'the social responsibility of business encompasses the economic, legal, ethical, and philanthropic expectations placed on organizations by society at a given point in time.' (Carroll 1979, p. 500). In other words, he posited that besides economic and legal responsibilities (that is, to be profitable and obey the law), companies are expected to satisfy other requirements, relevant to conformity to social norms and voluntary contributions to the community in which they operate. Another important CSR approach developed during the 1980s in the light of the growth of the stakeholder approach theory (Freeman 1984). According to this view, managers of firms have obligations to a broader group of stakeholders than the simple shareholders, where a stakeholder is 'any group or individual who can affect or is affected by the achievement of the firm's objectives' (Freeman 1984). Proposing a more radical perspective on corporations, Freeman added that 'business can be understood as a set of relationships among groups which have a stake in the activities that make up the business' (Freeman *et al.* 2004, p. 9).

Another significant research trend developed within the theoretical framework of CSR is the corporate social performance (CSP) perspective (Wood 1991). It can be considered as complementary to CSR, underlining the importance of developing a methodology to clearly measure societal performances. At the same time, CSP establishes a bridge between stakeholder management and CSR, in that managing stakeholders with only the traditional profit-maximization goal is not effective, and both the responsiveness to social pressure and the search for social legitimacy are measured by corporate social performance.

Finally, since the 1990s, CSR has continued to transform and enrich itself with new theories and themes like the integrative social contract theory (Donaldson and Preston 1995; Donaldson and Dunfee 1999), the corporate citizenship approach (Crane and Matten 2004), and research into measurement and reporting (Elkington 1997). The CSR concept has become the main managerial framework wherein the relationship between business and society are studied.

Although CS and CSR have different roots and have developed along diverse theoretical paths, they ultimately converged and overlapped from both the academic and practical perspectives. This strong complementarity is evident in some recent definitions of CSR provided by international organizations like the Prince of Wales International Business Leaders Forum: 'CSR means open and transparent business practices that are based on ethical values and respect for employees, communities, and the environment. It is designed to deliver sustainable value to society at large, as well as to shareholders.' Furthermore, this red line is strengthened in some institutional documents, including the European Union Green Paper *Promoting a European Framework for CSR,* ' which defines corporate responsibility as 'a concept whereby companies integrate social and environmental concerns in their business operations and in their interaction with their stakeholders on a voluntary basis' (CEC 2001c, p. 6).

II. FROM SD TO CS/CSR: THE TRADE-OFF

Management science began to include the concept of sustainable development in its theoretical framework in the 1990s. Organizations such as the Organization and Natural Environment (ONE), a specific interest group of the Academy of Management, were established in this decade to promote academic contributions and research on the topic. Special research forums and entire issues of management journals were devoted to the natural environment, social responsibility, and the stakeholders' perspective (*Academy of Management Journal; Strategic Management Journal*, etc.). In the same period, several new academic journals were launched to delve more deeply into the relationship between business, society, and ecosystems: *Business Strategy and the Environment, Organization and the Environment, Greener Management International,* and *Corporate Social Responsibility and Environmental Management* represent just a few. Over the years, numerous papers and articles have been published, with the goal of both building a systematic conceptual theory of corporate sustainability, and empirically exploring the phenomenon of 'going sustainable' with a set of methodological tools.

Although there was a strong infiltration of sustainability into the theoretical literature in organizational and managerial studies, the concepts of SD and CS/CSR discussed above still presented some relevant theoretical trade-offs. As Gladwin, Kennelly, and Krause (Gladwin *et al.* 1995, p. 875) very clearly pointed out, 'Most management theorizing and research continues to proceed as if organizations lack biophysical foundations'. This disassociation, in fact, seems to mark a variety of contributions that in the last decade explored the relations between business, society, and the natural environment. In particular, economic theory questioned some pillars of the discipline, delving into the implications of the SD concept for the notion of growth to the extent of developing new theoretical domains like bio-economics and ecological economics. In contrast, the managerial discipline seems unable to incorporate in its representations some key elements of the strong sustainability concept: the idea of physical limits to growth and limited substitutability—or outright non-substitutability—among the different forms of capital. Moreover, another difference is related to the interpretation of the word 'resource.' Resource scarcity, both in terms of source and sink, is at the basis of the concept of sustainability from a bio-economic view, setting normative boundaries to human economic growth (Daly 1992). But in the modern strategic management framework, the concept of 'resources' was assigned a totally different meaning, acquiring value only within the perspective of competitive advantage (Wernerfelt 1984; Prahalad and Hamel 1990; Barney 1991). These considerations will be discussed below.

The Resource Perspective

The term 'resource' may refer to different concepts, according to the theoretical 'milieu' in which it appears (for example, biology, ecology, economy, sociology, and so on). In the SD framework, resources are the means available for the development of a nation— or a population—and include natural resources (natural capital in terms of sources and sink), economic resources (like capital goods and other forms of economic capital), and human resources (like intellectual and social or relational capital). As noted above, ecological economics has stressed that natural resources have specific properties that differentiate them from other forms of capital and make them irreplaceable. Natural resources are often classified as renewable or non-renewable, according to the capacity to restock themselves and be used indefinitely. When resources are consumed at a rate faster than that of replacement, the stock diminishes and eventually extinguishes itself. This equilibrium is a key issue in sustainability theory. It depends on the relation between the behaviour of human organizations, including firms, and the biosphere. The SD concept conceived within the bio-economic theoretical framework internalizes the question of stocks and resource flows. The physical availability of commodities— oil, water, metals, and so on—and the absorptive capacity of sinks are the essence of environmental sustainability. The effectiveness of sustainable development is grounded in an understanding of the 'materiality' of natural resources, either as isolated parts or as systemic, and is tied to their intrinsic scarcity as much as to the economic and social value they generate.

A completely different view of the concept of resources has been contributed by management science. Researchers in the field of strategic management developed the resource-based view (RBV) theory (Wernerfelt 1984; Prahalad and Hamel 1990; Barney 1991) in response to the dominant structure-conduct-performance paradigm of the industrial organization (Bain 1959; Porter 1985). The RBV grew from the seminal work of Penrose (1959) and developed in the last two decades to the extent that it can probably be considered the most influential theoretical framework in management science

(Barney 2001). This theory posits that internal assets—resources and capabilities—are the basis of the firm's competitive advantage. Resources are classified into three main categories: tangible, intangible, and personnel-based. Tangible resources include physical resources such as plants, technological devices, raw materials, and financial reserves. Intangibles include reputation, loyalty, knowledge, and technology. Personnel-based resources consist of culture, expertise of workers and employees, and their commitment (Grant 1991).

According to the RBV, resources are not productive when considered in isolation. To be effective in generating competitive advantage, they must be assembled and integrated through the firm's organizational capabilities. The concept of resources, therefore, is linked to the notion of capabilities and both can be viewed as 'bundles of tangible and intangible assets, including a firm's management skills, its organizational processes and routines, and the information and knowledge it controls' (Barney 2001, p. 621). Moreover, according to this view, productive resources must be valuable (rent producing), irreplaceable, rare (or firm specific), or difficult to imitate (that is, causally ambiguous and socially complex) (Barney 1991). Starting from this compact and effective theoretical framework, as Russo and Fouts wrote in 1997 (p. 537), scholars in the strategic field 'expanded the RBV of the firm to include the constraints imposed and opportunities offered by biophysical environment.' Hart, who can be considered the father of the natural-resource-based view, stated in a popular article that probably gave birth to this approach: 'In the future, it appears inevitable that business (markets) will be constrained by and dependent upon ecosystems (nature). In other words, it is likely that strategy and competitive advantage in the coming years will be rooted in capabilities that facilitate environmentally sustainable economic activity—a natural-resource-based view of the firm.' (Hart 1995, p. 991)

RBV theory has occupied a position progressively more central to studies on corporate sustainability, providing a conceptual framework for incorporating environmental and social issues into strategic management and deeply influencing the last decade of research streams.[11] The main focus in this broad series of contributions has been to understand the role of specific corporate resources—and

[11]See Aragón-Correa 1998; Aragón-Correa and Sharma 2003; Christmann 2000; Russo and Fouts 1997; Sharma and Vredenburg 1998.

capabilities—in the development of proactive strategy based on sustainability leading to superior performance and competitive advantage. This conceptualization of resources has nothing to do with the notion of resources at the core of the bio-economic view of SD. Even the characteristics of 'scarcity' and 'non-substitutability' have different meanings, according to heterogeneous theoretical frameworks. As noted in the previous section, managerial science has internalized in its system of rules the concept of natural resources, as a means of attaining sustainable competitive advantage. Russo and Fouts stress that 'physical resources can be a source of competitive advantage if companies outperform equivalent assets within competitors' (Russo and Fouts 1997, p. 538). But when bio-economic theory deals with resources, they become physical inputs (or sinks) to transformation and consumption processes, and the focus is on how to preserve them (or preserve the services they provide).

Management scholars and theoreticians have thus modified the framework of organizational strategy to include the constant drive toward sustainability—at both the environmental and social levels. This effort to understand the mechanisms that link SD to CS/CSR and CS/CSR to competitive advantage is built into the theoretical framework of organizational science, which has in turn inspired an intensive amount of research that helped expand the definition of the challenges posed by sustainable development for companies and businesses. This focus encompasses more consensus than was previously possible (Shrivastava 1995b; Bansal 2002; Hart and Milstein 2002). But, according to this view, the scarcity of natural resources, which are an intrinsic component of natural capital and a pillar of SD from a bio-economic view, has been de-emphasized in CS/CSR models and strategies—which brings us to the second point of divergence in the level of analysis: hierarchies and capital substitutability.

Hierarchies and Capital Substitutability

Having advocated a strict and prescriptive view of sustainable development, aligned with the bio-economic theoretical framework (Daly and Cobb 1989; Costanza 1991, Köhn 1998), this chapter now turns to the question how these concepts are applied in management science, in the areas of CS and CSR. In terms of the definitions proposed above, in fact, a different conceptual approach seems to prevail at the firm level: that is, firms are most concerned with balancing in a contingent way the three dimensions—environmental, social, and economic—of sustainability (Elkington 1994 and 1997), or balancing different stakeholder needs and requests (Freeman 1984). For example, Post *et al.* (2002) emphasize how the capacity of a company to generate value over time, in the long run, depends on its relationship with the stakeholders, and that 'the stakeholder relationship may be the most critical one at a particular time or on a particular issue' (Post *et al.* 2002, p. 9).

If we consider the evolutionary path of the CS/CSR framework, it is possible to state that the 'triple-bottom-line' added a fresh and new flavour to the concept of firm sustainability, which up to a few years ago was perceived strictly as 'sustainable competitive advantage'. Of course, in practical terms, many scholars have observed that companies have difficulties in adopting a balanced view between environmental concerns, social issues, and economic value. In other words, economic sustainability is still the prevalent consideration, widely influencing organizational goals and decision-making (Bansal 2002). But a triple-bottom-line approach requires that the three forms of SD be addressed simultaneously. A CS- or CSR-oriented firm should consider: a) the environmental principle, which establishes that the consumption of natural resources should be (at the least) consistent with the rate of natural reproduction and the carrying capacity; b) the social principle, which ensures that companies respect and increase the human capital and the social capital of the communities where they operate; and c) the economic principle, which guarantees that companies create a wide-ranging value to shareholders and other stakeholders. However, if we accept the idea of strong sustainability at a macro level, even the triple-bottom-line view is probably not sufficient to transpose the concept of SD at the firm level. This argument is based on two main considerations.

First, the equitable integration of the three dimensions of sustainability in the long term is somehow dissociated from the assumption that economic, social, and environmental dimensions are interconnected. But according to a hierarchical model, the notion of SD requires prioritizing decisions consistently with a precise scale of values, which in turn is based on resource scarcity, resource boundaries, and contingent circumstances—for example, sudden and unexpected crises of the systems considered, whether ecological, social, or economic. Defining hierarchies allows for priorities and facilitates the management of structural trade-offs among different aspects of SD. For example, the problem of the ozone layer and chlorofluorocarbons (CFC) pollutants led to a phase-out regulation, prescribed at the international level by the Montreal Protocol. The global ban on these substances had a direct impact on industries, companies, and employees, generating a trade-off between environmental protection goals, economic value, and social issues. At the same time, the question of ozone depletion and the prioritization among the three aspects of sustainability obliged several companies to cease production and turn to other activities. Another example is the Kyoto Protocol and the enforcement of the emission trading system. Even in this case, the theoretical model sets limits on global emissions based on environmental boundaries. This priority conditions the other dimensions of sustainability, both the economic and the social.

At the company level, in order to comply with these binding regulations, strategic behaviours are required, involving trade-offs between the three domains. The issue of air quality is a case in point. If a company generates a certain amount of emissions per unit of product/service, and it is forced to respect the carrying capacity limits, its emissions must accumulate at a rate less than the absorption capacity of the natural system. If the balance between the accumulation rate of pollutants and the absorption capacity is not respected, it will run up against its carrying capacity and cease to grow. Therefore, either the technology efficiency improves enough to compensate for the growth of sales in absolute values to maintain the absolute quantity of emissions in the limits, or the company must no longer seek growth. Many firms must cope with this trade-off in their everyday activities in that the increase in technological efficiency and resource productivity cannot compensate for market growth.

Concerning the theoretical debate, the question that arises is whether management science will accept such physical limits to production, if not offset by increments in efficiency and productivity. In other words, as strong sustainability forces prioritizing among the different domains—natural, social, and economic—the pursuits of CS and CSR must adapt their own framework to include the principle of limits. A radical change in management science is thus obligatory; after all, value creation is the ultimate goal of companies (Jensen 2000); it follows that the notions of CS and CSR are consistent with the triple-bottom-line approach. The idea of balancing and harmonizing in a contingent way the different dimensions of sustainability coheres with the long-term capacity of the firm to generate and maintain a competitive advantage. But balancing different tasks according to the management framework involves the possibility of dissolving hierarchies and boundaries between systems, while strong sustainability might entail prioritizing environmental integrity over economic value creation.

The second consideration, decisively linked to the first, concerns the substitutability among various types of capital. As previously noted, according to CS/CSR management theory, it is possible to sacrifice a specific performance in one dimension for the sake of better performances in other dimensions of sustainability. In this view, different forms of capital—natural, social, and economic—are considered substitutable in the short term, thus contributing to sustainability in the long term. The idea is that different forms of capital compensate for each other. As an example, consider a company that develops new markets for its consumer goods in emerging countries, leveraging on a socially responsible business model that respects the existing social capital and improves the well-being of local communities. This company is probably creating economic value, reducing poverty, and increasing social equity. The same company, on the other hand, is probably indirectly modifying the environmental integrity of its surroundings, creating less environmentally sustainable consumption patterns, and increasing the amount of waste generated and dispersed in the natural environment or augmenting water pollution. The company probably considers its strategies responsible, in that several stakeholders are satisfied with this value-creation process. The firm is balancing different needs in order to preserve and improve its capacity to generate value. On the other hand, this behaviour works against the strong-sustainability model that considers different forms of capital only slightly interchangeable at best.

There are two main implications of this argument. First, at the theoretical level, managerial studies on CS and CSR are at odds with the strong-sustainability view. The inclusion of sustainable development in management literature responds to a different goal that definitely requires long-term corporate sustainability, and therefore accepts that specific expectations might be more important than others at certain times.

Moreover, these expectations depend not on the hierarchical view, but on contingent factors. Corporate-sustainability theory seeks to embrace environmental constraints and social issues, but when external prescriptions intrude, the fact must be faced that natural capital is not dispensable, and a disassociation between the macro SD concept promoted by bio-economic analysis and the management science approach to CS and CSR becomes evident. The second point, related to the practical implications of this conceptual divergence, refers back to the above example, where a number of large corporations, for contingent reasons, agree to sacrifice the same set of performances, thus making the whole system unsustainable. The exploitation of natural capital beyond its carrying capacity would be acceptable where a significant improvement in social conditions occurs and companies generate economic value for their shareholders. But, for bio-economists, natural capital is not interchangeable with other forms, and the time scale and velocity of its autonomous recovery are not comparable with the lifetime scale of such human organizations as companies.

CONCLUSION

The goal of this paper is to explore the reasons why the concept of sustainable development, after more than twenty years of policies and regulations at the international, national, and local levels which support the idea, is still so far from implementation. In exploring this question, the concept of sustainable development has been transposed from the macro to the corporate dimension. Companies, in fact, are a productive resource of our socio-economic system and key to the eventual implementation of sustainability (Schmidheiny 1992). According to management theory, the attempt to include sustainability issues in the managerial framework can be divided into two separate issues: CS and CSR. The actualization of the theoretical pillars of SD within CS/CSR seems crucial to effectively respond to the challenges posed by sustainability.

The first finding of the study is that between the macro and company dimensions, a significant theoretical gap persists due to the disparity between the disciplines in which the concepts of SD, CS, and CSR are grounded. The field of ecological economics has shaped the notion of SD, addressing the question of hierarchies and physical limits, and the non-substitutability of different forms of capital.

The strong version of sustainability has defined a new framework for economics, in which boundaries to growth are conceptually established and accepted. But such a version of sustainability is seen by many to be hardly practicable, complex to implement, and probably extremely costly (Sneddon et al. 2006). The *missing link*, however, can be found within the different perspectives of managerial science. Both the approaches of CS and CSR came to life within the paradigm of competitive advantage and the creation of economic value for shareholders. Therefore, when these theories have included environmental and social sustainability, they were easily absorbed into the existing framework of sustainable competitive advantage and value creation—a reality confirmed by the increasing number of articles and papers that have appeared in managerial literature since the mid-1990s.

Management theory has attempted to adapt the principles of sustainable development—for instance, the triple-bottom-line—and has explored the effects of environmental strategies and social strategies on competitive advantage. In other words, the management theoreticians have tried to explore and understand which company's capabilities and strategies optimize the environmental and social performance without resulting in economic underperformance. On the other hand, management theory has thus far been unable to include the concept of boundaries and the non-substitutability of different forms of capital as a prescriptive norm for strategic planning. Automakers, for example, are improving the environmental efficiency of cars through several innovations. However, they cannot give up on developing new markets (China, India, and so on), where the growth in demand will eclipse the gains achieved by improvements in the environmental efficiency of cars and their prioritization. Furthermore, the managerial approach to SD accepts short-term compromises among different sustainability goals, but these may lead to irreversible loss in certain forms of capital, which in the long run could compromise the efficiency of other systems.

The discussion in this chapter suggests the following **proposition**: *From a strong sustainability perspective, companies which seem to be CS- or CSR-oriented (according to the managerial theory) when considered separately, are not necessarily sustainable when considered all together.*

Strong sustainability requires that organizations understand the physical and social constraints to the creation of economic value. There is a critical need to bridge the theoretical distance between ecological economics and managerial science in order to better integrate these two domains. Research on the possibility of integrating such concepts as the physical limits to growth and carrying capacity, hierarchies, and non-substitutability of forms of capital into management theory should be carried out in the future.

Moreover, in order to bridge the gap between these two disciplines, by transferring boundaries from the macro to the micro dimension, new measurement techniques to assess the corporate contribution to sustainability must be explored. Practical tools to support decision-making processes are needed to systematically evaluate the impact of products and services on the natural environment and society. In particular, the transition from relative to absolute measures must be improved, in that absolute measures are essential to evaluate the effective contribution of a company to SD, linking the organizational system with the notion of limits and carrying capacity associated with its production activity. Interesting examples in this context have been proposed in economics (Callens and Tyteca 1999; Figge and Hahn 2004), management, and accounting (Dyllick and Hockerts 2002; Schaltegger and Wagner 2006) literature, but these methods have yet to achieve consensus among scholars and practitioners.

Along with the need for a more cohesive and integrated perspective on SD and CS/CSR, this study suggests another important issue. Companies behave according to strategic systems that are grounded in management theory, including the creation of economic value and competitive advantage. When structural trade-offs between natural capital preservation, social integrity maintenance, and economic growth take place, and no short-term compensation is accepted, SD requires external regulations to coerce and force firms to respond to specific external rules. Although individual firms are committed to promoting CS and CSR as a voluntary response to increasing pressures from different stakeholders, these efforts are probably inadequate compared to the challenges posed by SD, as these challenges require the acceptance of a long-term compromise between economic development, social well-being, and nature preservation.

Consequently, to address these challenges, a key step is the enforcement of regulations and norms at the international, national, and local levels. On the one hand, this enforcement must involve developing countries in equitable ways, in that probably one of the greatest social and environmental problems will occur as countries like China, India, Brazil continue their economic growth. Future regulations should include forms of economic compensation and redistribution of the environmental and social obligations that burden poor countries and as well as those specified as heavy polluters that have already achieved high levels of progress. On the other hand, effective control and sanction systems for rule-breaking organizations must be established. Whereas firms and markets cannot adopt limits and hierarchies that do not foster the creation of economic value, such external forces as regulations and norms become crucial to the improvement of the sustainability of production processes and consumption patterns.

REFERENCES

AccountAbility, *AccountAbility 2000 (AA1000) Framework. Standard, Guidelines and Professional Qualification*, London: Accountability, 1999, available at: *http://www.accountability.org.uk*

Aragón-Correa, J.A., S. Sharma, 'A Contingent Resource-based View of Proactive Environment Strategy', *Academy of Management Journal*, 28, 2003, pp. 71–88.

Aragón-Correa, J.A., 'Strategic Proactivity and Firm Approach to the Natural Environment', *Academy of Management Journal*, 41 (5), 1998, pp. 556–67.

Atkinson, G., T. Hett, J. Newcombe, 'Measuring 'Corporate Sustainability', CSERGE Working Paper, 1999, available at *http://www.uea.ac.uk/env/cserge/pub/wp/gec/gec_1999_01.pdf* accessed on 7 June 2007.

Bain, J.S., *Industrial organization*, New York: Wiley, 1959.

Bansal, P., 'Evolving Sustainably: 'A Longitudinal Study of Corporate Sustainable Development', *Strategic Management Journal*, 26 (3), 2005, pp. 197–218.

Bansal, P., 'The Corporate Challenges of Sustainable Development', Academy of Management Executive, 16 (2), 2002, pp. 122–31.

Barbier, E., 'The Concept of Sustainable Economic Development', *Environmental Conservation*, 14 (2), 1987, pp. 101–10.

Barney, J.B., 'Resource-based Theories of Competitive Advantage: A Ten-year Retrospective on the Resource-based View', *Journal of Management*, 27, 2001, pp. 643–50.

Barney, J.B., 'Firm Resources and Sustained Competitive Advantage', *Journal of Management*, 17 (1), 1991, pp. 99–120.

Bateson, G., *Steps to an Ecology of Mind*, New York: Ballantine, 1972.

Baumert, K.A., T. Herzog, J. Pershing, 'Navigating the Numbers: Greenhouse Gas Data and International Climate Change', Washington, DC: World Resources Institute, 2005.

Callens, I., D. Tyteca, 'Towards Indicators of Sustainable Development for Firms: A Productive Efficiency Perspective', *Ecological Economics*, 28, 1999, pp. 41–53.

Capra, F., *The Hidden Connections: Integrating the Biological, Cognitive and Social Dimensions of Life into a Science of Sustainability*, Toronto, ON: Doubleday, 2002.

Capra, F., *The Web of Life: A New Scientific Understanding of Living Systems*, New York: Anchor Books: 1996.

Carey, J., and S.R. Shapiro, 'Global Warming', Cover Story, *Business Week*, Issue 3896, August 16, 2004, pp. 60–9.

Carroll, A.B., 'The Pyramid of Corporate Social Responsibility: Towards the Moral Management of Organizational Stakeholders', *Business Horizons*, 34, 1991, pp. 39–48.

Carroll, A.B., 'A Three-dimensional Model of Corporate Social Performance', *Academic of Management Review*, 4, 1979, pp. 497–505.

Carroll, A.B., and A.K. Bucholtz, *Business & Society: Ethics and Stakeholder Management*, 5th edition, Mason, OH: Thomson—South Western, 2002.

Carson R., *Silent Spring*, Boston: Houghton Mifflin, 1962.

CEC (Commission of the European Communities), The Sixth European Community Environmental Action Programme 'Environment 2010: Our Future, Our Choice', 2001a. *http://ec.europa.eu/environment/newprg/pdf/6eapbooklet_en.pdf*, accessed on 5 June 2007.

CEC (Commission of the European Communities), *A Sustainable Europe for a Better World: A European Union Strategy for Sustainable Development*, 2001b, available at: *http://europa.eu/eur-lex/en/com/cnc/2001/com2001_0264en01.pdf*, accessed on 7 June 2007.

CEC (Commission of the European Communities), Green Paper 'Promoting a European Framework for Corporate Social Responsibility', 2001c, available at: *http://ec.europa.eu/employment_social/soc-dial/csr/greenpaper_en.pdf*, accessed on 5 June 2007.

CEC (Commission of the European Communities), *Corporate Social Responsibility: A Business Contribution to Sustainable Development*, 2002., available at: *http://ec.europa.eu/employment_social/publications/2002/ke4402488_en.pdf*, accessed on 5 June 2007.

Christmann, P., 'Effects of 'Best Practices' of Environmental Management on Cost Advantage: the Role of Complementary Assets', *Academy of Management Journal*, 43, 2000, pp. 663–80.

Commoner B., Making Peace with the Planet, New York: Phanteon, 1990.

Costanza, R. (ed), *Ecological Economics: The Science and Management of Sustainability*, New York: Columbia University Press, 1991.

Costanza, R., H. Daly, and J. Bartholomew, 'Goals, Agenda, and Policy Recommendations for Ecological Economics' in *Ecological Economics: The Science and Management of Sustainability*, R. Costanza (ed), New York: Columbia University Press, 1991.

Crane, A., and D. Matten, *Business Ethics*, Oxford: Oxford University Press, 2004.

Daly, H., *Steady-State Economics*, London: EarthScan Publications, 1992.

Daly, H., and J. Cobb, *For the Common Good: Redirecting the Economy Toward Community, the Environment, and a Sustainable Future*, Boston: Beacon Press, 1989.

Dasgupta, P., *Social Capital and Economic Performance: Analytics*, working paper. Stockholm: University of Cambridge and Beijer International Institute of Ecological Economics, 2002.

Donaldson, T., and T.W. Dunfee, *Ties that Bind: A Social Contract Approach to Business Ethics*, Cambridge: Harvard Business School Press, 1999.

Donaldson, T., and L. Preston, 'The Stakeholder Theory of the Corporation: Concepts, Evidence and Implications', *Academy of Management Review*, 20, 1995, pp. 65–91.

Dyllick, T., and K. Hockerts, 'Beyond the Business Case for Corporate Sustainability', Business Strategy and the Environment, 11, 2002, pp. 130–141.

Elkington, J., *Cannibals with Forks: The Triple-bottom-line of 21st Century Business*, Oxford: Capstone, 1997.

Elkington, J., 'Towards the Sustainable Corporation: Win-Win-Win: Business Strategies for Sustainable Development', *California Management Review*, 36, 1994, pp. 90–100.

Figge, F., and T. Hahn, 'Sustainable Value Added-measuring Corporate Contributions to Sustainability Beyond Eco-Efficiency', *Ecological Economics*, 48, 2004, pp. 173–87.

Freeman R.E., 'The Wall-Mart Effect and Business, Ethics, and Society', *The Academy of Management Perspectives*, 20 (3), 2006, pp. 38–41.

Freeman, R.E., *Strategic Management: A Stakeholder Approach*, Boston: Pitman Publishing, 1984.

Freeman, R.E., A. Wiks, B. Parmar, and J. McVea, 'Stakeholder Theory: the State of the Art and Future Perspectives', *Politeia*, 74, 2004, pp. 9–22.

Fussler, C., and P. James, *Driving Eco-Innovation: A Breakthrough Discipline for Innovation and Sustainability*, London: Pitman Publishing, 1996.

Gladwin, T.N., J.J. Kennelly, and T.S. Krause, 'Shifting Paradigms for Sustainable Development: Implications for Management Theory and Research', *Academy of Management Review*, 20, 1995, pp. 874–907.

Grant R.M., 'The Resource-Based Theory of Competition Advantage', *California Management Review*, 33 (3), 1991, pp. 114–35.

Gunther, M., D. Burke, and J.L. Yang, 'The Green Machine' (Cover story), *Fortune*, 154 (3), August 7, 2006, pp. 34–42.

Hall, J., and H. Vredenburg, 'The Challenges of Sustainable Development Innovation', *Sloan Management Review*, 45 (1), 2003, pp. 61–8.

Harrison, J.S., and R.E. Freeman, 'Stakeholders, Social Responsibility, and Performance: Empirical Evidence and Theoretical Perspectives', *Academy of Management Journal*, 42, 1999, pp. 479–85.

Hart, S.L., 'A Natural-Resource-Based Biew of the Firm', *Academy of Management Review*, 20, 1995, pp. 986–1014.

Hart, S.L., and M.B. Milstein, 'Creating Sustainable Value', *Academy of Management Executive*, 17 (2), 2003, pp. 56–67.

Hart, S.L., and M.B. Milstein, 'Global Sustainability and the Creative Destruction of Industries', *Sloan Management Review* 41 (1), 1999, pp. 23–33.

Hicks, J.R., *Value and Capital 2nd edition*, London: Oxford University Press, 1948.

Hoffman, A.J., 'Institutional Evolution and Change: Environmentalism and the U.S. Chemical Industry', *Academy of Management Journal*, 42 (4), 1999, pp. 351–71.

ISO, *The ISO Survey—2005*, 2005, available at *http://www.iso.org/iso/survey2005.pdf*, accessed on 6 June 2007.

Jonas H., 'The Imperative of Responsibility: In Search of an Ethics for the Technological Age', Chicago: University Of Chicago Press, 1985.

Köhn, J., 'Thinking in Terms of System Hierarchies and Velocities. What Makes Development Sustainable?', *Ecological Economics*, 26, 1998, pp. 173–87.

KPMG, KPMG International Survey of Corporate Responsibility Reporting 2005. June, available at: www.kpmg.com.au/Default.aspx?TabID= 1278&KPMGArticleItemID=1685, accessed on 22 May 2008.

Lehtonen, M., 'The Environmental-Social Interface of Sustainable Development: Capabilities, Social Capital, Institutions', *Ecological Economics*, 49, 2004, pp. 199–214.

Lovelock, J., *The Ages of Gaia: A Biography of Our Living Earth*, New York: W.W. Norton & Company, 1988.

Lovins, A.B., L.H. Lovins, and P. Hawken, 'A Road Map for Natural Capitalism', *Harvard Business Review* May-June, 1999, pp. 145–58.

Martinez-Alier, J., *Ecological Economics: Energy, Environment and Society*, Oxford: Basil Blackwell, 1987.

Morin, E., *L'écologie généralisée*, Paris: Edition de Seuil, 1980.

Naess A., and D. Rothenberg, Ecology, *Community and Lifestyle: Outline of an Ecosophy*, Cambridge: Cambridge University Press, 1990.

Norgaard, R.B. and Howarth, R.B., 'Sustainability and discounting the future', in *Ecological Economics: The Science and Management of Sustainability*, R. Costanza (ed), New York: Columbia University Press, 1991.

Odum, E.P., *Ecology and Our Endangered Live-Support Systems*. Sunderland, MA: Sinauer Associates, 1993.

Passet, R., *L'économique et le vivant*. Paris: Payot, 1996.

Pearce, D., E.B. Barbier, and A. Markandya, *Sustainable Development: Economics and Environment in the Third World*, London: Earthscan Publications, 1990.

Pearce, D.W., A. Markandya, and E. Barbier, *Blueprint for a Green Economy*, London: Earthscan Publications, 1989.

Pearce, D.W., and R.K. Turner, *Economics of Natural Resources and the Environment*, Brighton: Wheatsheaf, 1989.

Penrose, E.T., *The Theory of Growth of the Firm*, London: Blackwell, 1959.

Perrings, C., *Economics of Ecological Resources: Selected Essays*, London: Edward Elgar, 1997.

Porter, M.E., and C. van der Linde, 'Green and Competitive', *Harvard Business Review*, 73, 1995, pp. 120–34.

Post, J.E., L.E. Preston, and S. Sachs, *Redefining the Corporation: Stakeholder Management and Organizational Wealth*, Palo Alto: Stanford University Press, 2002.

Prahalad, C.K., and G. Hamel, 'The Core Competencies of the Corporation', *Harvard Business Review*, 68 (3), 1990, pp. 79–91.

Putnam, R.D., Bowling Alone: *The Collapse and Revival of American Community*, New York: Simon and Schuster, 2000.

Putnam, R.D., *Making Democracy Work: Civic Traditions in Modern Italy*, Princeton: Princeton University Press, 1993.

Rondinelli, D.A., and M.A. Berry, 'Environmental Citizenship in Multinational Corporation: Social Responsibility and Sustainable Development', *European Management Journal*, 18 (1), 2000, pp. 70–84.

Russo, M.V., and P.A. Fouts, 'A Resource-based Perspective on Corporate Environmental Performance and Profitability', *Academy of Management Journal*, 40 (3), 1997, pp. 534–59.

Schmidheiny, S., *Changing Course: A Global Business Perspective on Development and the Environment*, Cambridge, MA: MIT Press, 1992.

Schmidheiny, S., and F. Zorraquin, *Financing Change: The Financial Community, Eco-efficiency, and Sustainable development*, Cambridge, MA: MIT Press, 1996.

Sen, A., *Development as Freedom*, Oxford: Oxford University Press, 1999.

Sen, A., *On Ethics and Economics*, Oxford: Basil Blackwell, 1987.

Sharma, S., and H. Vredenburg, 'Proactive Corporate Environmental Strategy and the Development of Competitively Valuable Organizational Capabilities', *Strategic Management Journal*, 19 (8), 1998, pp. 729–53.

Shiva V. (ed), *Biodiversity: Social and Ecological Perspectives*, Zed Press, U.K: Zed Press, 1992.

Shrivastava, P., 'The Role of Corporations in Achieving Ecological Sustainability', *Academy of Management Review*, 20 (1), 1995a, pp. 936–60.

Shrivastava, P., 'Environmental Technologies and Competitive Advantage', *Strategic Management Journal*, 16, 1995b, pp. 183–200.

Shrivastava, P., and S. Hart, 'Creating Sustainable Corporations', *Business Strategy and the Environment* 4, 1995, pp. 154–65.

Small, B., and N. Jollands, 2006. 'Technology and Ecological Economics: Promethean Technology, Pandorian Potential', *Ecological Economics*, 56, 2006, pp. 343–58.

Sneddon, C., R.B. Howarth, and R.B. Norgaard, 'Sustainable Development in a Post-Brundtland World', *Ecological Economics* 57, 2006, pp. 253–68.

Solow, R.M., 'On the Intergenerational Allocation of Natural Resources', *Scandinavian Journal of Economics,* 88, 1986, pp. 141–9.

Starik, M., and A.A. Marcus, 'Introduction to the Special Research Forum on the Management of Organizations in the Natural Environment: A Field Emerging from Multiple Paths, with Many Challenges Ahead', *Academy of Management Journal*, 43, 2000, pp. 539–46.

Stiglitz, J., 'A New Agenda for Global Warming', *The Economists' Voice*, 3 (7), 2006, Article 3. available at: *http://www.bepress.com/ev/vol3/iss7/art3*, accessed on 5 June 2007.

The Economist, 'The Heat is on', Vol. 380, Issue 8494, September 9th–15th, 2006, pp. 11–12.

The Economist, 'Don't Despair: Grounds for Hope on Global Warming', Vol. 377, Issue 8456, December 10th–16th, 2005, pp. 11–12.

United Nations, European Commission, International Monetary Fund, Organization for Economic Co-operation and Development, World Bank, Handbook of National Accounting, Integrated Environmental and Economic Accounting, final draft circulated for information prior to official editing, 2003, *http://unstats.un.org/unsd/pubs/gesgrid.asp?ID=55*, accessed on 5 June 2007.

van Marrewijk, M., 2003. 'Concepts and Definitions of CSR and Corporate Sustainability: Between Agency and Communion', *Journal of Business Ethics*, 44, 2003, pp. 95–105, WCED (World Commission on Environment and Development), Our Common Future. Oxford: Oxford University Press, 1987.

Wally, N., and , B. Whitehead, 'It's Not Easy Being Green', *Harvard Business Review*, 72(3), 1994, pp. 46–52.

Wernerfelt, B., 'A Resource-based View of the Firm', *Strategic Management Journal*, 5, 1984, pp. 171–80.

Wood, D.J., 'Corporate Social Performance Revisited', *Academy of Management Review*, 16 (4), 1991, pp. 691–718.

WWF, Zoological Society of London, and Global Footprint Network, Living Planet Report 2006, 2006, available at: http://www.panda.org/news_facts/publications/living_planet_report/index.cfm, accessed on 22 May 2008.

3

Sustainability
The Need for Institutional Change[1]

ARILD VATN

INTRODUCTION

How can we make our societies more sustainable? Many have been engaged in studying how the course of development of our societies could be changed to secure life conditions for future generations that are at least as good as those experienced by much of humanity today. Certainly, the fact that the quality of the environment is still deteriorating is of great concern. The United Nations Environment Programme Millennium Ecosystem Assessment concludes that approximately 60 per cent of the world ecosystem services examined are being degraded or used unsustainably (UNEP 2005). The ongoing climatic change is particularly disturbing, as is the present rate of biodiversity loss. The depletion of the world's fishing stocks, growing water shortage, salination problems, and increased desertification are additional elements of a depressing story. The same goes for the increased use and therefore loss of nutrients in various environments. The cycle of organic compounds has doubled in the last forty years. Such changes are of a magnitude that is likely to change the dynamics of any ecosystem. Finally, the sustained production and release of new substances into various ecosystems at almost inconceivable levels increase uncertainty concerning the long-run functioning of these systems.

The social dimension of sustainable development is also extremely worrisome. Poverty alleviation across the globe is slow. World economies are growing at a rate of almost 2.5 per cent per year on an average. In sub-Saharan Africa, the growth rate is negative. In contrast, India,

[1]The author would like to thank Valborg Kvakkestad, Jouni Paavola, and Clive Spash for comments on a draft of the paper.

and more so China, have economies that are growing especially fast with stunning growth rates of 8–10 per cent. However, even in the case of growing economies, large segments of the population are left outside the growth process (UNDP 2003), and there are strong indications that growth rates of this magnitude have very negative environmental impacts.

Growth is hence both a blessing and a curse. It may alleviate poverty and produce decent living conditions. However, as far as economic growth demands increased use of material resources, it also creates pressures on the long-run capacity to sustain these living conditions. In this situation, it is paramount that growth should foremost be directed towards the needs of the poorer sections of the world's population. What we observe, however, is that the fruits of growth are not so directed. We also see that there is nothing in the present system that makes it possible to make a distinction between growth that demands increased throughput and conversion of matter, and growth that does not. Rather, growth under present conditions has an important role in just 'keeping the system going'.

The way we organize much of our production decisions seems to demand growth. The dominant logic of our economic system is that of producing profits for capital accumulation. With low or no growth, investment decisions would be much more unsafe. As a consequence, capital would be wasted and people would risk losing their jobs. Capital accumulation is adversely affected in a maintenance-oriented economy. It needs a continuous creation of new 'frontiers' from which to extract (Princen 1997). As has been observed over and over again since the creation of the institutions of the 'self-regulated' markets in the early nineteenth century, if growth fades, a negative spiral starts, threatening to ruin society.

The same economic system tends to produce huge inequalities. While most of the population in the West are quite rich, the majority of the world's population is always 'relatively' poor. This creates discontent. Hence, the ongoing spiral of increased consumption may persist without reaching any level of saturation (Hirsch 1976). This is a great motor for economic growth, but not for welfare or for sustainable consumption. Recent research confirms that beyond a certain level of GDP per capita, people do not seem to be happier with increasing per capita GDP (Inglehart and Klingemann 2000). While one should certainly be very careful with interpreting the results of such analyses, it seems as if there is fairly little to gain by expanding yearly per capita income beyond US$ 10,000–15,000. If, therefore, poverty eradication and long-run ecological sustainability are at stake, halting capital accumulation and consumption in the rich countries seems to be wise. The problem is that under present institutions, this is not a feasible strategy. The system would break down.

Rather, as we face more and more problems with sustaining our resource base, it is more likely that the system will descend into a very oppressive regime to guard the rich and powerful against the (immediate) consequences of various problems. Looking at past patterns of reactions, the most expected prognosis would be that the rich would detach themselves from the fortunes of the poor. Physical barriers in wealthy regions against, for example, increasing sea level, and physical, legal, and mental barriers against increasing migration pressures will be what we should expect.

To deal with this scenario, we need to think seriously about fundamental institutional reforms. While this concern has been around for decades, we have fallen short in developing and delivering concrete ideas. The magnitude of the issues facing us may have thrown us all back into digging smaller holes. In this chapter, I argue that we also need to dig deep. We need to think innovatively and engage in developing new institutional structures. We need to think about how to change a system based on individualism, restricted responsibility or even irresponsibility, to one of cooperation and extended responsibility.

This chapter is divided into three main parts. Part I emphasizes some core messages concerning the role of institutions in directing and coordinating choices. Part II offers a brief analysis of the way the present system motivates behaviour. Part III looks at some generic principles that could guide the needed institutional change and discusses briefly ways of operationalizing these principles. While quite general, the discussion is hopefully concrete enough to have the potential to create engagement by the wider social and political agents themselves.

I. THE ROLE OF INSTITUTIONS

To be able to discuss which types of institutional change are needed, it is necessary to have a common understanding of what institutions are and what they do, and then to develop insights about how they motivate choice.

Understanding Institutions

Institutions are the conventions, norms, and formal rules of a society. They are hence both formal and informal structures. Some look at them just as constraints, as the 'rules of the game', so to speak. This is typically the perspective taken by the tradition of 'new' institutional economics (North 1990). Here the individual is seen as an autonomous utility maximizer operating under the constraints of institutions. The alternative is to look at institutions also as forming the individual and as creating meaning. They are not just constraints. They are better viewed as *rationality contexts*. This is a core aspect of institutions and is reflected in the works of many authors belonging to the 'classical' tradition of institutional economics (from Veblen and Commons to Bromley and Hodgson).

Certainly, institutions define choice sets and simplify transactions. They do, however, also define the motivation structures pertinent to a certain issue, situation or relationship. The individual has the capacity to act both in individualistic and socially responsible ways (Etzioni 1988; Sen 1977). Therefore, rationality is better understood as a plural concept. Where the neoclassical economists/new institutionalists only see individual and calculative/strategic rationality—maximization of individual utility ('I' rationality)—the classic institutionalists also observe the capacity to act cooperatively and engage in the fortune of the group or of other people—social rationality. The role of institutions is not the least to signal which kind of behaviour—which kind of rationality—is expected and to support us in undertaking accepted acts. They have the capacity to define whether the logic of a specific situation or relation should be of individual or of social rationality (Vatn 2005).

Social rationality may take various forms. Two generic classes may be defined: a) those where the rationale is about the needs or interests of the group to which one belongs ('We' rationality), and b) care for the other ('They' rationality). In the first case, institutions help individuals solving dilemmas that emerge when acts are interdependent. In such situations what is individually rational to do is typically quite different from what is collectively wise. By solving such coordination problems for the group, 'We' rationality, actually, is also favourable for the individual. Certainly, defecting when all others cooperate will offer the highest individual gain. Hence, 'We' rationality implies a certain level of individual restraint necessary to produce the solution that is collectively wise (cooperation) and avoid the detrimental result of widespread defection. It can be viewed as a form of solidarity, or reciprocal altruism as denoted by Crowards (1997).

In the second case—that of 'They' rationality—we encounter genuine care for the other. There is no personal gain involved, rather a loss. Such behaviour is governed by norms about helping people who are in situations defined as difficult, inhumane, etc. This kind of behaviour covers what can be termed 'true' altruism or according to Crowards, 'selfless' altruism.

Institutions are collectively developed rules that tell us when we may take only individual consequences into account, and when we are expected to include wider considerations. Certainly, there are many reasons why we would want institutions to do exactly this. It would first simplify our lives by defining some situations where the individual is free to choose what it prefers (the 'I' logic).[2] Next, it could solve a lot of coordination problems, which would be hard for the individual to handle (the 'We' logic). Finally, it would have the capacity to support us in acting respectfully or helpfully towards others (the 'They' logic).

Concerning the 'We' logic more specifically, a lot of conflict, stress, and wasteful resource use could be avoided if we were not always forced into the Nash equilibrium of all potential 'public goods games' or 'prisoners' dilemma situations' we encounter when our choices are interdependent—that is, when one person's behaviour influences other peoples' opportunities. Hence, there are strong motivations for developing rules defining the cooperative solution as the norm. We observe this in diverse situations, from various sharing strategies found among hunting tribes to the different forms of rules governing how people manage common pool resources (Ostrom 1990). Generally all environmental resources are best understood as interlinked and complex processes. Because of interlinkages, use is interdependent, with all kinds of cooperation problems attached. Because of complexity, potential consequences of what we do are often very hard to foresee.

The problem current generations face, is that we are caught between two developments. On the one hand, institutional change over the last two centuries has to a large extent been directed to foster 'I'

[2]Even in these cases we are not free to do whatever we may like towards others. Certainly, acting in a market implies following a lot of norms and rules concerning, say, 'good business conduct'. This is so despite the fact that markets are established to handle free exchanges.

rationality, as examined by Polanyi (1944). On the other hand, we are confronted with increasing environmental degradation and social despair. The latter developments demand increased capacity to act cooperatively. In simple terms: as the threat to sustainability is institutional, the response must certainly be institutional too, but based on a different direction than the present.

Observing the Various Rationalities

The standard response to the above idea of plural rationality is that it goes against human nature. The human being is fundamentally egoistic. Certainly, the modern developments of Western civilization implied a shift towards increased emphasis on the individual. The development of the discipline of economics is a very clear illustration of this. It is captured both in the way this discipline describes our motivation—characterized by the maximization of individual utility only—and in the institutions it favours—individual property rights and markets. Nevertheless, these institutions are historical constructs. They are characterizing a certain stage of human development, and are not an inevitable consequence of human nature.

Following Polanyi (1944), we would rather conclude that various forms of social rationality appeared prior to 'individualism'. He emphasizes that *reciprocity and redistribution* have been the dominating principles of behaviour across all kinds of societies. It was not until the seventeenth and eighteenth centuries that a gradual process of establishing hedonistic individualism as a dominating logic took place in Western Europe.

Even Adam Smith in his '*Moral Sentiment*' (Smith 1976a [1759])—standing in the middle of this change—emphasized the need for society and community—the need of assisting each other. Hence, there was a duality in his work. On the one hand he saw the great potential in the institutional reorganization of the economy towards an increased role for markets and trade and the possibilities for increased wealth creation therein (Smith 1976b [1776]). He also expressed a fear that this development would favour a kind of 'narrow' individualism that could ruin the reciprocity necessary to keep society flourishing.

Mainstream economics gradually lost touch with these issues and ideas which were instead studied within the confines of such disciplines as sociology and anthropology. These disciplines emphasize a wider understanding of human interaction and capabilities. Moreover, the role institutions play in forming the individual is very prominent. Therefore, the idea of plural rationalities as presented here is not at all new. Concerning the role institutions play in resource management, not least, the work of Elinor Ostrom and colleagues is revealing and offers similar insights.[3] It shows that people managing common resources are able and willing to cooperate and that institutional structures matter for the ability and willingness to do so.

Lately, support for the ideas presented here also comes from a rather unexpected source—that of experimental economics. The findings from ultimatum games,[4] dictator games,[5] public goods games[6] and wage experiments[7] document that people are willing to cooperate even in situations where the expectation, given the logic of individual rationality, would be defection. In ultimatum games, many proposers offer sums to receivers far beyond what one should expect from standard theory about utility maximization—e.g., the dominating divide is 50–50.[8] In these games respondents, moreover, start to refuse splits lower than 70–30. Hence, they punish despite the fact that they lose from doing so. They act reciprocally by being nice to those who are nice to you and by punishing those who act in a non-cooperative way (Gintis 2000).

In dictator games, proposers do not need to offer anything to responders. Still, 70–30 is the dominant divide in many experiments. This indicates the existence of 'They' rationality/'true' altruism. In public goods games, cooperation levels are far above what could be expected, again on the basis of individual rationality. Large fractions cooperate despite the fact that the game is only run once, that participants change if the game is run more than once and so on. If explicit punishment options are available, they tend to be used, despite the fact that it is costly for the individual, and the effect is

[3]See for example, Ostrom (1990, 2000, 2005); Agrawal and Gibson (2001); National Research Council (2002).

[4]See for example, Güth *et al.* (1982); Roth *et al.* (1991); Heinrich *et al.* (2001).

[5]See for example, Forsythe *et al.* (1994); Eckel and Grossmann (1995); Ben-Ner *et al.* (2004).

[6]See for example, Sato (1987); Ledyard (1995); Fehr and Gächter (2000); Ostrom (2000).

[7]See for example, Fehr *et al.* (1997); Fehr and Falk (2002).

[8]In such a game, the so-called proposer gets a sum of money to divide between herself and a receiver. If the receiver, who is unknown to the proposer, accepts the split, both get the money as divided. If the receiver turns the offer down, the two get nothing.

increased cooperation over the rounds in repeated public goods games. Finally, wage games show that employees deliver proportional to what is contracted even though employers do not execute any controls. Under certain conditions, incentive wage structures may even result in less effort, as compared to 'no incentive' (Fehr and Falk 2002). There is evidence that incentives tend to change the logic of the situation from voluntary cooperation to strategic behaviour.[9]

The observation that people behave in ways distinctly different from what could be expected using standard models of individual rationality is now quite commonly accepted also among many mainstream economists. Less acknowledged is the idea that what motivates behaviour varies across institutional contexts. More specifically, we observe that there are actually two types of variation. First, there is substantial individual variation in the experiments. Some act more individualistically than others. Part of this variation might be genetic; part may be due to different upbringing and internalization of norms. Second, we observe variation across institutional contexts. In some situations or contexts, 'I' rationality seems to dominate; in others, various forms of social rationality are key in determining behaviour.

Few experiments are constructed to explicitly bring forward insights about the latter relationship. Nevertheless, it is supported by many observations. First, experiments show that people under certain circumstances act in ways which come quite close to that of individual utility maximization (Holt *et al.* 1986; Davis and Holt 1993). There is, moreover, a growing literature emphasizing that people become individually rational in specific institutional contexts. Shogren (2006, p. 1147) points out that 'Markets create rationality in the population by putting a cost on irrational behavior'[10] While according to Shogren there is only one kind of rationality—that of maximizing individual utility—he refers to a series of studies where experimenters have been able to create situations supporting people in avoiding 'irrational' behaviour. What is needed is simply to make the institutional context or signals 'strong enough'.

---

[9]To get en overview of many of the results obtained in the above type of research see Gintis (2000); Gintis *et al.* (2005); Vatn (2005); Vatn (2006; 2007).

[10]Much of the research in this field seem motivated by various findings indicating that people act in 'irrational ways'; for instance, prospect theory and preference reversals.

Irrationality, however, is not the only alternative to 'rationality'. For example, acting kindly does not have to be seen as some kind of irrationality or weakness of will. Thinking of rationality as plural, and of institutions as capable of supporting different types of rationalities, avoids such miserable conclusions. In some situations, the main problem may be envisioned to be deficient individual capacity to maximize utility or profits. In such contexts, institutions may be created to support that logic. That is what Shogren and others have proposed. In other situations, social rationality could be supported.

While quite obvious to the sociologist, most economists are quite unfamiliar to this approach and would rather go to great lengths, if necessary, to show that what seems to be 'We' or 'They' rationality, is in fact individual maximization. Nevertheless, there are findings also within the experimental and behavioural literature supporting the ideas presented here (Fehr and Falk 2002; Batson 1991; Sober and Wilson 1998).[11] The famous 'Wall Street Game' vs. 'Community Game' as documented in Ross and Ward (1996), is another illuminating example. A public goods game was set up with identical pay-offs. It was, however, run by alluding to two different institutional settings. Calling it the 'Wall Street Game' resulted in significantly lower cooperation than calling it the 'Community Game'. So, even a weak form of institutionalization like naming seems to evoke different norms.

A similar result was found in Hoffman *et al.* (1994). They report results from an ultimatum game where a set of proposers were asked to 'divide' the sum they had received between him-/herself and the respondents. This set of games was compared to another where the splitting of the sum was formulated as an 'exchange' between the proposer and the respondent. Again, different naming resulted in significantly different splits. Relating the game to the market (exchange) increased the level of self-regarding acts. The results of other studies associated with payment for day-care point in the same direction; such as, Gneezy and Rustichini (2000) and Eek *et al.* (2001). In the latter cases people were asked about their perception of private vs. public day-care. While private provisioning resulted in an expectation of treatment relative to the level of payment, public provisioning created expectations about equal treatment independent

---

[11]There is no room to present the findings of these rather complex literatures here. For a more thorough analysis, see Vatn, forthcoming.

of pay (that is, payment differentiated by income). What was considered 'right' was again a function of the institutional context.

Resource Regimes

Institutions can operate as single rules, or they can be combined in systems of rules linked together. A very important set of such connected rules is the *resource regime* (Vatn 2005). This concept covers institutional structures distributing access to resources and regulating their uses. They consist of: a) the property regime governing the use and transfer of the resources themselves (property right), and b) the rules and norms that govern the transactions concerning the products made from the resources (product transfer).

The literature distinguishes between four types of property regimes: a) private property, b) state or public property, c) common property, and d) open access (Bromley 1991). While each type has some clear distinctive characteristics, every one of them also covers quite a large variation of institutional structures. This also implies that some may generate rather similar types of behaviour—for instance, a private corporation and a state-owned stock company—while in other situations the differences are quite distinct as in the case of a private firm and a publicly managed entity such as a hospital (Vatn 2001; Vatn 2007).

State or public property might be viewed as a special form of common property (Vatn 2005). Following Paavola (2007), drawing the main distinction between private and common property with public property as a sub-group of the latter makes sense. This brings the definition of regimes clearer in line with the distinction between 'I' and 'We' rationality. Moreover, a state regulation of externalities through, for example, environmental taxes or emission licenses can be compared to the rules established by a common property regime concerning, for example, access to water in a common irrigation system. Certainly, the level of action and the number of people involved differs. So, too, does access to formal power. But there are also many similarities. An elaboration of what this may mean for policy follows in later sections.

Looking next at the systems for product transfers, these may take the form of market exchanges, various forms of public rationing or community-based distribution—for example, following Polanyi, redistribution or reciprocity. Private firms generally sell their products in markets, but they may also be involved in producing goods like health care distributed under a state license, which implies that social criteria and not purchasing power may govern distribution. States/ public owners often allot their products to the citizen on the basis of social principles such as giving priority to certain age classes, health status, and so on, or they are offered for free, as in the case of public schools and hospitals. The state however, may also engage in market transactions. Moving to co-owners of a commons, their products are often transferred via market transactions. In this sense, individual co-owners may act like ordinary firms, even though they may also be involved in community-based forms of distribution, sharing, and so on. Again, the mix is influenced by the wider institutional context.

II. INSTITUTIONALIZING SEPARATION AND ONE-DIMENSIONALITY

The basic institutional issue is the balance between the 'I', the 'We', and the 'They' rationalities. Major problems may arise if the individual is subordinated to a common rationality in all instances. There is also a problem if the collective is too weak. Moreover, the way the 'I' or the 'We' rationality is instituted is important. This section will briefly look at the construction of a specific form of 'I' rationality— that of corporate capitalism.

The Creation of Corporate Capitalism

Western modernization and with it the creation of individualism, involved a long process that included the establishment of the economy as a separate sphere. According to Polanyi, the fundamental transformation taking place through the formation of the capitalistic market was to institute the motive of 'gain' and to transform land, labour, and money into the commodity form. Through these changes, all 'inputs' to production could be measured in one dimension— monetary value—and a complete definition of 'gain' or profits became possible. While labour and land had always been involved in human production, Polanyi emphasizes that they were not produced for exchange. 'Labour is only another name for a human activity which goes with life itself, which in its turn is not produced for sale but for entirely different reasons ...; land is only another name for nature, which is not produced by man' (Polanyi 1944, p. 72).

The above process led to the creation of the modern form of individual property rights. Looking at how this concept developed is very illustrative of how social construction comes about. It shows how what were initially controversial issues tend to vanish into a forgotten past. The solution to a contentious issue tends to become an objective fact as materialized through the institutions it produced. When new rules are instituted, this happens on the basis of these institutions constituting 'given facts' and not on the prior—often very conflicting—constructs.

In Locke's time—the late seventeenth century—developing a legitimacy for private property was important, particularly in a context where the enclosure movement was underway in England and Europeans were settling in America. What was demanded was a justification for why someone should have the right to exclude others from a piece of land. Locke argued that the individual creates a property right when he mixes his labour with the products of nature (Locke 1994). Locke, like Adam Smith later, looked at nature as abundant, making exclusion rather unproblematic. Those excluded could always find other pieces of land with which to mix their labour. Nevertheless, Locke emphasized that what was beyond what a man could fix as property by his own labour should belong to others.

When there was no more land to turn to—when economics in the early twentieth century became the 'science' of scarcity—the modern idea of private property was well established, and the initial worries of Locke were totally forgotten. This was partly due also to a belief in technological development making scarcity just a relative and not an absolute concept. Hence again, the potential worry of inequality—both inter- and intra-generational—could be buried in the belief that through material output growth, all of us would in the end be well off.

Moving to the history of a certain form of private property— that of the corporation—we see even more strongly how the construction process had to fight its way through various quite serious counter arguments. When, however, these were defeated, they were generally forgotten.

Bakan offers an analysis of the rise of the corporation. Up until the end of the nineteenth century, the family firm and the partnership dominated economic life. Thereafter, corporations became the dominant way of organizing economic activity. This was not something that could be expected. Bakan writes: 'The corporation's dramatic rise to dominance is one of the remarkable events in modern history, not least because of the institution's inauspicious beginnings' (Bakan 2004, p. 5).

The first joint-stock company was established in England in 1564—the Company of the Mines Royal—based on the need to raise capital for activities of a size beyond that which was possible even for partnerships. By 1688, fifteen such firms with split management and ownership existed. There was a lot of opposition to this institution, not least because of worries concerning the opportunities for fraud. Scandals followed, and in 1720, the right to establish corporate bodies was banned in England by the Bubble Act. This law was in place until 1825.

Meanwhile, the development of the corporation shifted to the United States. Corporations were established to raise enough capital to build railways, and they were looked upon as instruments of government. Moreover, a lot of restrictions were put upon the corporate body. The stockholders had full liability. Corporations could only operate for narrowly defined purposes, for a limited amount of time, and in certain locations. Hence, there were a lot of deliberate restrictions on the growth of a corporation. These were defined on the basis of protecting society against corporate dominance. They reflected the need for taking a multiplicity of interests and values into account.

The first restriction to fall was that of full liability. The idea of limited liability was instituted in England in 1851, substantially lowering the risks of investing in corporations and boosting their growth. Throughout the rest of the century, a process towards establishing the corporation as a legal person was completed. According to Bakan, this happened 'through a bizarre legal alchemy, [where] courts had fully transformed the corporation into a 'person" (ibid., p. 16). The corporate person had taken the place of its owner. Gone was the 'grant theory' of corporations as instruments for governments.

As important were the changes undertaken in the 1890s by the states of New Jersey and Delaware—emphasizing corporations as 'free individuals'. The rules requiring businesses to incorporate only for narrowly defined purposes, to exist only for a limited time, and to operate only in particular locations, were repealed. The rules concerning controls on mergers and acquisitions were also loosened. Finally, the rule against a company holding stocks in other companies was eliminated. Other states had to follow, and the number of corporations in the United States fell from 1800 in 1898 to 157 in 1904.

The concentration of corporate power challenged the legitimacy of the corporation and provoked a social reaction, reflected, for example, in the Trust Buster movement and the demand that corporations act in socially responsible ways. Some corporations were broken up. Some also changed their wage policies in response to this critique. In the 1930s, the concept of corporate social responsibility appeared in parallel to the New Deal policy, which reflected an ideology that remained dominant for several decades. This was superseded by neoliberalism that gained in strength from the late 1970s, changing the role of governments and reducing the power of labour unions as the process of economic globalization accelerated. Even China now embraces corporate economics and we observe how the combination of a powerful one-party state and a corporate business structure is able to foster growth in a magnitude never before observed.

Corporate Economics and Sustainability

In this modern era, the corporation has also been haunted by scandals—for example, the rise and fall of Enron. Our main concern, however, is not with this type of issue, but rather with the consequences of the system for sustainability when operating legally. In relation to this aspect, I will moreover restrict myself to looking primarily at that part of the sustainability triad that is concerned with the environmental resource base.

The history of the corporation is embedded in the wider history of detaching economic activity from the various social relationships within which it used to be embedded (Polanyi 1944). It was a way to institute rationality as maximizing, this time not in the form of utility, in this case, but in the narrower form of returns to invested capital. This construct demanded that numerous instruments be in place to become complete. Many, of course, were in place long before the corporation came into existence. They included, for example, the concept of money, which ensured that every value could be calculated in one dimension, the technology of double book-keeping, and the concept of capital. Taken together, the construction of the bottom line—the one-dimensional measurement of success—became the driving force of the system. To make that possible, one had to institute which consequences should be taken into account—that is, which costs the firm or corporation was responsible for and which were to be carried by the workers or by society. Moreover, all the consequences taken into account had to be measured along the same dimension.

Two consequences of this are important for our discussion. First, the corporate form of capitalism both fosters and depends on economic growth. As emphasized by O'Connor (1994), there is little profit in maintenance. What motivates investment is its return. Growth creates more revenue and it strengthens the expectation of positive returns. Low or zero growth threatens the system by the uncertainty it creates concerning the return on investment. Therefore, the system will restlessly look for new opportunities— new frontiers (Princen 1997). These may be found in the form of new land to exploit. Over time, however, some such 'frontiers' have diminished, intensifying economic and social pressures on those that remain, as well as the search for modern frontiers, found, not the least, in new technologies.

Second, simplifying assessments to one dimension makes decision-making much easier. The creation of the one-dimensional bottom line with its necessary constructs is perhaps the largest revolution in history. It has tremendous power. There are, however, also problems. There are two ways of earning money: that of increasing revenues and that of reducing costs. Costs can be reduced by more efficient resource use, but also by 'cost shifting' (Kapp 1971). At a stage where cost shifting causes minor problems, one could easily support such a growth-creating machine. The situation becomes quite different if we are in a world where the foremost problem is that of escalating 'external effects'. Some of the cost shifting is explicitly illegal as in unlawful dumping and safety violations. Some are legal, but still problematic, as when firms move to countries with weaker restrictions on dumping and safety. Some are legal because they are as yet unobserved or not (yet) regulated. These costs are shifted to the future. Hence, we observe a *systems-dependent displacement of costs* in time and space, a process that is accelerating both because of technological development and the complex patterns of material flows created by the distancing implied by the globalized economy. More fundamentally, if we look at the environment, we observe complexity. We see a system of interlinked processes and feedback loops roughly maintaining their internal and external balances as matter and energy flows through it. The system is basically self-organized—developed over vast time spans where biological and geochemical processes have evolved in gigantic 'experiments' of trial and error. In the long run, only those processes that support each other have survived.

A tremendous amount of information is therefore stored in such a system. Even when exempting all the social dimensions involved in decision-making, we see that the loss of information when simplifying this spectrum of relationships down to one dimension is vast. One must ask: Can a system based on a single bottom line be able to capture what is going on? Can it be made sensitive enough to capture all the various consequences of the behaviour it motivates? Isn't the very logic of the system instead that of 'throwing away' information so that the goal of profit maximization can be made operational?

Bakan (2004) is bothered by these questions. He recognizes that the corporation is in legal terms a 'person'. However, what kind of 'person' is the corporation? To find the answer, he asks a psychologist—Dr. Robert Hare. Using psychological terminology, Hare concludes that the corporation has strong psychopathic characteristics. It is singularly self-interested. It is irresponsible in the sense that 'in an attempt to satisfy the corporate goal, everybody else is put at risk.' It lacks empathy and is unable to feel remorse: 'if (corporations) get caught (breaking the law), they pay big fines and they ... continue doing what they did before' (ibid., p. 57). Hence, they relate superficially or instrumentally to others.

Nevertheless, Bakan insists that managers of corporations are not psychopaths. They may also be caring fathers or mothers, be active in local organizations, and pay a lot of money to civic organizations. This illustrates quite starkly that we simply have to act differently in different institutional contexts. Different institutions are based on different logics or ideas about 'what is right'. The capacity to compartmentalize our lives this way is exactly what makes it possible to live under such quite conflicting demands as that of the CEO and that of a father. One may ask if modernization would have been a possible project without this capacity.

Finally, the issues of growth and multi-dimensionality are interlinked. The basic argument is very simple: the smaller the economy, the fewer the potential impacts on the environment and hence the fewer conflicting issues or dimensions. A one-dimensional system, therefore, serves us better, the less expansive the economy is. On the other hand, the more simplified economic decisions are, the more expansive the system also tends to be. There are just fewer obstacles or interests to be taken into account. The consequence of expansion, however, is higher demands on the information systems we use to direct its development. The success of the system of one-dimensional evaluations tends to ruin its own logical base.

III. CREATING INTEGRATION AND MULTI-DIMENSIONALITY INSTITUTIONS

We face, then, some very difficult decisions. On the basis of the above discussion, I offer a simple thought experiment. Let us assume that with the present organization of the economy, we need a growth rate within the range of 2–2.5 per cent—that is, the average growth rate of the Western countries in the nineteenth century—to avoid economic crises.[12] A sustainable economy in this sense, implies that it must grow approximately eight times in 100 years, more than 60 times in 200 years, and about 500 times in 300 years. Looking back, 300 years is about the age of the corporation as an institutional system. Observe moreover, that institutional change takes time. Observe also, while the creation of the corporation eliminated various social and politically motivated ties and restrictions, creating a more socially responsible system is a far more complex endeavour. Observe finally, that the structure of prevailing institutions has created a series of strong interests that are tied to the structure of the system. On the basis of the data on 'GDP and happiness', referred to in the Introduction, and on the basis of the environmental crises we observe today, we might agree that economic growth should not be an important goal among rich countries any more. Nevertheless, when acting on behalf of firms or governments, this becomes a dangerous position to hold. What is objectively true becomes subjectively impossible to pursue given the structures we have to operate within. Changing these structures is both a necessary and a very demanding task.

Can Self-Correcting Forces Save Us?

One could reasonably argue that technological development will have the capacity to reduce substantially the relative need for material inputs. Competition will be helpful in achieving this, but given the existing institutions, the mechanism only works for priced inputs. Moreover, will we—following our example—be able to reduce inputs per unit of GDP to less than 2 per cent of today's use in 200 years to keep input levels stable over that time span? Following the Millennium Ecosystem Assessment, it seems reasonable to conclude

[12]Since there were several crises in that period, one might ask what growth rate could avoid that fact. The point here is that the lower the rate, the more endemic the problem seems to be.

that we even need to reduce substantially the impact below today's level. Furthermore, even if to some extent this is technically possible, what would really be the effect on the qualitative aspects of materials and products? We will most certainly need to produce a lot of new substances to make such a development even thinkable, multiplying today's problems concerning this issue many times. A specific aspect of this is our capacity to maintain the resilience of the ecological systems on which the economy is dependent (Perrings 1997). This is related to the various qualitative ways by which the economy influences the dynamics of ecosystems.

What, then, about changes in consumption patterns? One might argue that we will not be able to increase consumption by the above magnitude. Actually, the present knowledge about this tells us that any form of 'natural' saturation is a long way off, if it at all exists. The social construction of insaturation seems to be quite 'effective'. Moreover, if it were to materialize, the system would be driven into a crisis. The only chance is that most growth in consumption comes in some kind of dematerialized cultural activities and maintenance.

A third 'solution', related to the latter and actually the most plausible, is that of continuing on the growth-based path. For example, on increased demand for repair of environmental services, and curing health problems following environmental degradation or direct exposure to toxins. This could create a big market for the bottom-line to exploit. This is exactly what should be expected and is already anticipated by some within the corporate world itself. As Hertsgaard (1999, p. 19) emphasizes: 'A growing minority of experts within corporate and government circles believes that restoration of the environment could become a source of virtually limitless profit for consumers and companies alike in the coming century.'[13] How it could offer gains for consumers, though, is a mystery. We might, nevertheless, accept it as a necessary cost of 'progress' (Norgaard 1994). While growth can continue, the issue is about the meaning and price thereof. So, the larger economy may mostly be engaged in repair and consequently not offer a better world to live in. Most probably we move ourselves onto a 'slippery slope' due to the fact that the repair itself will demand environmental resources, the creation of new uncertainties, and so forth.

[13]I am indebted to Lux (2003) for this reference.

Would More of Today's Remedies Do?

A lot of institutional change has already been undertaken. Since these changes have been rather systems-compatible, it would be much easier to look for ways that could strengthen these existing remedies. These can be divided in two. First, we have the idea that if all resources were privately owned, then the market could solve the problems. Second, we have the idea that the state—through various *ex post* regulations—is able to correct the missing signals from markets to firms and establish conditions for a sustainable future.

According to the first solution, the problem is not seen as a result of separation and one-dimensionality. It is rather that there is too little of it. While politically a favourite of neo-liberal thinking, it is as a general strategy fundamentally at odds with the problems we face. The existing and pervasive interrelationships across environmental resources and processes will not disappear by just assuming that the environment can be further divided into pieces that have to be individually controlled and exchanged in the market. The physical characteristics of environmental resources create one kind of limit. The high level of transaction costs following from this solution represents another. Issuing more individual property rights is not always an incorrect remedy. Local ownership—also in the private form—may under certain conditions sustain resources. But, by no means can it constitute the overall solution.

Privatization of information and knowledge is an important part of this story and needs to be commented on. Such a development is expected since research is currently the main basis for creating new opportunities or 'frontiers' for corporate growth. Turning knowledge into a private good implies, however, secrecy and restrictions on general use. This, in itself, creates a social loss. It also increases the uncertainty concerning the quality of the knowledge that becomes available. A temptation to withhold or even manipulate knowledge is created to avoid public awareness of facts that are negative for a certain product or production process.

What, then, about *ex post* state regulations? Certainly, these can be based on multi-dimensional evaluations. The state is not bound by the bottom-line assessment. State regulations, like taxes, are rather directed towards influencing the evaluation by making it costly to pollute. Nevertheless, the bottom line is influential in ways that we rarely think about. This is reflected in the way that state regulations interact with the dynamics of the corporate economic system. Regulations are dominantly *ex post*. They are a reaction to observed and proven external effects. That is, they are instituted many years, often many decennia, after the practices causing the problem started. This relates to the way the burden of proof must be instituted in a world where free entrepreneurship is a fundamental system's value and characteristic.

What is created, therefore, is a public authority—a state—that is running after a moving target. Moreover, the costs of regulation must appear much higher and the level of 'optimal abatement' must be correspondingly much lower in such a system compared to one where actions are *ex ante*. This is because all costs related to readjustments will appear in the calculation of abatement costs in the *ex post* state evaluation. If a firm has invested in a product/production process that later is shown to create harm, the prior investments undertaken as if no harm were to happen will influence the measurement of abatement costs. If regulations instead were *ex ante*, the cost structure would be different. In a fast growing economy, the difference between *ex post* and *ex ante* regulation/measurements could be substantial, indeed. Furthermore, in the period a certain production process and/ or consumption pattern has been accepted to lead to a belief that no harm would occur and strong interests connected to this development will be produced. These interests will demand protection and, through lobbying, do what they can to defend the existing processes/consumption patterns and opt for mild reactions. Certainly, these interests are a creation of the system and the path it is on. If the system were different, so would be the interests involved.

Finally, it is a problem that states must look into and conduct localized analyses. Their jurisdiction is geographically bound, while corporations, under the present regime, may move where they find conditions to be the best. The rights of the corporations create a vast imbalance. While based on the (unfounded) thought that the gains of free movement of capital are greater than its costs, this asymmetry in power is a tremendous challenge to sustainability. It reduces drastically the action potential of states.

Ex-ante Regulations

How can we get around the above problems? One way would be to institute *ex ante* regulations. We already observe some tendencies towards introducing such regulations. The precautionary principle is an example. It was emphasized in the United Nations Earth Summit processes and included in the Cartagena Protocol on biosafety. While still playing a minor or unclear role, the concept is emphasized in national policies as well.

A first step would, therefore, be to develop the system of *ex ante* regulations further. Herman Daly (1977; 1997) has been a strong advocate for implementing a system of input regulations to restrict throughput levels. This implies that quotas are set on how much physical resources can be taken into the economy. This system could offer a strong incentive to shift the direction of growth—to boost re-circulation and dematerialization.

Such a regulation would also have to include a systematic change in the burden of proof requirement from having to prove harm to proving no (serious) harm. This would be necessary to handle the qualitative aspects of throughput since fewer throughputs—*ceteris paribus*—would most probably increase the incentive to convert more of the materials available for the economy. It is not given that the net effect of lower throughput and higher materials transformation offers a better result in the end. If firms were obliged to prove that their materials transformations/new products would not be harmful to the environment, one could in principle also be able to handle the aspect of qualitative shifts in a positive way.

Cooperative and Integrative Institutions

While more *ex ante* regulations could offer progress in the wanted direction, we also recognize that it will be difficult to integrate into today's institutional structures. Taken seriously, it would—due to the existence of irreducible ignorance—imply that the introduction of new technologies in most situations would have to be refused. No proof of safety could be produced. This would endanger the motion of the system and instead of balanced growth, we would see collapse. Insights of this kind explain why the introduction of the precautionary principle has been so restricted. This is easily shown by the strong position of the WTO demanding victims' burden of proof and the limited attempts to introduce the precautionary principle, as in the Biodiversity Convention.

Moreover, policy reforms narrowly focused on reduced throughput and regulations of quality changes would increase distributional problems substantially again, given the characteristics of the system. Reducing throughput would make capital more valuable than before.

Hence, people relying only on their labour would be forced into an even more difficult position. Remember that our present system is at best a 'trickle down system' when it comes to income development. The way productive assets are controlled demands necessary return to investment in those assets for the system to work properly. Consequently, growth in the South will demand growth also in the North, since most assets are controlled from there. If the basis for this accumulation is restricted, the asymmetry in power between those owning capital and those not would actually be strengthened. There is a danger that the idea of environmental sustainability will foster an oppressive social and political system, ruining the capacity to maintain social sustainability.

My point is that it is very hard to produce a system dealing well with sustainability issues if we do not also include changes in the basic motivation structures of economic decisions. What seems to be needed is an institutional reform where the role of social rationality is strengthened and where multi-dimensional and multi-functional assessments are instituted as part of this. Moreover, these considerations must be instituted at the core of the system and not as correcting forces operating at various, continuously changing margins. We need to go from a system based on separation to one based on integration. More completely, we need to go from a system favouring separation, individual rationality, and strategic interaction to one favouring integration, social rationality, and communicative interaction. While separation has been instrumental in boosting growth, it is incompatible with sustainability.

The demand for integration follows from the fact that natural resources and resource flows are interacting in complex processes of various magnitudes and at different scales of time and space. Separation simplifies decision-making, but must inevitably create decisions that are incompatible with the motions of the natural systems and must systematically end up with 'exporting' or displacing the costs of their actions upon other agents.

Increasing the role of social rationality is both a great possibility and a necessity. The positive message from the new research on economic behaviour is that it confirms that social rationality is a fact and that it can be developed and sustained through institutional change. Communicative interaction is finally an important part of making social rationality viable. It fosters such rationality. It fosters cooperative outcomes through establishing increased group solidarity, through supporting the development of consensus, and finally it seems to strengthen the commitments to cooperate (Kopelman *et al.* 2002).

Developing the principles for integrative institutions at the level we are considering here is obviously very demanding. We know that humanity has created a lot of cooperative institutions. Common property regimes are of this kind. They have proven to be successful, but exist mainly for the management of local resources and hence involve rather small groups where it is easier to develop social cohesion and solidarity (Ostrom 1990; National Research Council 2002). Expanding solidarity beyond the local level is a challenge. It is also a necessity when building a new level of civilization—that of integrative cooperation.

To do this, we need to undertake two fundamental changes of the system. First, we need to change the operating principles of the basic unit of the economy—'the firm'. Second, we need to build a governance structure above that level that is able to communicate between these reorganized economic 'going concerns' in ways that: a) facilitate and support their pursuit of sustainability, and b) link decisions at different levels of impact. Some issues can be decided upon locally— that is, where consequences are only local and no higher-level structures are needed. Other decisions affect higher-scale processes due to various interlinkages in scale and time, as in the case of fishing regimes, regional or global pollution, regional or global biodiversity concerns, and climate change.

Concerning principles for linking decisions at different levels, we observe a growing literature—for example, Berkes (2002); Young (2002a and b). While it is very demanding to organize well-functioning hierarchies, we are beginning to understand how it could be done. As Young (2002b) emphasizes, 'the key to success lies in allocating specific tasks to the appropriate level of social organization and then taking steps to ensure that cross-scale interaction produce complementary rather than conflicting actions' (ibid., p. 266). Such an approach is particularly demanding in many cases where important resource dynamics cross national borders—for example, climate change, global biodiversity preservation, and fish species management. It is also a great challenge to civilize and democratize the role of nation-state governments. Certainly, where corruption dominates, where the state is 'owned' by some leaders and not controlled by the citizens, the basic foundation for creating the necessary processes to build well-functioning hierarchies does not exist.

Moreover, many see the state more as part of the problem than a necessary part of the solution. Certainly, there are many occasions where state property has had negative influence on resource use. Local interests and needs may be overridden. It may be viewed as a means to boost export-led economic growth. The phenomenon of 'crony capitalism' has been observed in many countries of South-East Asia (Dauvergne 1997). In reviewing this situation, Young (2002b) emphasized that local people have much greater incentives to sustain the resource base. Therefore, local ownership would be positive.

Whilst one can agree with this, it is nevertheless important to recognize that the state must constitute a core level in the hierarchy. What is needed is not only to move decisions down to the lowest level possible. The structure of the hierarchy is as important. Instead of viewing the state as something qualitatively different from other cooperative structures, one should utilize the potential in such a structure to develop its capacity to coordinate activities at lower levels and take part in regional and global coordination activities. The state is a public body and state property could be viewed, hence governed, as a form of common property. The key point is which rules and rationales are instituted. While local users have much better capacities to evaluate consequences of various use and preservation strategies at the local level, coordinating between different local and sub-national decision-making units is also a very important task. Here we need to involve structures like the state. The state must, however, be made accountable both to its citizens and to the international community in ways that go far beyond what exists today.

What, then, about changes in the way we organize economic activity? Such activities take place within various structures—for example, the family, the family firm, small businesses, non-profit organizations, locally-owned stock holding companies to large, often multinational corporations. It is the corporate organization that represents the greatest challenge for sustainability. This institutional structure has accumulated such great power and is led by principles that are so contradictory to those that are demanded by sustainable development, that it is hard to envision sustainability without a reform process aimed at including social rationality and responsibility at this level. The search must be for institutions that are also adaptive to local circumstances. Establishing the basis for diversity in adaptations (Norgaard 1994) is extremely important.

In doing this, we will first face the problem of circumventing the power of these structures. While arguments for institutional change are overwhelming, the power to implement such change is not yet there. Nevertheless, we need to start thinking more systematically about what such a reform could look like. To engage in that endeavour, I see two principal ways in which social rationality and multi-dimensionality could be instituted at the heart of economic life. The first would be to reduce the direct power of the corporation by embedding it within socio-political structures that are themselves built on social rationality. The second would be to institute social rationality at the basis of the firms themselves. While the latter would essentially remove the corporation as an economic entity from the scene, the former would imply changing its power and dynamics.

Looking at the first option, it could simply mean reinventing some of the context in which the corporation operated in its youth. For example, instituting full or at least increased responsibility, restricting its existence in time, and restricting its geographic domain to secure community ties. Restricting existence in time would be a core element. It could involve, for example, a social contract between the firm and society implying, the setting of goals concerning social and environmental standards. A full evaluation of the corporation could take place, say, every ten years where it would have to show how it had been able to fulfil the wider demands set by society. While its bottom line would be that of maximizing profits, the firm would have to meet a wider set of explicit demands to survive such an evaluation. To avoid opportunistic behaviour, the corporation could be legally responsible for setting aside funds to support its employees for a defined period of time and take care of other contracted responsibilities if its contract with society was not renewed. Increasing owners' responsibility would have to be an important element in this.

Concerning the second option, instituting social rationality within the firm could take several directions. As Lux (2003) proposes, firms could 'simply' be turned into non-profit organizations by law. There would then be no stockholders or stock markets and all participants in the firm would be both owners and salaried employees. This solution is based on the idea that excluding the profit motive would alone solve the problem of social and environmental sustainability. It would reduce the impetus for firms to grow, but not necessarily secure the multi-dimensional evaluation we are also looking for.

Another alternative would be to make corporations operate on the basis of an institutionalized triple-bottom-line approach—one including market revenues and costs, one including social goals, and finally, one related to environmental impacts. Ownership should be distributed along these three dimensions, implying that individuals could still hold shares, but that proceeds would depend not only on market revenues and costs, but also on the ability to fulfil social and environmental goals as well. A core issue to decide would be who should represent the social and environmental interests and how their ownership in the firm should be instituted.

Finally, one could envision that beyond a certain size, maybe within certain sectors, the public should control firms. The dominant form of ownership would be either public or community ownership— the latter making it potentially more like a co-operative or non-profit firm. Some would argue that demanding public ownership for large businesses would not work. While I think sustainability demands breaking down the size of large firms to smaller entities, there would still be variations in size and geographical scale. In that situation, public or community ownership offers an interesting alternative to the solution of a triple-bottom-line corporation also because it offers more flexibility. What is observed, from studying the operation of common property, is that the ability to adapt as new challenges or problems appear, without getting 'stuck' in all types of protected rights that must be compensated, is of great value. In an environment of uncertainty, this offers a necessary flexibility. This adaptability can also be a source of abuse. It is observed that community values like fairness and reciprocity have strong standing in such systems, probably because otherwise they would collapse.

None of the above changes would demand abolishing the market institution. Some markets would disappear—like the stock market in some proposals. Moreover, the importance of markets would be reduced and changed since allocations would now be built on a mix of market signals and other, broader, evaluations. Changing the form and logic of the firm would moreover open up for a new way of governing world trade. We have already emphasized the need for a political structure linking decisions at different geographical scales. Changing the logic of the basic economic unit as sketched above, opens the floor for thinking very differently about trade and trade regimes.

I mentioned earlier that in the present system, instituting the precautionary principle in a workable way would be difficult, if not impossible. What would happen, however, if the institutions of the economy were changed as above? Certainly, the fundamental issue of what to do in a situation characterized by uncertainty/irreducible ignorance is not altered. But what would change is the way the problem appears and can be treated. First, the different growth patterns established will create less uncertainty. Second, and most important for the argument here, precaution will not be counter to the goal of the firms—their need to continuously open new 'frontiers' is greatly relaxed. The evaluation of whether to take the chance or not can be based much more on arguments about what characterizes the problem at hand and less on the problems that precaution may cause for the development or survival of the firms involved. While we cannot know the unknown, our capacity to envision what the consequences of moving in different directions may be, will not be hampered by systematic wishful thinking emanating from a 'blind' search for new profit-making frontiers. Responsibility will be much more real.

CONCLUSION

While the creation of individualism has freed humanity from one type of oppression, for example, feudalism and slavery, it has created new forms of domination—that of separation over cooperation and that of the present over the future. Individualism alone is not a proper response to oppression. Individualism can itself be oppressive. What is needed is to balance freedom of choice with real responsibility for the consequences. This is what social rationality is about.

Present development trends are worrying. Moreover, the present ways of correcting these seem both wrong and too weak compared to the challenges we face. As long as sustainability is a core goal, a search for integrative institutions is needed both at the basic level of the economy—its 'going concerns'—and across the various levels of time and space. We need to institute social rationality and multi-dimensional evaluation procedures both at the level of the basic economic units and at the level of social and political hierarchies. While easy to see and easy to say, such a reform is not at all easy to make.

We have to search for institutional structures not seen before. While new, they must build on what is learned from various present and earlier institutional structures. While we have a lot of insight already in relation to this, further research is needed. A crucial point is to develop the most productive and relevant perspectives to guide this kind of research. This chapter can be seen as a response to that question. It represents an effort to clarify what are the questions we should ask when evaluating institutional structures.

I have, however, gone one step further, proposing to transform the ideas of integration, social rationality, and multi-dimensional evaluation into specific institutional structures. The results are certainly quite sketchy. One challenge is therefore to develop the above type of ideas in different directions and in more detail. This is necessary to evaluate potential internal inconsistencies and to make the proposals more concrete. Developing institutional structures never seen before represents a great intellectual challenge. Maybe more important still is to engage in the process of creating a public debate about the need to change direction. This is important both for raising awareness, to signal that there are alternatives, and to foster change. Engagement from the citizens is necessary. While the large corporations in a sense developed 'against the tide', they are now themselves forming the tide. Creating the grand corporations is much more demanding and it works against a tide that has now grown to immense proportions. To act in this environment demands a high level of integrity, ingenuity, and creativity.

REFERENCES

Agrawal, A. and C.C. Gibson (eds), *Communities and the Environment. Ethnicity, Gender, and the State in Community-Based Conservation*, New Brunswick: Rutgers University Press, 2001.

Bakan, J., *The Corporation—the Pathological Pursuit of Profit and Power*, New York: Free Press, 2004.

Batson, C.D., *The Altruism Question. Toward a Social-psychological Answer*, Hilldale, New Jersey: Lawrence Elbaum Associates, Publishers, 1991.

Ben-Ner, A, L. Putterman, F. Kong, and D. Magan, 'Reciprocity in a two-part Dictator Game'. *Journal of Economic Behavior & Organization*, 53(3), 2004, pp. 333–52.

Berkes, F., 'Cross-scale institutional linkages: Perspectives from the bottom up' in National Research Council, 2002, pp. 293–321.

Bromley, D.W., *Environment and Economy: Property Rights and Public Policy*, Oxford: Basil Blackwell, 1991.

Crowards, T., 'Nonuse Values and the Environment: Economic and Ethical Motivations', *Environmental Values*, 6, 1997, pp. 143–67.

Daly, H., *Steady-State Economics*, San Francisco: W.H. Freeman and Company, 1977.

Daly, H., 'Reconciling Internal and External Policies for Sustainable Development', in *Sustainability and Global Environmental Policy*, O.K. Dragun, and Kim Jacobsson (eds) Edward Elgar, 1997, pp. 11–32.

Dauvergne, P., *Shadows in the Forest: Japan and the Politics of Timber in Southeast Asia*, Cambridge: MIT Press, 1997.

Davis, D.D. and C.A. Holt, *Experimental Economics*, Princeton NJ: Princeton University Press, 1993.

Eek, D., A. Biel, and T Gärling, 'Cooperation in Asymmetric Social Dilemmas When Equality is Perceived as Unfair', *Journal of Applied Social Psychology*, 31, 2001, pp. 649–66.

Eckel, C.C. and P.J. Grossman, 'Altruism in Anonymous Dictator Games', *Games and Economic Behavior*, 16, 1995, pp. 181–91.

Etzioni, A., *The Moral Dimension: Toward a new Economics*, New York: The Free Press, 1988.

Fehr, E., S. Gächter, and G. Kirchsteiger, 'Reciprocity as a Contract Enforcement Device: Experimental Evidence', *Econometrica*, 65(4), 1997, pp. 833–60.

Fehr, E., and S. Gächter, 'Cooperation and Punishment', *American Economic Review*, 90, 2000, pp. 980–94.

Fehr, E. and A. Falk, 'Psychological Foundations of Incentives. Joseph Schumpeter Lecture', *European Economic Review*, 46, 2002, pp. 687–724

Forsythe, R., J.L. Horowitz, N.E. Savin, and M. Sefton, 'Fairness in Simple Bargaining Experiments', *Games and Economic Behavior*, 6, 1994, pp. 347–69.

Gintis, H., 'Beyond 'Homo Economicus': Evidence from Experimental Economics', *Ecological Economics,* 35, 2000, pp. 311–22.

Gintis, H., S. Bowles, R. Boyd, and E. Fehr, *Moral Sentiments and Material Interests. The Foundations of Cooperation in Economic Life*, Cambridge, Massachusetts: The MIT Press, 2005.

Gneezy, U. and A. Rustichini, 'A Fine is a Price', *The Journal of Legal Studies*, 29, 2000, pp. 1–17.

Güth, W., R. Schmittberger and B. Schwarze, 'An Experimental Analysis of Ultimatum Bargaining', *Journal of Economic Behavior and* Organization, 3, 1982, pp. 367–88.

Henrich, J.R., B.S. Bowles, C. Camerer, E. Fehr, H. Gintis, and R. McElrath, 'In Search of Homo Economicus: Behavioral Experiments in 15 Small-Scale Societies', *American Economic Review Papers and Proceedings*, 91(2), 2001, pp. 73–8.

Hertsgaard, M., 'A Global Green Deal', *The Nation*, 1, 1999, pp. 18–23.

Hirsch, F., *Social Limits to Growth*, Cambridge MA: Harvard University Press, 1976

Hoffman, E., K. McCabe, K. Shachat, and V. Smith, 'Preferences, Property Rights, and Anonymity in Bargaining Games', *Games and Economic Behavior*, 7, 1994, pp. 346–80.

Holt, C.A., L. Langan, and A.P. Villamil, 'Market Power in Oral Double Auctions', *Economic Inquiry*, 24, 1986, pp. 107–23.

Inglehart, R. and H.D. Klingemann, 'Genes, Culture, Democracy and Happiness' in *Culture and subjective well-being*, E.Diener and E.M. Suh (eds), Cambridge MA: MIT Press, 2000, pp. 165–83.

Kapp, K.W., *The Social Costs of Private Enterprise*, New York: Schoken Books, 1971.

Kopelman, S., J.M. Weber, and D.M. Messick, 'Factors Influencing Cooperation in Commons Dilemmas: A Review of Experimental Psychological Research', in National Research Council, 2002, pp. 113–56.

Ledyard, J.O., 'Public Goods: A Survey of Experimental Research', in *The Handbook of Experimental Economics*, J.H. Kagel and A.E. Roth (eds), Princeton NJ: Princeton University Press, 1995, pp. 111–94.

Locke, J., *Two Treatises of Government*, Cambridge: Cambridge University Press, 1690 (1994).

Lux, K., 'The Failure of the Profit Motive' *Ecological economics*, 44, 2003, pp. 1–9.

National Research Council, *The Drama of the Commons*, Committee on the Human Dimension of Global Change, E. Ostrom, T. Dietz, N. Dolsak, P.C. Stern, S. Stovich, and E.U. Weber (eds), Division of Behavioral and Social Sciences and Education. Washington DC: National Academy Press, 2002.

Norgaard, R.B., *Development Betrayed. The end of Progress and a Coevolutionary Revisioning of the Future*, New York: Routledge, 1994.

North, D.C., *Institutions, Institutional Change and Economic Performance*, Cambridge: Cambridge University Press, 1990.

O'Connor, J., 'Is Sustainable Capitalism Possible?' in *Is Capitalism Sustainable?*, M. O'Connor (ed), New York/London: The Guilford Press, 1994, pp. 152–175.

Ostrom, E., *Governing the Commons: The Evolution of for Collective Action*, Cambridge University Press, 1990.

Ostrom, E., 'Collective Action and the Evolution of Social Norms', *Journal of Economic Perspectives*, 14(3), 2000, pp. 137–58.

Ostrom, E., *Understanding Institutional Diversity*, Princeton and Oxford: Princeton University Press, 2005.

Paavola, J., 'Institutions and Environmental Governance: A Reconceptualization', *Ecological Economics*, 63, 2007, pp. 93–103.

Perrings, C., 'Ecological Resilience in the Sustainability of Economic Development', *Economics of Ecological Resources. Selected Essays*, in C. Perrings, Cheltenham: Edward Elgar, 1997, pp. 45–63.

Polanyi, K., *The Great Transformation. The Political and Economic Origins of our Time*, Boston: Beacon Press, 1944 (1957).

Princen, T., 'The Shading and Distancing of Commerce: When Internalization is not Enough', *Ecological economics*, 20, 1997, pp. 235–53.

Ross, L. and A. Ward, 'Naïve Realism: Implications for Social Conflict and Misunderstanding', in *Values and Knowledge*, E.S. Reed, E. Turiel and T. Brown (eds) Mahwah, NJ: Lawrence Erlbaum Associates, 1996.

Roth, A.E., V. Prasnikar, M. Okuna-Fujiwara, and S. Zamir, 'Bargaining and Market Behavior in Jerusalem, Ljubljana, Pittsburg and Tokyo: an Experimental Study', *American Economic Review*, 81, 1991, pp. 1068–95.

Sato, K., 'Distribution and the Cost of Maintaining Common Property Resources', *Journal of Experimental Social Psychology*, 23, 1987, pp. 19–31.

Sen, A., 'Rational Fools: A Critique of the Behavioral Foundations of Economic Theory', *Philosophy and Public Affairs*, 6 (4), 1977, pp. 317–44.

Shogren, J., A Rule of One, *American Journal of Agricultural Economics*, 88(5), 2006, pp. 1147–59.

Smith, A., *The Theory of Moral Sentiments* (edited by E. Cannan), London: Methuen, 1759 (1976a).

Smith, A., *An Inquiry into the Nature and Causes of the Wealth of Nations*, Chicago: University of Chicago Press, 1776 (1976b).

Sober, E. and D.S. Wilson, *Onto Others. The Evolution and Psychology of Unselfish Behavior*, Cambridge, Massachusetts: Harvard University Press, 1998.

UNDP, *Human Development Report 2003—Millennium Development Goals: A Compact Among Nations To End Human Poverty*, Oxford: Oxford University Press, 2003.

UNEP, *Millennium Ecosystem Assessment*, Washington D.C.: Island Press, 2005.

Vatn, A., 'Environmental Resources, Property Regimes and Efficiency', *Environment and Planning C: Government and Policy*, 19(5), 2001, pp. 681–93.

Vatn, A., *Institutions and the Environment*, Cheltenham: Edward Elgar, 2005.

Vatn, A., 'Explaining Cooperative Behavior', paper presented at the First Nordic Workshop in Behavioral and Experimental Economics, 9–10 November 2006, Oslo.

Vatn, A., 'Resource Regimes and Cooperation', *Land Use Policy*, 24(4), 2007, pp. 624–32.

Vatn, A., 'Institutions and Rationality', in *Assessing the Evolution and Impact of Alternative Institutional Structures*, S. Batie, and N. Mercuro (eds), Routledge Press, forthcoming.

Young, O.R., 'Institutional Interplay: The Environmental Consequences of Cross-Scale Interactions', in National Research Council, 2002a, pp. 263–91.

Young, O.R., *The Institutional Dimension of Environmental Change. Fit, Interplay, and Scale,* Cambridge MA: The MIT Press, 2002b.

4

Social and Environmental Liabilities of Transnational Corporations
New Directions, Opportunities, and Constraints
PETER UTTING[1]

INTRODUCTION

In recent decades there has been a marked change in the regulatory context that attempts to shape the social and environmental performance of business enterprises, in particular transnational corporations (TNCs). The terms neoliberalism, embedded liberalism, and alternative globalization capture the very different regulatory approaches that exist (Utting 2005). While economic globalization and liberalization associated with neoliberalism sought to secure corporate rights through 'hard' law and ushered in various forms of 'de-regulation' and 'corporate self-regulation', 'embedded liberalism' has promoted an increasingly diverse range of voluntary initiatives associated with corporate social responsibility (CSR). More recently, a 'corporate accountability movement' (Broad and Cavanagh 1999) has refocused attention on the roles of law and the state in regulating business, as well as on promoting alternative models of enterprise and 'local' development that contrast sharply with 'corporate globalization'.

This chapter examines the evolving nature of business regulation associated with environmental, social, and human rights dimensions of development. It focuses on key developments that have taken place in relation to the social and environmental liabilities of TNCs in recent years and reflects on their significance from the perspective of social and environmental justice. In both accounting and law, liability generally refers to a situation where an entity has certain obligations. Legal liability implies that a party that has committed a wrong can

[1]I would like to thank José Carlos Marques for research assistance.

be punished or restrained from doing further wrong, and that a victim can receive compensation. During the 1980s, it became widely recognized that policies and processes associated with economic globalization and liberalization were strengthening the rights of TNCs to expand their operations globally. The necessary counterbalance of corporate obligations related to social, human rights, and environmental dimensions of business activities was far less in evidence (UNRISD 1995). Instead, the attention of a growing number of large TNCs, business associations, multilateral organizations, and some governments and NGOs focused on the discourse and practice of CSR, which aimed to improve the social and environmental performance of companies through normative and institutional arrangements associated with voluntary initiatives.

When the CSR agenda took off internationally following the Earth Summit in 1992, its limitations and contradictions soon became apparent. By the time of the World Summit for Sustainable Development ten years later, a new concept had gained currency, namely that of 'corporate accountability'. In contrast to CSR, corporate accountability implied that corporations should not only be obliged to answer to different actors or 'stakeholders' affected by their operations, but should also incur some sort of penalty in cases of non-compliance with agreed standards of behaviour. The corporate accountability movement has refocused attention on the question of legal liability of corporations in the social, human rights, and environmental domains, as well as the role of state institutions and public policy in transforming corporate behaviour in these areas. While much of this attention has focused fairly narrowly on the need for new institutions and legal mechanisms that have 'teeth', various developments have in fact been occurring in the realm of corporate legal liability, which in practice, or potentially, bode well for corporate accountability.

The chapter pays particular attention to three aspects of regulation related to legal liability. The first involves hybrid or 'articulated regulation', that is, the coming together of quite different regulatory approaches in ways that are complementary and synergistic (Utting 2005). This involves both laws and public policy that promote corporate 'voluntary' initiatives, and the gradual hardening or ratcheting-up of corporate voluntarism to a point where the arenas of voluntary and legalistic regulation connect and merge. The second concerns the expanding body of international law that relates more directly to TNCs. Such a body of law is characterized by two distinctive features, namely, the fact that it 'fixes' not only on states but also corporations, and the proliferation of so-called soft law involving normative instruments. The latter does not impose penalties in the conventional sense but, in practice or potentially, aims to modify or restrain corporate malpractice. The third aspect involves 'subaltern legality', where spaces exist or are expanded for victims, disadvantaged groups, and activists to take advantage of existing laws and jurisdictions to seek redress for social and environmental wrongs committed by corporate interests, and pursue other causes associated with environmental and social justice. The chapter cautions against over-stating the potential of legalistic approaches, and discusses the constraints associated with 'hegemonic' legality, involving myriad ways and means by which powerful interests shape law and law enforcement in a manner conducive to corporate interests and 'business-as-usual'. It concludes by identifying some key challenges facing the corporate accountability movement.

I. REGULATORY TRENDS

Neoliberalism—the ideology and policy framework that has shaped patterns of economic globalization—is often associated with transformations in state-market relations that involve de-regulation, the liberalization of labour and capital markets, and trade policy. Such trends are particularly apparent in developing countries where concerns are prevalent about the weakening of certain labour market institutions as well as of state capacity to protect the environment. This is in addition to a lopsided opening up of trade and investment regimes in contexts where developing countries are constrained by ongoing protectionist tendencies in the North and the so-called unlevel playing field that characterizes international trade (International Forum on Globalization 2002). Responsibility for regulation under neoliberalism has been diffused with not only state institutions but also firms, business, and non-governmental organizations, so-called multi-stakeholder entities and international bodies assuming prominent roles. In relation to the environmental and social responsibilities of corporations, 'corporate self-regulation', and voluntary initiatives, as well as privatized forms of governance have emerged as prominent institutional approaches (Cutler *et al.* 1999; Cashore 2002).

Neoliberalism should not be simply equated, however, with de-regulation and self-regulation. Various aspects of so-called 'hard law' have also been strengthened. This may occur to secure corporate rights through what has been called the New Constitutionalism (Gill 1995), which strengthens, *inter alia*, laws protecting property rights and the investments of TNCs in host countries. But some aspects of environmental regulation at both national and international levels have also been strengthened, particularly in the more developed economies (Braithwaite and Drahos 2000). In many developing countries, new laws associated with environmental and social protection have been added to the books, but the so-called rolling-back or down-sizing of state institutions that has been a core feature of neoliberalism often ensures that state regulatory capacity is diminished. The nature of the state is also said to be changing with the emergence of the so-called 'intermediary' state (Kaul 2006)[2] or 'regulatory' state, which is expected to set the rules of the game in contexts where extensive privatization is taking place (Amann 2006). A key concern in this context is not only that of weak regulatory capacity but also institutional 'capture' by corporate interests that come to exert undue influence over state or independent regulatory bodies (Baldwin and Cave 1999; Ugaz and Waddams Price 2003).

Hard law related to environmental protection or corporate behaviour also often follows in the wake of crises of various sorts. This is particularly apparent in countries like the United States where state-business relations, in what have been termed 'liberal' regimes or varieties of capitalism (Esping-Andersen 1990; Hall and Soskice 2001), have historically involved a compromise. Under such a pact, business is given considerable free rein within certain basic rules of the game regarding corporate environmental and social behaviour and fiscal responsibility, as well as on the understanding that corporations should give something back to the community via philanthropic activities. When such a bargain goes very wrong, the state often responds through the imposition of hard law, which happened, for

[2]Kaul describes the roles of the intermediary state in terms of 'blending domestic and external policy preferences, correcting markets and standing corrected by non-state actors (business and civil society), exerting coercive powers and being compelled to compete with other states for mobile resources (finance and skills).' (Kaul 2006, p. 73).

example, in the wake of the Exxon Valdez oil spill and the financial scandals of the late 1990s that resulted in the collapse of Enron and several other large corporations. In these particular instances, the state responded with the 1990 Oil Pollution Act (see Chapter 9) and 2002 Sarbanes-Oxley Act, respectively.

Litigiousness has also increased, particularly in the United States (US) and Europe. A study by SustainAbility argues that 'companies are at greater risk from litigation and liability more generally as a result of a well-funded litigation industry; highly motivated legal activists; expanding boundaries of liability in both legal and accounting terms; and a decline in trust in business reflected in new governance and disclosure requirements.' (Sustainability 2004, p. 6). The study notes that companies are being increasingly sued by different 'stakeholders' including consumers, workers, local communities, non-governmental organizations (NGOs), and investors. Furthermore, settlements for (all) tort cases in the United States increased steadily from the late 1970s, reaching more than US$ 200 billion in 2001. In the United States, much of the recent growth in tort litigation targets companies (ibid., p. 10).

In the 1990s, the reaction to the negative social and environmental implications and impacts of neoliberalism gathered force. This response manifested itself in terms of two broad ideological currents. The first, associated with 'embedded liberalism', acknowledges the reality of economic globalization and liberalization, but seeks to contain, mitigate or compensate perverse effects of corporate power and the freeing-up of markets, often through 'softer' normative arrangements (Ruggie 2003). The other, 'alternative globalization', seeks to 'delink', roll-back or reform policies, institutions, and processes associated with neoliberalism and corporate globalization, often via law, redistribution, and empowerment (Broad 2002).

A prominent feature of embedded liberalism has been a panoply of CSR initiatives and institutions that aim to address the downside to 'corporate globalization'. These include codes of conduct, company 'sustainability' or 'triple-bottom-line' reporting, and schemes like ISO14001 certification for environmental management, SA8000 certification for labour standards, and Forest Stewardship Council (FSC) certification for the forestry sector. Such schemes and several other initiatives aimed at improving corporate performance, have increasingly assumed the form of 'multi-stakeholder initiatives' where some combination of business interests, NGOs, trade unions, government, and international organizations collaborate in the design of standards and the promotion and oversight of implementation (Cashore 2002; Utting 2002).

While this approach challenged some aspects of neoliberal and management orthodoxy that had disregarded the reality of market failure and the complex determinants of successful enterprise and market economies, it was rife with problems of free-riding, weak or non-implementation of principles and policies, window-dressing or outright 'greenwash' (Greer and Bruno 1996). It also failed to question structural changes that were fundamental to understanding global trends associated with rising inequality, ongoing mass poverty, and unsustainable development. These changes included, for example, labour market flexibilization, structural adjustment, free trade and investment, the downsizing of the state, and corporate-driven globalization and shareholder capitalism.

The limitations of corporate self-regulation and voluntary initiatives—both core features of CSR—prompted a variety of proposals, demands, campaigns, and institutional reforms associated with 'corporate accountability'. These initiatives were often led by civil society organizations. In contrast to CSR, the concept of corporate accountability places greater emphasis on corporate obligations, compliance, penalties in cases of non-compliance, grievance procedures, and redress (Bendell 2004; Newell 2002). Corporate accountability initiatives include, for example, the following (Utting 2005):

- Friends of the Earth International proposed that the 2002 World Summit on Sustainable Development (WSSD) consider a Corporate Accountability Convention that would establish and enforce minimum environmental and social standards, encourage effective reporting and provide incentives for TNCs to take steps to avoid negative impacts. In the build-up to the Summit, Greenpeace had also proposed the Bhopal Principles on Corporate Accountability and Liability.
- The International Forum on Globalization has advocated the creation of a United Nations Organization for Corporate Accountability that would provide information on corporate practices as a basis for legal actions and consumer boycotts.
- Christian Aid has proposed the establishment of a Global Regulation Authority that would establish norms for TNC conduct, monitor compliance, and deal with breaches.
- Several trade union and non-governmental organizations in the United States have launched the 'International Right to Know'

campaign to demand legislation that would oblige US companies, or foreign companies traded on the US stock exchanges, to disclose information on the operations of their overseas affiliates and major contractors.

- There have been calls, particularly in the United States, for the 're-chartering' of corporations, to revive a system whereby states granted corporations a charter. This license to operate stipulated certain responsibilities and obligations and, periodically, had to be renewed (see Chapter 3).

- In the United Kingdom (UK), over 100 civil society organizations and political parties have joined the Corporate Responsibility Coalition (CORE), which is calling for mandatory triple bottom-line reporting; legal liability for human rights, and environmental abuses committed by UK companies abroad; and extending the company directors' duties so that they take into account not only the impact of decisions on shareholders but also on other stakeholders.

- Various NGOs and lawyers have called not only for extending international legal obligations to TNCs in the field of human rights but also for bringing corporations under the jurisdiction of the International Criminal Court.

- In 2002, a coalition of civil society organizations and the financier George Soros, launched the 'Publish What You Pay Campaign', which calls for a regulatory approach to ensure that extractive companies in the oil and mining industries disclose the net amount of payments made to national governments.

- Several Global Union Federations have promoted International Framework Agreements with TNCs that not only establish a set of standards that the corporation agrees to apply throughout its global structure, but also reassert the role of industrial relations as a mechanism to ensure the application of international labour law, monitor corporate social performance, and deal with grievances.

Such initiatives have served to refocus attention on the obligations and legal liability of corporations. The following sections describe three significant developments of the past decade related to corporate social and environmental liability. They include first, the ratcheting-up of voluntarism to an extent that the boundary between voluntary and legalistic institutional arrangements becomes a much greyer area where some 'soft' and 'hard' approaches or instruments coexist and fuse in ways that may be complementary; second, the strengthening of certain strands of international law that have a bearing on corporate social and environmental performance; and third, the rise of 'subaltern' or 'counter-hegemonic' legality (Santos and Rodríguez-Garavito 2005).

II. RATCHETING-UP VOLUNTARISM

Why should voluntarism feature in an analysis of legal liability? Since the 1990s, when CSR discourse took off internationally, there has been a heated 'voluntary versus legal' debate, with these forms of 'regulation' sometimes seen as polar opposites or mutually exclusive. There are still numerous areas of regulation where this may indeed be the case but with the gradual hardening of certain voluntary initiatives, the boundaries separating these two approaches have become more blurred.[3] This is apparent where voluntary and legalistic approaches are complementary or synergistic, and where hybrid forms of regulation emerge that combine elements of both.[4] Such developments point to the emergence of more coherent systems of institutions, rather than a collection of fragmented, competing or contradictory instruments and regulatory approaches.

The concept of corporate accountability, and what has been referred to as the 'corporate accountability movement' (Bendell 2004; Broad and Cavanagh 1999) have played an important role in these developments. Institutionalist perspectives that emphasize the importance of path dependency and organizational learning are also relevant, revealing how organizations—both public and private—adapt and evolve, learn by doing, and, in the case of companies, may ratchet-up regulatory approaches once they become accustomed to certain norms and procedures. Corporate accountability discourse and activism related to the social and environmental impacts of TNCs have attempted to reconnect the issue of institutional reform with the notion of obligations, compliance and redress; as well as the key roles of national and international law and states.

In terms of proposals for policy and institutional reform, there is a considerable area of overlap between the CSR and corporate accountability approaches. This is apparent in relation to the ratcheting-

---

[3]For a systematic analysis of the relationship between CSR and law, see McBarnet *et al.* 2007.

[4]Conceptual analysis and empirical evidence of such complementarity and hybridity can be found in Gunningham and Sinclair 2002, McBarnet 2007, SRSG 2007, Utting 2005, Ward 2003.

up of voluntary initiatives that has occurred particularly since the turn of the millennium. It manifests itself in the adaptation of existing voluntary initiatives so that they address loopholes and other weaknesses related to disclosure, monitoring, and supply chain management. Ratcheting-up is also apparent in terms of new codes and guidelines that extend the arena of corporate social responsibility to include areas hitherto excluded. Such is the case, for example, with the Principles for Responsible Investment (PRI) that provide a framework that aims to encourage institutional investors to address certain environmental, social, and corporate governance issues. Promoted by the United Nations, in particular the United Nations Environment Programme Finance Initiative (UNEP FI) and the UN Global Compact, the Principles were launched in 2006. By June 2007, some 200 companies and institutions had formally adhered to the Principles. While 'voluntary and aspirational', the PRI could well follow the path of other multi-stakeholder initiatives like the UN Global Compact, where an initial focus on dialogue and 'learning by doing' is later complemented by monitoring and/or reporting. As in the case of the Fair Labor Association and the Global Compact, some sort of complaints procedure often follows.

The complementarities and synergies that are a feature of ratcheting-up are also apparent in relation to the gradual shift from proliferation and fragmentation that characterized early developments in codes of conduct and other standard-setting initiatives, to cooperation and mutually reinforcing relations. This is apparent, for example, in the case of the UN Global Compact. Closer ties have emerged between the Global Compact and other standard-setting initiatives such as the Global Reporting Initiative, the Organization for Economic Co-operation and Development (OECD) Guidelines for Multinational Enterprises (MNEs), the International Labour Organization's (ILO) Tripartite Declaration of Principles Concerning MNEs and Social Policy, and Transparency International's Business Principles for Countering Bribery. It is also evident in Global Compact's role in launching, with the United Nations Environment Programme (UNEP), the Principles for Responsible Investment, mentioned above.

In some cases, the 'voluntary' initiative later becomes articulated with the legal domain. This is apparent in the case of the Voluntary Principles on Security and Human Rights, which have been incorporated into legal agreements involving host governments and oil companies (Commission on Human Rights 2006). These principles were launched by the US and UK governments in 2000. Supported by several NGOs and companies in the extractive industries, as well as the governments of Norway and the Netherlands, they aim to facilitate risk assessments, strengthen human rights safeguards in security arrangements, improve company relations with local communities, and mitigate any potential for conflict. Another example involves the attempts in some countries to embed the norms and procedures promoted by the Extractive Industry Transparency Initiative (EITI) in statutory law. In Nigeria and Ghana, bills are being considered that would institutionalize the EITI in binding legislation (PWYP and Revenue Watch Institute 2006).

The articulation of CSR with legal instruments is occurring in many other respects as well. Hard law, for example, may require companies to be more transparent and to report on their social or environmental performance, but not specify what that performance should be. If performance standards are found to be low, then it is up to such actors and entities as civil society organizations, the media, and public opinion to expose, name, and shame or otherwise bring pressure to bear on a company to improve its performance. Pollutant Release and Transfer Registers (PRTRs), which impose reporting obligations on companies producing toxic substances, now exist in certain countries, as well as internationally through the PRTR Protocol signed in 2003. Other laws, related, for example, to freedom of association and freedom of information, pave the way for CSR by creating an enabling institutional environment, which safeguards and facilitates the role of actors and organizations that can exert pressures on companies, such as trade unions, NGOs, and the media. Furthermore, laws on misrepresentation and false advertising frame voluntary reporting by companies (Ward 2003, p. 5). Forms of 'negotiated agreements', which are sometimes used in the field of waste management and other areas of environmental protection, establish legally grounded objectives or targets, and involve some element of sanction in cases of non-compliance. These agreements, however, grant the companies involved the flexibility to decide how to comply in the most cost-effective way (Hanks 2002).

Specific laws that mandate CSR practices include, for example, a UK law that requires pension funds to report on social and environmental aspects; French laws that require companies to produce a sustainability report and provide information on their social and environmental impact; a Belgian law that requires Belgian TNCs and subsidiaries to include a *Bilan Social* in their annual reports

(Abrahams 2004). In South Africa, the Mineral and Petroleum Resources Development Act of 2002 stipulates that mining companies must re-apply for mining permits and demonstrate due diligence in relation to social and environmental matters, and that directors may be held liable for environmental damage (Hamann and Bezuidenhout 2007).

There are, then, various areas of regulation where the divide between voluntary and legalistic approaches is becoming more blurred. Whereas in the 1990s there was a strand of CSR that evolved from 'corporate self-regulation' to 'co-regulation', defined in terms of different actors coming together to collaborate in the design and implementation of voluntary initiatives, in the 2000s there are some signs of what can be called institutional complementarity (Hollingsworth and Boyer 1997) or 'articulated regulation' (Utting 2005; 2007) This refers to a situation where quite different regulatory approaches come together in a more complementary and synergistic way, and where hybrid forms of regulation emerge that comprise both voluntary and legalistic elements.

III. INTERNATIONAL LAW

An essential feature of global governance is the increasing reliance on international law to deal with the processes of transnationalization and the reconfiguration of power that characterizes globalization. In relation to the environmental, social, and human rights dimensions of corporate performance, there are two important developments in the arena of international law.

The first relates to the fact that international law increasingly identifies corporations as the bearers of obligations (Muchlinsky 2007). The traditional 'fixation' of public international law on states, and to a lesser extent individuals, has broadened to include non-state actors (Clapham 2006, p. 28). Referring to international human rights law, Clapham notes that 'the existing general rules ... now fix on non-state actors so that they may be held accountable for violations of this law' (ibid. p. 28). He further adds: 'The paradigm shift is coming as businesses are treated, not only as partners, but as having responsibilities under the international law of human rights' (ibid. p. 270).

While legal obligations under international law are extending to corporations, the institutional processes and infrastructure to try corporations is lacking (ibid. 267). This has been a major concern of the corporate accountability movement that, as noted above, has put forward or supported various proposals to strengthen institutions that can hear and prosecute complaints, impose penalties, and seek redress for victims. These range from the UN Norms to expanding the remit of the International Criminal Court, or establishing an International Court for Corporate Crimes (Anderson 2007).

Since the mid-1990s, there has been renewed dynamism in the international law arena related to social and environmental justice and the operations of TNCs. For example, the treaty of African nations known as the Bamako Convention, entered into force in 1996 in an attempt to halt the import into Africa and control the movement of hazardous wastes across borders. Building upon the Food and Agricultural Organization of the United Nations' (FAO) Voluntary International Code of Conduct on the Distribution and Use of Pesticides, the Rotterdam Convention on Prior Informed Consent, which aims to regulate the export of hazardous chemicals, was adopted in 1998 and entered into force in 2004. The Convention on Access to Information, Public Participation in Decision-making, and Access to Justice in Environmental Matters, also known as the Aarhus Convention, was adopted in 1998. A compliance procedure was adopted in 2002, and in 2004, the Complaints Committee began to hear submissions from NGOs alleging non-compliance with the Convention (Abrahams 2004). A legally-binding Pollutant Release and Transfer Register Protocol was also adopted in 2003. While focusing attention on environmental matters in Europe, the Aarhus Convention also relates to the rights of communities in other regions affected by European investments. For example, in April 2006, the Finnish government responded to a request for information from the Argentinean NGO, Center for Human Rights and Environment, concerning the activities of the Finnish firm Botnia and the Finnish Export Credit Agency and their controversial investment in a cellulose plant in Uruguay (CEDHA 2006). The first public health treaty negotiated by the World Health Organization (WHO), the Framework Convention on Tobacco Control, was adopted in 2003, targeting the activities of the tobacco industry and what the WHO regarded as 'the single biggest preventable cause of death.' (Sagafi-nejad 2006).

The second major development in the arena of international law that relates to corporate behaviour, involves so-called soft law. Much of the dynamism associated with strengthening the connections between international law and business corporations centres on a growing body of norms and standards derived from declarations, resolutions, recommendations, guidelines, principles and codes adopted by United Nations entities, the Organization for Economic Co-operation and Development (OECD), the European Union and other multilateral bodies (ICHRP 2002). While the term soft law is disputed in legal circles, it has often been used to refer to the non-binding character of the instruments themselves. Some also employ the term to convey the fact that the substance of even formally-binding treaty provisions is soft, in terms of 'evasive prescriptions' and vague wording that fails to create 'a precise obligation or burden ...' (D'Amato and Engel 1997, p. 56)

By definition, international soft law is a form of articulated regulation, as defined above. It carries no penalties in the conventional sense of imprisonment, fines or payment of compensation but it nevertheless carries moral authority. It is also universal, in the sense that it is applicable to a broader universe of agents (for example, governments or corporations). As Muchlinsky explains, soft law can harden and become part of international customary law 'if a consensus develops that the principle in question should be viewed as an obligatory standard by reason of subsequent practice' (Muchlinsky 2003). Some would argue that the Universal Declaration of Human Rights and certain ILO labour conventions have achieved this status. Soft law can also encourage national governments to incorporate its provisions in legislation at the national level, as is the case of the International Code of Marketing of Breastmilk Substitutes (Abrahams 2004, Clapham 2006).

Various international soft law instruments related to social and environmental dimensions of TNC activities emerged in the 1970s and 1980s, in a context where activists or some governments were pushing for tougher regulatory measures, and where international norm-setting organizations like the United Nations Environment Programme (UNEP) had been established.[5] Like voluntary CSR initiatives, soft law proposals have long been a compromise solution for accommodating demands for tougher international regulation of business. During the 1970s, for example, there were increasing calls from the non-aligned movement and others for a New International

---

[5]The creation of UNEP arose out of the 1972 United Nations (Stockholm) Conference on the Human Environment.

Economic Order (NIEO) and binding regulations on TNCs. Against this backdrop, the UN began drafting a comprehensive code of conduct for TNCs. The code process ran into opposition and was eventually scuppered. What did emerge, however, was a series of international agreements in the shape and form of non-binding principles and guidelines for TNCs. The OECD Guidelines for Multinational Enterprises adopted in 1976, the ILO's Tripartite Declaration of Principles Concerning Multinational Enterprises and Social Policy adopted in 1977, and codes related to the marketing and use of specific products such as breast-milk substitutes, medicinal drugs, and pesticides adopted by certain UN agencies in the 1980s were crucial in this context. More recently, use of the soft law to displace the hard law was seen clearly at the 2002 Word Summit for Sustainable Development in Johannesburg, when business interests rallied against certain proposals for corporate accountability, arguing that their involvement in company reporting and public-private partnerships obviated the need for harder regulatory action (Utting 2006). While the term 'corporate accountability' did find its way into the WSSD Plan of Implementation, substantive corporate accountability reforms, as proposed by some civil society organizations during the WSSD preparatory process, were ignored. Instead, attention focused mainly on voluntary initiatives, dialogue, partnerships, and learning about best practices.[6]

Potentially, one of the most significant developments in the arena of international soft law relates to the OECD Guidelines for Multinational Enterprises. Revisions that took place in 2000 strengthened certain aspects related to internal environmental management systems and greater disclosure of environmental information. They also enhanced the role of 'national contact points' (NCPs) that constitute a form of complaints procedure. This procedure allows third parties, such as trade unions and NGOs, to file a complaint. The number of complaints is increasing. By June 2005, over 100 complaints had been filed by NGOs and trade unions. (OECD Watch 2005, p. 5). Between June 2004 and June 2006, 74 cases were considered by NCPs in 19 of 39 countries that have adopted the Guidelines (OECD 2006).

New proposals have also emerged. A working group of experts

established in 1999 by the United Nations Sub-Commission on the Promotion and Protection of Human Rights drafted the UN Norms on the Responsibilities of Transnational Corporations and other Business Enterprises with regard to Human Rights (hereafter referred to as the UN Norms), which were adopted in their draft form by the Sub-Commission in August 2003, and then submitted to the Commission on Human Rights for approval. The UN Norms, in fact, went beyond norm-setting and monitoring, and contained harder elements related to redress and compensation. They failed to get the political backing from the Commission on Human Rights, which was required for them to become international law. At its April 2005 session, the Commission did, however, call on the United Nations Secretary-General to appoint a Special Representative to organize further consultations on the issue of TNC responsibility for human rights and to report back to the Commission (now the Human Rights Council) with recommendations in 2007.[7] A group of ten companies also joined the Business Leaders Initiative on Human Rights to trial test the Norms (BLIHR 2006).

IV. SUBALTERN LEGALITY

From the perspective of progressive institutional reform and social justice, one of the most significant developments related to the social and environmental liability of corporations relates to what can be called 'subaltern' or 'counter-hegemonic' legality (Santos and Rodríguez-Garavito 2005). This involves efforts on the part of social groups and communities whose livelihoods, identity, rights and quality of life are negatively affected by states and corporations to use the existing legal apparatus to seek redress for injustice, and to participate in struggles and processes associated with accountability. As Martinez-Alier observes, such conflicts also 'may help to move society and economy in the direction of ecological sustainability' (Martinez-Alier 2002, p. 270). Different strands of subaltern legality can be observed.

'Subaltern cosmopolitan legality' is the term used by Santos and Rodríguez-Garavito to refer to such bottom-up approaches, and more specifically to the role of political mobilization in rights-based and grassroots legal strategies. It also refers to multi-scalar strategies that connect actors at local, national, regional, and global levels through

[7]In 2007, the report-back period was extended until 2008.

social movements and transnational activist networks, and employ existing political and legal tools at different levels (Santos and Rodríguez-Garavito 2005, pp. 15–16). A significant legal instrument in this regard involves the use of national law to prosecute TNCs for their activities in host countries that have caused injury and harm. The term 'foreign direct liability' has been used by Halina Ward to refer to this legal procedure (Ward 2003).

Such use of the courts in the home country of a corporation has increased particularly in the United States with the revival of the Alien Tort Claims Act (ATCA). Originally passed in 1789, ATCA laid dormant until the 1980s when several cases were brought against foreign governments, dictators and military personnel accused of torture, murder and other human rights abuses. In the 1990s, the law was also used to prosecute US companies for socio-environmental damage and complicity in human rights violations.

In one of the earliest cases brought against a TNC, the oil company Unocal (now part of Chevron Corporation) was accused of complicity in human rights abuses in Burma. The use of ATCA to prosecute TNCs has increased since 2000 and some thirty ATCA cases have involved corporations. Of these, however, only two have been settled. By end-2006, thirteen were ongoing and fourteen had been dismissed (see Table 4.1). Corporations involved in the ongoing cases include: Royal Dutch Petroleum (Shell) for alleged complicity with the Nigerian military government and security forces in committing human rights violations, including torture and murder; Pfizer for allegedly using untested drugs in its biomedical experiments on children suffering from brain infections; Rio Tinto for allegedly conspiring with the government of Papua New Guinea to violently suppress civil resistance to a mining operation; ExxonMobil for its alleged complicity with acts of violence committed by the Indonesian military on the local population.[8]

More recently, in July 2007, some 5,000 agricultural workers from Nicaragua, Guatemala, Honduras, Costa Rica, and Panama brought five lawsuits against US companies associated with the manufacture and use of the chemical Nemagon (DBCP). They accused Dole (which incorporated Standard Fruit Company in the 1990s), Dow Chemical Co, and Amvrac Chemical Corp of concealing the dangers posed by Nemagon. The pesticide, which allegedly causes serious health problems, was used on banana plantations in Central America and

[8]See Stephens 2006, Hagens 2006, BBC News 2001, Webb 2004.

Table 4.1   ATCA Court Cases Involving TNCs

Plaintiff	Defendant	Year	Country of operation	Status[1]
Eastman Kodak	Kavlin	1997	Bolivia	settled
Bodner	Banque Paribas	2000		settled
Wiwa	Royal Dutch Petroleum Co.	2002	Nigeria	ongoing
John Doe I.	Exxon Mobil Corp.	2001	Indonesia	ongoing
Arias	DynCorp.	2001	Ecuador	ongoing
Sarei	RioTinto	2000	Papua New Guinea	ongoing
Brown	Amdahl Corp.	2002	South Africa	ongoing
Khulumani	Barclays	2002	South Africa	ongoing
Estate of Rodriguez	Drumond Co., Inc.	2003	Colombia	ongoing
Digwamaje	Bank of America	2003	South Africa	ongoing
Abdullah	Pfizer Inc.	2003	Nigeria	ongoing
Bauman	Daimler-Chrysler A.G.	2003	Argentina	ongoing
Mujica	Occidental Petroleum	2003	Colombia	ongoing
Al Rawi	Titan	2004	Iraq	ongoing
Bowoto	Chevron	2004	Nigeria	ongoing
Hamid	Price Waterhouse	1995		dismissed
Doe	Unocal Corp.	1996	Burma	dismissed
Beanal	Freeport-McMoran	1998	Indonesia	dismissed
Carmichael	United Technologies Corp.	1998	Saudi Arabia	dismissed
Iwanowa	Ford Motor Co.	1999	Germany	dismissed
Bigio	Coca-Cola Co.	2000	Egypt	dismissed
Mendonca	Tidewater, Inc.	2001		dismissed
Bano	Union Carbide Corp.	2001	India	dismissed
Numerous plaintiffs	Japanese Corporations	2001	Japan, Philippines, Korea, China	dismissed
Villeda Aldana	Del Monte	2003	Guatemala	dismissed
Flores	S. Peru Copper Corp.	2003	Peru	dismissed
Presbyterian Church of Sudan	Talisman Energy, Inc. (Canada)	2003	Sudan	dismissed
Aguinda	Chevron-Texaco	2001	Ecuador	dismissed[2]
Sinaltrainal	Coca-Cola Co.	2003	Colombia	dismissed
Maugein	Newmont Mining Corp.	2004		dismissed

Sources: Apple, Bruno, Herz, and Redford 2004.
Neumeister 2006.
Kay 2006.
Lifsher 2005.
Business and Human Rights Resource Centre 2007.
Notes: [1]as of end 2006.
        [2]in 2007 the case was being heard in Ecuador.

elsewhere in the 1970s. In November 2007, a Los Angeles jury that had heard the first case, awarded US$ 3.3 million in compensatory damages to six workers who claimed they were left sterile from contact with Nemagon. Dole was ordered to pay most of the awards that ranged from US$ 311,200 to US$ 834,000 (BBC 2007). A verdict of punitive damages of US$ 2.5 million for malice was also brought against Dole with the jury refusing to accept the argument that the 'new Dole', which projects itself as a leader in the field of corporate social responsibility, should not be punished for the transgressions of the 'old Dole'.[9] Although many similar lawsuits have been filed in the US, this case was unusual in that it had gone before a jury. Amvrac had previously reached an out-of-court settlement amounting to US$ 300,000.

In South Africa, the post-apartheid Truth and Reconciliation Commission, which had recommended the payment of reparations to apartheid victims, provided an impetus to litigation. The Apartheid Claims Taskforce and Jubilee 2000 South Africa brought cases in the United States against certain TNCs (Hamann and Bezuidenhout 2007). Similar cases were brought in the United Kingdom. Some 7,500 South Africans, suffering from asbestos-related diseases, sued the UK-based company Cape plc. In South Africa, a case was also brought by asbestosis sufferers against Gencor. Both Gencor and Cape plc eventually agreed to make a contribution to a trust fund to aid those suffering from asbestos-related diseases (ibid.)

Subaltern legality has attracted considerable attention in India as a result of 'public interest litigation' (PIL). PIL emerged in 1977 when two Supreme Court justices proposed an extraordinary form of litigation aimed at allowing subordinated groups the possibility to seek redress, as well at fast-tracking the legal process, which tends to be extremely protracted in the conventional court system. While PIL was formally a top-down initiative, it was partly a response to social movement activism and the high profile which abusive practices received when the free press reasserted itself following the Emergency period that had lasted from 1975 to 1977 (Dasgupta 2002). As one advocate to the Delhi High Court explains: 'PIL emerged as a result of an informal nexus of pro-active judges, media persons, and social activists' (George 2005: 2). PIL has provided not only victims, but also activists, with a key instrument to promote their concerns. It is these features of PIL that lead some to refer to it as 'social action litigation' (Baxi 1987).

[9]See *www.bananalink.org.uk*, accessed on 25 November 2007.

The discourse and procedures associated with PIL appear quite different to the features of 'legal centralism' and 'legal formalism' associated with the system of Anglo-Saxon law established by the British during the colonial period. Such a system had the effect of limiting access to the courts to the advantaged and denying justice to the disadvantaged (George 2005, pp. 1–2). Under PIL, rules of representation are relaxed, allowing 'public-spirited' persons or organizations, such as NGOs, to file petitions and not only the aggrieved parties or those directly affected.[10] Another distinguishing feature of PIL is 'collaborative' and 'investigative' litigation (ibid., p. 5). Rather than simply listening to evidence, making a judgement and sentencing, 'the claimant, the court and the Government or the public official, all are in collaboration ... to see that basic human rights become meaningful for the large masses of the population.' (ibid.) In practice, the court acts as ombudsman, a discussion forum, provider of emergency relief through interim orders, mediator, and investigator (ibid.). PIL has also attempted to fast-track the dispensation of justice, which is notoriously slow in the conventional legal system. Social Watch India reports that over 20 million cases were pending in the subordinate courts in 2002, and that the pendency rate in the High Courts increased from 2.6 million cases in 1993 to 3.6 million in 2002, with approximately 17 per cent more than 10 years old (Social Watch India 2003; 2004).

Recent PIL cases that relate to or affect the social and environmental performance of firms include a petition filed by the Centre for Public Interest Litigation that aims to oblige Coca-Cola and PepsiCo to list all chemicals present in their bottled drinks (Reuters India 2006), as well as the filing of a petition to halt the alleged practice of companies like Tata and Reliance and others to acquire land from farmers for setting up Special Economic Zones (The Hindu 2006). Monsanto has been targeted several times, first by the Research Foundation for Science Technology and Ecology (RFSTE). The foundation unsuccessfully attempted to stop the company from obtaining a European patent for an Indian variety of wheat which the foundation claimed would cause great harm to Indian farmers (The Tribune 2004). More recently, Monsanto and other manufacturers of bio-agricultural products have witnessed leading anti-genetic modification organizations

[10]See *www.supremecourtofindia.nic.in/new_links/speech.htm.*

convince India's Supreme Court to issue an interim order to halt future trials of transgenic crops pending a PIL hearing (Suresh 2006).

In 1994, PIL took on a regional dimension when the Supreme Court in Bangladesh entertained a petition related to air and noise pollution. The court agreed with the argument that the right to life, stipulated in the Constitution, extends to include the right to a safe and healthy environment (Sabharwal 2005).

V. HEGEMONIC LEGALITY

The above discussion of contemporary developments associated with articulated regulation, international soft law, and subaltern legality point to a situation that appears to augur well for environmental and social justice. Such developments suggest that institutional reforms and innovations associated with both 'embedded liberalism', with its more normative and reformist approach, and 'alternative globalization', with its more legalistic and transformative approach, are gaining ground. The reality, however, is far more complex, contradictory, and uncertain. As this section illustrates, the route to justice through liability is fraught with obstacles that derive from institutional processes, and the capacity of corporate interests and political elites, and mainstream development ideologies and narratives, to shape outcomes. The term 'hegemonic legality' is used here to refer to a variety of ways in which powerful actors, institutions, and discourses counteract or dilute the progressive potential of institutional and legal reforms, promote 'soft' or normative alternatives to deflect harder ones, and assume leadership positions in reform movements.

Corporations have at their disposal a legal industry that exists largely to enhance their ability to circumvent the law or render it impotent. Through so-called 'creative compliance' and 'legal gamesmanship', which deflects attention from the intentions or the spirit of the law to the details of the 'letter of the law', companies can often rely on loopholes and technicalities to get them off the hook (McBarnet 2007, pp. 48–9). Governments, political leaders, and corporate interests will sometimes attempt to reverse or overturn legal reforms as part of their political strategizing. This appears to have been the case, for example, in the decision of the UK Chancellor— announced at the annual conference of the Confederation of British Industry in 2005—not to go ahead with a plan, which had considerable civil society and parliamentary backing, that would require publicly-listed companies in the United Kingdom to submit to shareholders an Operating and Financial Review outlining social, environmental, and other issues in their operating environment that may affect future operations (Kuszewski 2006). Similarly, in the United States, the Bush administration and corporate interests have attempted to repeal or restrict the scope of ATCA, now that it is being used not only to seek redress for cruel and inhumane acts committed by dictators and repressive regimes, but also to sue TNCs (Hermer and Day 2004). A Supreme Court decision in 2004 emphasized that only a 'very limited category' of cases could be brought under ATCA but left the door open for cases against corporations which allege gross human rights abuses (Apple *et al.*

Case studies of the determinants of 'success' or 'failure' of PIL cases from the perspective of environmental justice reveal the considerable challenges that judicial activism confronts. A study of a successful PIL case related to vehicular air pollution in Delhi illustrates the panoply of tactics and their relationships that eventually convinced the public and the judiciary that compressed natural gas (CNG) should be used, prompting the state and federal governments to undertake the conversion of Delhi's public transport fleet to CNG between 2001 and 2003 (Sarma 2006). Despite strong opposition, this significant policy change took place as a result of a multi-faceted approach that included legal action; influencing public opinion, particularly through the media and advertising, as well as public campaigns that included gathering signatures; generating, gathering, and disseminating evidence-based knowledge both within India and abroad; active participation in so-called epistemic communities of 'experts' organically linked to the policy process; and petitioning and otherwise communicating with government officials and politicians (ibid.).

In relation to another PIL case—the attempt to halt construction of the Sardar Sarovar dam and the displacement of people affected by the project, and to force a comprehensive review of the project—the outcome was quite different. In the mid-1990s, the Supreme Court took a number of decisions that boded well for the 'Save the Narmada', movement. As Rajagopal explains, the situation began to change, however, in the late 1990s in a context where nationalist and developmentalist sentiments were gaining ground, political supporters of the dam ascended to power at both state and federal levels, activist participation in the struggle was waning, and where 'the juggernaut of construction of the dam and displacement could not be stopped' (Rajagopal 2005, p. 213). In 2000, the Supreme Court issued an order that allowed construction to continue and 'left no doubt that the final decision-making authority belonged to the political arena ...' (ibid., p. 202).

Another feature of hegemonic legality relates to situations where soft or hard law is rendered ineffective from the perspective of social and environmental justice. Such concerns have arisen in relation, for example, to the OECD Guidelines for Multinational Enterprises. According to OECD Watch, an international network of forty-seven NGOs whose work focuses on the OECD Guidelines and the OECD Investment Committee, the implementation of the guidelines leaves much to be desired: '.... In a handful of cases, NCPs have sought to issue useful or meaningful recommendations that could guide and improve corporate behaviour.' But the general conclusion is that: 'Five years on, there is no conclusive evidence that the Guidelines have helped reduce the number of conflicts between local communities, civil society groups and foreign investors ... As a global mechanism to improve the operation of multinationals, the Guidelines are simply inadequate and deficient.' (OECD Watch 2005, p. 7,5) This conclusion was reached after an evaluation of the performance of NCPs in twenty-two countries and consultations with NGOs in seven developing countries that do not adhere to the Guidelines.

The concerns of the NGOs consulted centred on:

- 'The unequal and unfair treatment of NGOs in the process;
- A lack of investigative or fact-finding capacity of NCPs;
- The unwillingness to assess alleged breaches of the Guidelines;
- Attempts to exclude cases dealing with supply chain responsibility;
- The weakness of many NCP statements;
- A failure to communicate properly with complainants and inordinate delays in dealing with cases; and
- The failure to investigate fully the alleged illegal exploitation of the natural resources of the Democratic Republic of Congo by OECD companies.' (ibid., p. 7)

OECD Watch recommendations called for the strengthening of aspects related to impartiality, sanctions, parliamentary oversight, the scope of the Guidelines, the role of judges and ombudsmen, investigative capacity, and redress for affected communities. (ibid., pp. 8–9)

In addition to rolling back progressive reforms or constraining the progressive potential of existing institutions, another aspect of hegemonic legality consists of promoting softer regulatory alternatives. This can have the effect of crowding out harder institutional arrangements. Such a scenario is currently being played out in relation to the UN Norms, referred to above.[11] The UN Norms attempt to address some of the weaknesses that characterize the Global Compact and CSR initiatives more generally, namely picking and choosing among standards, weak compliance with agreed standards, and free riders. They pull together a wide range of standards that are derived from international law that apply to states, but which are commonly found in multi-stakeholder CSR initiatives. They state that all TNCs and related companies have an obligation to uphold such standards, and they propose an implementation and monitoring mechanism. The Norms push the envelope even further by stipulating 'adequate reparation' in cases of stakeholders affected by non-compliance.

Some of these harder aspects of the UN Norms were anathema to certain business interests and governments, and the 2004 session of the UN Commission on Human Rights, which considered the draft Norms, not only reminded the Sub-Commission on the Promotion and Protection of Human Rights that the Norms had no legal status and that it was not to perform any monitoring function, but also that it had never been asked to draft any such norms in the first place (ECOSOC 2004). The opponents of the Norms argued that they were essentially unnecessary since voluntary instruments associated with corporate self-regulation and international standard-setting already exist. This was the position, for example, of the International Chamber of Commerce (ICC) and the International Organization of Employers (IOE): 'The binding and legalistic approach of the draft norms will not meet the diverse needs and circumstances of companies and will limit the innovation and creativity shown by companies in addressing human rights issues in the context of their efforts to find practical and workable solutions to corporate responsibility challenges ... To be effective and relevant to a company's specific circumstances, business principles and responsibilities should be developed and implemented by the companies themselves. Indeed,

[11]The Norms were drafted by a working group of experts established in 1999 by the United Nations Sub-Commission on the Promotion and Protection of Human Rights, adopted in their draft form by the Sub-Commission in August 2003, and submitted to the Commission on Human Rights.

the IOE, ICC, and their member companies are already demonstrating their commitment to encourage good corporate practice and responsible business conduct through actions taken by individual companies— as well as through their participation in the Global Compact, their constructive contribution to the revised OECD Guidelines for Multinational Enterprises, and various other initiatives such as the Global Sullivan Principles.' (ICC and IOE 2003).

At the April 2005 session of the Commission on Human Rights, there was a new twist in the process of considering the UN Norms. A resolution, originally proposed by the United Kingdom and several other governments, that omitted all reference to the Norms, was passed. The Norms were seen as divisive and an obstacle to achieving the type of broad-based consensus needed to move forward. It was agreed, however, to continue the dialogue on business and human rights via the appointment by the United Nations Secretary-General of a Special Representative. A block of mainly developing countries, which included South Africa, Egypt and Cuba, as well as several NGOs, pushed unsuccessfully for an amended resolution that not only acknowledged the groundwork that had already been done via the Norms, but also incorporated references to regulatory and developmental problems associated with TNCs and corporate power.[12] While most governments and NGOs welcomed the appointment of a Special Representative, there were concerns that an agreement to keep talking and not to build on the Norms represented a step backwards.

The interim report of the Special Representative, published in February 2006, appeared to side with the opinion of the ICC and some business leaders by dismissing the Norms as a 'distraction'. Even the wording coincided with that apparently used by one of industry's most prominent proponents of voluntary CSR approaches in a consultation organized three months earlier.[13] Instead, the way

[12]The author participated in two of the meetings that considered the draft resolution.

[13]In the consultation on Human Rights and the Extractive Industry, organized in November 2005 by the United Nations High Commissioner for Human Rights in cooperation with the Special Representative on Human Rights and TNCs, Sir Mark Moody Stuart, former Chairman of Royal Dutch/Shell and currently Chairman of Anglo American reportedly stated: '... the draft Norms ... were a distraction in improving national legislation and building respect for human rights across the world. He said that we did not need more high-level norms, but detailed multi-stakeholder work on how principles could be put into operating practice.' (ECOSOC 2005, p. 6)

forward lay with 'principled pragmatism' (Commission on Human Rights 2006), an approach that would essentially continue the process of scaling-up and ratcheting-up existing voluntary initiatives, and expanding forms of 'collaborative governance' involving co-regulatory or multi-stakeholder initiatives, as well as some of the regulatory initiatives referred to above that operate at the interface of voluntary and legalistic approaches. Specific reference was made to such aspects as extending the extraterritorial application of some home countries' jurisdiction for the extreme human rights abuses committed by their firms abroad; best practice learning and capacity-building in developing countries; the development of effective impact assessment tools; and extending CSR and monitoring initiatives to state-owned enterprises.

Another dimension of hegemonic legality relates to the establishment or strengthening of certain institutions at the supranational or multilateral level that, in effect, constitute trump cards that can be used to overrule progressive reforms and regulations at the national level. The Agreement on Trade Related Aspects of Intellectual Property Rights (TRIPs), that introduced intellectual property law into the world trading system via the General Agreement on Tariffs and Trade (GATT) in 1994, has received most attention. Administered by the World Trade Organization (WTO), TRIPs also contains enforcement, redress, and dispute resolution procedures. In practice, corporate interests and states have had to tread carefully in invoking the TRIPs Agreement given the opposition from many developing country governments and advocacy groups that followed attempts to prevent certain governments in developing countries such as South Africa and Brazil, from producing generic drugs to combat HIV/AIDS (Sell 2004).

Other institutions associated with bilateral and regional trade and investment agreements have not been noticed as much. The proliferation of international investment agreements, in particular bilateral investment treaties (BITs), which aim to create an enabling environment for foreign direct investment, has added weight to the role of international arbitration tribunals. Such agreements include, amongst other things, dispute settlement provisions. Playing a key role in this regard is the International Centre for Settlement of Investment Disputes (ICSID), an entity of the World Bank Group that was established in 1965, to facilitate the arbitration of investment disputes between states and foreign investors, in order to create an environment conducive to the flow of private international investment.[14]

ICSID heard few cases for over two decades, a fact that led some commentators to dismiss its significance (Vernon 1998). The situation changed, however, with the rise in the numbers of BITs, which increased from 385 in 1989 to 2,181 by 2002 (UNCTAD 2003, p. 89). Whereas only 35 cases were heard in ICSID's first 25 years of existence (Vernon 1998, p. 193), this number had increased to 215 by late 2006.[15] Of the cases registered, 110 had been concluded and 105 were pending.

From the perspective of developing countries, various concerns have arisen with international arbitration (UNCTAD 2003, pp. 117–18). These include the impartiality and even-handedness of the ICSID process, the cost of settlements for developing countries, the limited ability of some developing countries to muster the resources and expertise needed for arbitration, and bypassing and weakening local settlement dispute institutions. From a legal perspective, there are concerns that while the ICSID Convention does leave open the possibility that rules of international law can be taken into account, 'so far, there is little consideration of environmental and human rights obligations' (Clapham 2006, p. 156).

One of the most recent cases to be registered with ICSID— Shell Brands International AG and Shell Nicaragua S.A. v. Republic of Nicaragua (Case No. ARB/06/14)—illustrates some of the issues involved for those seeking environmental and social justice. It concerns the case, referred to earlier, of Nicaraguan agricultural workers whose health suffered as a result of contact with the pesticide Nemagon.

Legal proceedings against several companies began in the 1990s in the United States and in 2001, the Nicaraguan National Assembly passed a law backing the lawsuits brought by Nicaraguan victims against Dole, Dow Chemical, and Shell. In December 2002, a Nicaraguan court ordered these corporations to pay US$ 489 million to 583 workers. A subsequent ruling added another US$ 64 million to the compensation bill. Several cases brought against companies in the United States were ruled to be inadmissible due to legal

[14]See *www.worldbank.org/icsid/basicdoc/partB-section03.htm.*
[15]See *www.worldbank.org/icsid/cases/cases.htm,* accessed 10 October 2006.

irregularities. Following lengthy protests by Nemagon victims, the Nicaraguan government eventually agreed in 2004 to provide legal and social support to those affected and to present the case to the Human Rights Commission in Geneva. A number of environmental protection measures were also agreed (ENVIO 2005).

In December 2005, a Nicaraguan judge ordered economic restrictions to be imposed on Shell Oil until it paid part of the US$ 489 million. In May 2006, Shell Brands countersued the Nicaraguan government for the same amount, in compensation for lost profits. Bringing such a case before ICSID is made possible by investment safeguards contained in the bilateral investment agreement signed by the governments of Nicaragua and the Netherlands. Questions arise regarding the capacity of cash-strapped developing country governments to successfully fight such cases. Apart from the US$ 60,000 that must be put up by parties to a dispute, in October 2006 the Nicaraguan government reportedly had to allocate US$ three million for legal fees (El Nuevo Diario 2006, p. 14).

The capacity of transnational legal structures to trump national policy and institutional reforms is also apparent in relation to regional trade agreements. Several cases heard under ICSID include those brought under Chapter 11 of the North American Free Trade Agreement (NAFTA). This clause of the regional accord provides a mechanism that allows companies and other investors to sue national governments that impose regulations or privilege national investors in violation of the rights and privileges of foreign investors that are enshrined in NAFTA. Chapter 11 has enhanced the role of arbitral tribunals that operate outside of national court systems (Public Citizen 2005). Of the eleven cases that had been completed by 2005, six were won by governments and five by investors who were awarded 35 million dollars (ibid., p.v). A study of forty-two cases and claims that emerged from 1994 to 2005 identifies various instances where the environmental policies and regulations of local, state, and national governments have been challenged by corporate investors. These include the successful challenge by the US company Metaclad, which won a US$ 15.6 million compensation award with respect to decisions made by municipal and state authorities in San Luis Potosí, Mexico, to refuse a permit for the construction of a toxic waste dump and to establish an ecological preserve around the site. Cases have also been brought against governments that take actions consistent with international environmental agreements. A successful challenge was brought by the United States waste treatment company S.D. Myers against the Canadian government when it closed its border to trade in toxic PCBs, which is discouraged under the Basel Convention (ibid., pp. ix–x). Other concerns raised in relation to these institutional arrangements include the fact that they can inhibit policy making in the public interest, and that citizens and democratically-elected local and state-level public officials have 'no avenue of meaningful participation ...' (ibid., p.vii).

CONCLUSION

The analysis in this paper suggests that a number of important developments have occurred in the past decade in relation to the social and environmental liabilities of TNCs—developments that appear to bode well for environmental and social justice. The ratcheting-up of some areas of voluntarism and CSR has reached a stage where responsibilities start to merge with obligations that fix on a broader universe of corporate actors, and penalties start to be applied for non-compliance with agreed standards. The expanding body of international law that has a bearing on the environment and human rights performance of TNCs also suggests a degree of institutional thickening conducive to taming corporate capitalism. And the discussion of subaltern legality suggests that victims of injustice and activists are using the legal system to greater effect.

Corporate and other powerful actors and institutions have at their disposal, however, a variety of tactical and strategic options to counter institutional and legal developments associated with progressivity and corporate accountability. In comparison with local victims, NGOs and even governments, corporate interests can muster considerable economic and human resources in their defence. Legal and institutional reforms can be rolled back, laws and institutions can be stripped of their progressive potential, and the legal architecture can be redesigned to give greater power to supranational or multilateral institutions that can suppress challenges to corporate interests that arise at the national level. We have also seen that normative approaches associated with 'embedded liberalism' and CSR can sometimes have the effect of crowding out regulatory approaches associated with corporate accountability.

This analysis indicates that there are no quick institutional fixes to minimize injustice and ensure compliance with agreed standards, or for redress. It would seem, however, that both social contestation and institutions concerned with environmental, social, and human rights aspects of business performance are being consolidated at multiple levels. These developments associated with the ratcheting-up of voluntarism, international soft law, and subaltern legality depend crucially on the correlation of social forces, formal and informal coalitions of actors, and the broader political and ideological context and narratives shaping patterns of national development and policy-making. The ideological underpinnings of neoliberalism are now being questioned on two fronts, namely 'embedded liberalism' and alternative globalization'. Such approaches sometimes work in tandem to promote the ratcheting-up of voluntary initiatives and international soft law, and the type of institutional thickening and policy coherence needed to tame markets and corporate capitalism. But there are also clear tensions involved given the harder regulatory and redistributive options associated with alternative globalization. In this context, the struggle for environmental and social justice involves not only a struggle to redesign and harness the potential of certain institutions, but also to reconfigure social and political alliances and mainstream development discourse.

Herein seems to lie the greatest challenge for the corporate accountability movement and 'alternative globalization'. Agendas associated with neoliberalism and embedded liberalism are politically strong, with support constituencies involving state institutions, international organizations and influential non-state actors. In contrast, the corporate accountability movement is a fledgling movement that needs to mobilize social and political forces from outside the narrow ranks of its immediate constituency. It needs to build the broad-based coalitions and networks that are required to promote progressive institutional change (Utting 2005). This means identifying potential allies within both state and business circles. It also requires reconnecting civil society activism with democratic party politics. And it means overcoming key divisions within civil society, notably between trade unions and NGOs; 'purist' and 'collaborationist' NGOs; as well as NGOs from North and South.

REFERENCES

Abrahams, Désirée, *Regulating Corporations: A Resource Guide,* Geneva: UNRISD, 2004.

Amann, Edmund, *Regulating Development: Evidence from Africa and Latin America*, Cheltenham, Edward Elgar, 2006.

Anderson, Sara, 'Transnational Corporations', in *How to Regulate and Control Neo-liberal Globalization: Workshop on International Regulations 2003–2006)*, Kitazawa Yoko (ed), Tokyo/Paris, Pacific Asia Resource Center/ Foundation Charles Leopold Mayer for the Progress of Humanity, 2007.

Apple, Betsy, K. Bruno, R. Herz, and K. Redford, *In Our Court: ATCA, SOSA and the Triumph of Human Rights. A Report about the Alien Tort Claims Act by Earth Rights International*, Washington DC: Earth Rights International, 2004.

Baldwin, R. and M. Cave, *Understanding Regulation*, Oxford: Oxford University Press, 1999.

Baxi, U. 'Taking Suffering Seriously: Social Action Litigation', in *The Role of the Judiciary in Plural Societies*, Tiruchelvam and Coomaraswamy (eds), New York: St. Martin's Press, 1987.

BBC News, '*US payout awarded over pesticide*', 2007, available at *http:// news.bbc.co.uk/2/hi/americas/7080143.stm*, accessed on 15 November 2007.

BBC News, *Exxon 'helped torture in Indonesia'*, 2001. Available at *http:// news.bbc.co.uk/2/hi/asia-pacific/1401733.stm*, accessed on 1 November 2006.

Bendell, Jem, *Barricades and Boardrooms: A Contemporary History of the Corporate Accountability Movement. Programme on Technology, Business and Society.* Programme Paper, No. 13, Geneva: UNRISD, 2004.

BLIHR (Business Leaders Initiative on Human Rights), *Report 3: Towards a 'Common Framework' on Business and Human Rights: Identifying Components*, London: BLIHR, 2006.

Braithwaite, John and Peter Drahos, *Global Business Regulation*. Cambridge: Cambridge University Press, 2000.

Broad, Robin (ed), *Global Backlash: Citizen Initiatives for a Just World Economy*, New York: Rowman and Littlefield, 2002.

Broad, Robin and John Cavanagh, 'The corporate accountability movement: Lessons and opportunities', *The Fletcher Forum of World Affairs*, 23 (2), 1999, pp. 151–69.

Business and Human Rights Resource Centre, '*Apartheid reparations lawsuits*' 2007,
available at *http://www.business-humanrights.org/ Categories/Lawlawsuits/Lawsuitsregulatoryaction/ LawsuitsSelectedcases/ApartheidreparationslawsuitsreSoAfrica*, accessed on 26 June 2007.

CEDHA (Center for Human Rights and Environment), *Aarhus Convention Enforced for Outside EU Inquiry*, 2006, available at *www.cedha.org.ar/ en/more_information/aarhus-convention.php*, accessed on 2 November 2006.

Cashore, Ben, 'Legitimacy and the Privatization of Environmental Governance: How Non-State Market-Driven (NSMD) Governance Systems Gain Rule-Making Authority', *Governance: An International Journal of Policy, Administration and Institutions*, 15(4), p. 503, 29 October 2002.

Clapham, Andrew, *Human Rights Obligations of Non-State Actors,* Oxford: Oxford University Press, 2006.

Commission on Human Rights, *Promotion and protection of human rights: Interim report of the Special Representative of the Secretary-General on the issue of human rights and transnational corporations and other business enterprises, Sixty-second session, UN Doc. E/CN.4/2006/97, February 22,* New York: United Nations, 2006.

Cutler, Claire, V. Haufler, and T. Porter (eds) *Private Authority and International Affairs*, State University of New York (SUNY) Series in Global Politics, Suny, Albany, 1999.

D'Amato, Anthony and Kirsten Engel, 'Soft Law', in *International Environmental Law Anthology,* Anthony D'Amato and Kirsten Engel (eds), Ohio: Anderson Publishing Company Cincinnati, 1997.

Dasgupta, M., 'Social Action for Women? Public Interest Litigation in India's Supreme Court' *Law, Social Justice & Global Development Journal (LGD)*, 2002, available at *http://elj.warwick.ac.uk/global/02–1/dasgupta.html.*

ECOSOC (United Nations Economic and Social Council), *Promotion and protection of human rights. Report of the United Nations High Commissioner for Human Rights on the Sectoral Consultation entitled 'Human rights and the extractive industry', 10–11 November 2005. UN Doc. E/CN.4/2006/ 92, December 19,* New York: United Nations, 2005.

ECOSOC (United Nations Economic and Social Council), *Report to the Economic and Social Council of the Sixtieth Session of the Commission. UN Doc. E/CN.4/2004/L.11/Add.7, 22 April 2004,* New York: United Nations, 2004.

El Nuevo Diario, 'Paul Richter nuevamente en defensa de Nicaragua', *El Nuevo Diario*, 20 October 2006.

ENVIO, 'Victims of Nemagon Hit the Road', *Envio*, Managua, 287, 2005, pp. 11–17.

Esping-Andersen, G., *Three Worlds of Welfare Capitalism*, Princeton: Princeton University Press, 1990.

George, Jasper Vikas, 'Social Change and Public Interest Litigation in India', *Independant Media Center*, 2005, available at *http://india.indymedia.org/ en/2005/03/210205.shtm*, accessed on 2 November 2006.

Gill, Stephen, 'Globalisation, Market Civilization, and Disciplinary Neoliberalism', *Millennium: Journal of International Studies*, 24(3), 1995, pp. 399–423.

Greer, Jed and Kenny Bruno, *Greenwash: The Reality Behind Corporate Environmentalism*, Penang: Third World Network, 1996.

Gunningham, Neil and Darren Sinclair, *Leaders and Laggards: Next Generation Environmental Regulation*, Sheffield: Greenleaf, 2002.

Hagens Berman Sobol Shapiro LLP, *Oceanic Islanders Win Appeal in Massive Claim against Mining Giant Rio Tinto for Alleged Ecocide and Human Rights Crime*, available at *http://www.hagens-berman.com/ press_release_riotinto.htm*, accessed on 1 November 2006.

Hall, Peter A. and David Soskice, 'An Introduction to Varieties of Capitalism', in *Varieties of Capitalism: The Institutional Foundations of Comparative Advantage*, Peter A. Hall and David Soskice (eds), Oxford: Oxford University Press, 2001.

Hamann, Ralph and Andries Bezuidenhout, 'Corporate Social Responsibility in the South African Mining Industry', in *Staking their Claims: Corporate Social and Environmental Responsibility in South Africa.*, David Fig (ed), Scottsville, South Africa: University of KwaZuluNatal Press, 2007.

Hanks, J., 'Promoting corporate environmental responsibility: What role for 'self-regulatory' and 'co-regulatory' policy instruments in South Africa?', in *The Greening of Business in Developing Countries: Rhetoric, Reality and Prospects*, Peter Utting (ed), London: Zed Books, 2002.

Hermer, Richard and Martyn Day, 'Helping Bush bushwhack justice: The most progressive law on the US statute books delivers justice to victims of human rights violations. Now the Bush regime is trying to scrap it—and the UK government is backing him', *Guardian*, Tuesday 27 April 2004.

Hollingsworth Roger J. and Robert Boyer (eds), *Contemporary Capitalism: The Embeddedness of Institutions*, Cambridge: Cambridge University Press, 1997.

ICHRP (International Council on Human Rights Policy), *Beyond Voluntarism: Human Rights and the Developing Legal Obligations of Companies*. Versoix, Switzerland: ICHRP, 2002.

ICC (International Chamber of Commerce) and (IOE) International Organization of Employers, *Joint written statement submitted by the International Chamber of Commerce and the International Organization of Employers, non-governmental organizations in general consultative status*, Commission on Human Rights, Sub-Commission on the Promotion and Protection of Human Rights, E/CN.4/Sub.2/2003/ NGO/44, 2003

International Forum on Globalization, *Alternatives to Economic Globalization: A Better World is Possible*, San Francisco: Berret-Koehler Publishers, 2002.

Kaul, Inge, 'Blending External and Domestic Policy Demands: The Rise of the Intermediary State', in *The New Public Finance: Responding to Global*

Chalenges, Inge Kaul and Pedro Conceição (eds), Oxford: Oxford University Press, 2006.

Kay, Julie, '11th Circuit to Clarify Liability', *Daily Business Review*, 30 October 2006.

Kuszewski, Judy, *Wither the OFR?*, SustainAbility, 2006, available at *http:// www.sustainability.com/insight/article.asp?id=405*, accessed on 2 November 2006.

Lifsher, Marc, 'Unocal Settles Human Rights Lawsuit over Alleged Abuses at Myanmar Pipeline' *Los Angeles Times*, 22 March 2005.

McBarnet D., A. Voiculescu and T. Campbell (eds), *The New Corporate Accountability: Corporate Social Responsibility and the Law*, Cambridge: Cambridge University Press, 2007

McBarnet, D. 'Corporate social responsibility beyond law, through law, for law: the new corporate accountability' in McBarnet D., A. Voiculescu and T. Campbell (eds), *The New Corporate Accountability: Corporate Social Responsibility and the Law*, Cambridge: Cambridge University Press, 2007.

Martinez-Alier, Joan, *The Environmentalism of the Poor: A Study of Ecological Conflicts and Valuation*, Cheltenham: Edward Elgar, 2002.

Muchlinsky, Peter, 'Human rights, social responsibility and the regulation of international business: The development of international standards by intergovernmental organisations', *Non-state Actors and International Law*, 3, 2003, pp. 123–52.

Muchlinsky, Peter, *Multinational Enterprises and the Law*, Oxford: Oxford University Press, 2007.

Neumeister, Larry, 'Talisman Released from Genocide Case', *Guardian*, 12 September 2006.

Newell, P., 'From responsibility to citizenship: Corporate accountability for development' *IDS Bulletin*, 33 (2), 2002, pp. 91–100.

OECD (Organisation for Economic Co-operation and Development), *OECD Guidelines for Multinational Enterprises: Specific Instances Considered by National Contact Points*, Paris: OECD, 2006.

OECDWatch, *Five Years On: A Review of the OECD Guidelines and National Contact Points*, Amsterdam: SOMO—Centre for Research on Multinational Corporations, 2005.

Public Citizen, *NAFTA's Threat to Sovereignty and Democracy: The Record of NAFTA Chapter 11 Investor-State Cases 1994–2005*. Washington DC: Public Citizen, 2005.

PWYP (Publish What You Pay) and Revenue Watch Institute, *Eye on EITI: Civil Society Perspectives and Recommendations on the Extractive Industries Transparency Initiative*, London and New York: PWYP/Revenue Watch Institute, 2006.

Rajagopal, Balakrishnan, 'Limits of Law in Counter-Hegemonic Globalization: The Indian Supreme Court and the Narmada Valley

Struggle', in *Law and Globalization from Below: Towards a Cosmopolitan Legality*, Boaventura de Souza Santos and César A. Rodríguez-Garavito (eds), Cambridge: Cambridge University Press, 2005.

Reuters India, *India:* 'Court seeks Coke, Pepsi reply to additives petition', 2006, available at *www.corpwatch.org/article.php?id=13981*, accessed on 2 November 2006.

Ruggie, John Gerard, 'Taking embedded liberalism global: The corporate connection', in *Taming Globalization: Frontiers of Governance*, David Held and Mathias Koenig-Archibugi (eds), Cambridge: Polity Press, 2003.

Sabharwal, Y.K. *Human Rights and the Environment*, 2005, available at *www.supremecourtofindia.nic.in/new_links/speach.htm*, accessed on 10 October 2006.

Sagafi-nejad, Tagi, 'Should Global Rules Have Legal Teeth? Policing (WHO Framework Convention on Tobacco Control) vs. Good Citizenship (UN Global Compact)', *International Journal of Business*, 11 (1), 2006.

Santos, Boaventura de Souza and César A. Rodríguez-Garavito (eds), *Law and Globalization from Below: Towards a Cosmopolitan Legality*, Cambridge: Cambridge University Press, 2005.

Sarma, B. Mahesh, *CSO CASE STUDY 11—Contending paradigms for contested public spaces: role of CSOs in shaping Delhi's transport policy*. London: Overseas Development Institute (ODI), 2006

Sell, Susan, *The Quest for Global Governance in Intellectual Property and Public Health: Structural, Discursive and Institutional Dimensions*, Paper prepared for 'SARS, Public Health, and Global Governance', Institute for International Law and Public Policy, Temple University Beasley School of Law, Philadelphia, Pa. 24 March 2004.

Social Watch India, *Citizens Report 2004: Making Democracy Work—Deficits of Democracy and Governance*, New Delhi: Social Watch India, 2004.

Social Watch India, *Social Watch India: Citizens Report on Governance and Development 2003*. New Delhi: Social Watch India, 2003.

Special Representative of the United Nations Secretary-General (SRSG), *Business and Human Rights: Mapping International Standards of Responsibility and Accountability for Corporate Acts*, United Nations Human Rights Council, A/HRC/4/035, 2007.

Stephens, Joe, 'Panel Faults Pfizer in '96 Clinical Trial In Nigeria—Unapproved Drug Tested on Children', *Washington Post*, Sunday, 7 May 2006, pp. A01.

Suresh, Narayanan, *Monsanto's Transgenic Cross, Editorial*, available at *http://www.biospectrumindia.com/content/editorial/10610201.asp*, accessed on 1 November 2006.

SustainAbility. 2004. *The Changing Landscape of Liability: A Director's Guide to Trends in Corporate Environmental, Social and Economic Liability*, London: SustainAbility, 2004.

The Hindu, 'SEZs: PIL filed in Supreme Court' *The Hindu*, 30 September 2006.

The Tribune, 'Indian wheat patented by Monsanto flayed', *The Tribune*, Thursday 29 January 2004.

Ugaz, Cecilia and Catherine Waddams Price (eds), *Utility Privatisation and Regulation: Fair deal for consumers?* Cheltenham: Edward Elgar, 2003.

UNCTAD (United Nations Conference on Trade and Development), *World Investment Report: FDI policies for development: National and international perspectives*, Geneva: UNCTAD, 2003.

UNRISD (United Nations Research Institute for Social Development), *States of Disarray: The social effects of globalization*, Geneva: UNRISD, 1995.

Utting, Peter, Regulating Business for Sustainable Development', in Sanjay Sharma, Mark Starik and Bryan Husted (eds), *Organizations and the Sustainability Mosaic: Crafting Long-Term Ecological and Societal Solutions*, Cheltenham: Edward Elgar, 2007.

Utting, Peter, 'Corporate Responsibility and the Movement of Business' in *Development and the Private Sector: Consuming Interests*, John Sayer and Deborah Eade (eds). Bloomfield CT: Kumarian Press, 2006.

Utting, Peter, *Rethinking Business Regulation: From Self-Regulation to Social Control*. Programme Paper, No. 15, Geneva: UNRISD, 2005.

Utting, Peter, 'Regulating Business via Multistakeholder Initiatives', in NGLS/UNRISD (eds), *Voluntary Approaches to Corporate Responsibility: Readings and a Resource Guide*, Geneva, NGLS/UNRISD, 2002.

Vernon, Raymond, *In the Hurricane's Eye: The Troubled Prospects of Multinational Enterprises*, Cambridge MA: Harvard University Press, 1998.

Ward, Halina, *Legal Issues in Corporate Citizenship*. Stockholm/London: Swedish Partnership for Global Responsibility/IIED, 2003.

Webb, Tim, 'Shell faces human rights grilling', *The Independent*, 11 April 2004.

5

Corporate Accountability in the Agro-Food Sector
The Case of Illegal GMO Releases

JENNIFER CLAPP[1]

INTRODUCTION

The promotion of responsibility and accountability amongst transnational corporations (TNCs) has become an important topic of debate in recent years. In terms of environmental sustainability, there has been a push for the internalization of environmental costs and application of the precautionary principle as measures that firms can and should take to make themselves more responsible, and accountable, for the environmental impacts of their activities. But while these goals might be agreed upon—indeed they are highlighted as key principles in the Rio Declaration of the UN Conference on Environment and Development—the choice of governance mechanism to best achieve them is less clear. Should accountability measures be imposed on firms from the outside, by the state or an international treaty? Or should it be left to firms to work out on their own, through voluntary measures? Or is there some middle ground where voluntary and mandatory measures can work together in an effective way? This basic policy debate has been a central feature of global discussions on environmental protection since the Stockholm Conference in 1972 (see Utting 2000; 2005). While the 1970s saw an approach that preferred to enforce accountability on transnational corporations through a global regulatory mechanism, the emphasis shifted in the

[1]I would like to thank the Social Sciences and Humanities Research Council of Canada for financial support for this research. I would also like to thank Dave Campanella, Justin Williams, and Candace Wormsbecker for research assistance. A different version of this article has been accepted for publication in *Ecological Economics*.

1980s and 1990s to one of voluntary corporate measures. This voluntary approach was endorsed by the Earth Summit in 1992, and was recently boosted by the World Summit on Sustainable Development (WSSD) in 2002. We have now had at least fifteen years of corporate voluntary measures as the principal mechanism by which to achieve cost internalization and precaution amongst firms. But have these measures lived up to their promises with respect to environmental issues?

This chapter explores transnational corporate responsibility and accountability in the agro-food sector. In particular, it looks at the agricultural input industry and the global implications of 'accidental' releases of genetically modified organisms (GMOs). Recent years have seen a number of cases of 'accidental' or 'unintentional' releases of these organisms that were not approved for human consumption or in some cases even for commercial planting. In at least three of these cases, crops produced with the unapproved seeds entered into the global food system via international shipments. Because of the ongoing debates surrounding the environmental impact of GMOs when released into the environment, there have been differing interpretations as to what course of action should be taken, if any, in response. Corporate responses to these incidents have stressed that there is no need for concern, environmental or otherwise, from these releases. At the same time, environmental groups have complained about the potential environmental harm caused by accidental releases of GMOs.

In addition to the requirement that they meet with existing government regulations in the country in which they operate, a growing number of agricultural input corporations follow some sort of voluntary measure for the promotion of environmental and social responsibility. The agricultural input industry has embraced corporate social responsibility (CSR) reporting in recent years and some of its major players are members of the UN's Global Compact, who advertise that they abide by the OECD Guidelines on Multinational Enterprises (MNEs). And in some countries, such as the US, self-monitoring, as required by some of these voluntary measures, is relied upon for the enforcement of some government regulations, including those in the agricultural input industry. Voluntary measures can go some way to help improve corporate environmental responsibility, especially in cases where the economic goals of industry mesh closely with certain environmental goals, such as energy-use reduction and waste management.

But broader environmental goals that many would like to see firms achieve, such as the application of the precautionary principle and internalization of environmental costs, might not have the same effect on a firm's bottom line, especially where debate is rife over the environmental impact of the product the firm is seeking to market. In this chapter I argue that voluntary measures thus far have not been enough to encourage environmental accountability in the agricultural biotechnology sector where there is a heated debate over the environmental impact of the product the firm is attempting to market. In the case of illegal GMO releases, firms have openly attempted to avoid responsibility and liability for the environmental impact of the release of their products. In particular, they used their privileged access to information about the impacts of GMOs to assert their position that their products, even if illegally released, are safe. Asserting the safety of GMOs can be seen as a means by which firms seek to minimize their legal liability.

An implication of this finding is that in cases where firms' economic goals do not align with environmental responsibility, voluntary measures are likely to be weak in their impact. In this case, holding transnational agricultural biotechnology firms accountable for their environmental actions through more stringently monitored government regulations, or via externally-imposed governance mechanisms such as a legally binding treaty, are likely to be more effective ways to get firms to minimize environmental risks and the potential environmental costs associated with those risks. Indeed, the need to assign liability in the cases of unintentional transboundary movements of GMOs has been recognized. Work has recently begun on the negotiation of a liability protocol that will be attached to the Cartagena Protocol on Biosafety[2] to address issues of accountability when GMOs make their way into international shipments to countries where they are not approved. Talks on a protocol on liability began in 2005 and have been mired in debate. It is unclear what the final agreement will look like, or which actors (firms or states) will ultimately be held liable. To be sure, corporations themselves are actively involved in these negotiations, and are arguing strongly that firms not be held liable for damages that may result from such instances.

[2]The Cartagena Protocol is a global agreement which aims to regulate the trade in genetically modified organisms (GMOs), including bio-engineered seeds and foods. It was negotiated over the 1996–2000 period, and came into force in 2003.

This chapter first provides a brief review of corporate environmental responsibility and accountability and their relationship to the global food and agriculture industry. It then examines the case of accidental releases of GMOs and the lack of effective mechanisms to ensure corporate accountability in such instances. The chapter concludes with a discussion of the need for stronger international measures to impose accountability in the agricultural input industry, particularly with respect to genetically modified seeds, as a necessary complement to corporate voluntary measures.

I. AGRO-FOOD TNCs AND CORPORATE RESPONSIBILITY AND ACCOUNTABILITY

CSR measures, as explained in the first chapter of this book, incorporate a range of activities and organizations, from company codes of conduct to CSR reporting and participation in international initiatives such as the Global Compact. There has been some variation in terms of the timing of different sectors with respect to the adoption of voluntary measures. TNCs in high environmental impact sectors, such as chemicals, forestry and heavy industry, were early to sign up to a number of the voluntary corporate environmental measures outlined above, as a way to minimize liability and improve their public image. The chemical industry, for example, developed its own corporate standard in Responsible Care in the 1980s, and widely adopted ISO 14000 environmental management standards for their plant operations when that standard was introduced in the 1990s (Prakash 2000). Most such firms also engage in CSR reporting. Where environmental impact of an industry is high and public reputation is important, most firms have their bases covered in terms of one or more voluntary measures.

Large firms operating at various points along the global food production and marketing chain were relatively slow to adopt voluntary measures for corporate responsibility (Action Aid International 2005). The slow up-take of CSR measures in the agro-food industry can perhaps be explained by the fact that the environmental and social impacts of their activities are more obscure than is the case in high environmental impact sectors. Most consumers are not aware of the TNCs responsible for the production and processing of the food they purchase, typically at a large retail outlet—also large TNCs themselves. The source of food for most consumers starts and ends at the supermarket. The agro-food sector is characterized by corporate

Table 5.1   Key Players at Various Stages of Food Production Chain in
CSR Initiatives

Sector	Company	CSR reports produced regularly	Follows GRI guidelines*	Global Compact participant
Agricultural inputs	Monsanto (US)		No	No
	DuPont (US)	Yes	Yes (2002 CI)	Yes, since 2001
	Bayer (Germany)	Yes (2002 CI)	Yes	Yes, since 2000
	Syngenta (Switzerland)	Yes	No	No
	Dow (US)	Yes	Yes (2002 CI)	Yes, since 2007
	Aventis (France)	Yes	Yes	Yes, since 2000 (purchased by Bayer in 2002)
	BASF (Germany)	Yes	Yes (2002 CI)	Yes, since 2000
Food production and processing	Cargill (US)	Yes	No	Only Argentina affiliate, since 2004
	Archer Daniels Midland (US)	Yes	No	No
	ConAgra (US)	Yes	No	No
	Pepsico (US)	Yes	Yes (2002 CI)	No
	Tyson (US)	Yes	Yes (2002 CI)	No
	Nestle SA (Switzerland)	Yes	No	Yes, since 2001
Retail	Walmart (US)	No	No	No
	Carrefour (France)	Yes	Yes (G3—B+ Self Declared)	Yes, since 2001
	Tesco (UK)	Yes	Yes (2002 CI)	No

* GRI has three levels of adherence, AI = in accordance with external verification (highest rating); CI = Content Index—that is, report indexed for GRI categories (middle rating) and Reference = report made with reference to guidelines but not externally verified (lowest rating); 2002 is the second version of GRI guidelines and G3 is the most recent (2006) version of the guidelines. The G3 adherence is ranked by a self-declared system from A (highest) to C (lowest).
Sources: GRI Website; Global Compact Website; Company Websites.

concentration of globally connected firms, and is segmented into distinct activities, even though some of the same corporations often operate at one or more levels of these differentiated activities (McMichael 2005; Lang and Heasman 2004). The stages along the chain include agricultural inputs, food production and processing, as well as food retailing. Table 5.1 outlines the participation of the key players at these various stages of the food production chain in several of the key CSR initiatives.

II. CSR AND VOLUNTARY INITIATIVES STATUS FOR MAJOR CORPORATIONS IN THE FOOD AND AGRICULTURE SECTOR

Although initially slow to adopt voluntary measures, recent years have seen a proliferation of non-state market driven measures for certification to specific standards at the retail end of the agro-food sector—that which is most distanced from the environmental impact, but on the other hand is closest to the consumer (Busch 2000; Konefal *et al.*, 2005; Tallontire 2007). Typically, such standards are primarily for food safety and quality, and the responsibility—that is, the need to certify to standards—is pushed back to farmers as the producers of the food. The chain of responsibility for these quality and safety standards does not extend to the other side of the farmers—that is, the agricultural input corporations. In other words, it is the suppliers of the food who must certify to these standards, not the large corporations that supply the farmers with the inputs—the seeds and the chemicals—to produce that food. These retail standards have been subject to some debate as there is widespread concern that small farmers, particularly those in the developing world, might be squeezed out of markets because of the high costs associated with certification (Hatanaka *et al.*, 2005).

At the same time that the safety and quality certification schemes for produce were emerging as private standards set by large food retailers, a growing number of consumers also began to demand products that are not only safe and of good quality, but which also meet environmental and social standards. The market for organically-produced food products, for example, is growing enormously all around the world (Raynolds 2004). Similarly, the market for fair trade products has also expanded (ibid. 2000; Goodman 2004). This growing market for organic and fair trade products has given rise to other sorts of private market-driven certification schemes to verify that the products are indeed environmentally and socially sound, including certification of GMO-free products. The certification of these products is run by third-party groups and independently monitored, bringing a level of assurance to consumers that the products meet the required standard.

Firms at the agricultural input end of the global agro-food chain have also taken on voluntary CSR activities. Agricultural pesticides have long been associated with environmental problems. Thus, as mentioned above, most pesticide producers have now signed on to the chemical industry standard 'Responsible Care'. This standard is set and overseen by the chemical industry itself, which has raised concerns about its weak terms and lack of external enforcement (Prakash 2000). In response to critics' claims of pesticide misuse and lack of labeling of these products in the developing world, leading industry players have also promoted global 'safe use' educational initiatives as means by which to demonstrate their commitment to environmental and social responsibility. These campaigns have also been widely criticized for inflating their impact (Murray and Taylor 2000).

Large transnational seed companies also began to engage in voluntary corporate measures over the past decade. The first genetically modified crops intended for sale as food items were approved in the mid-1990s in the US, and in a number of countries after that. Before that time, there was little effort or need for seed companies to sign on to voluntary corporate responsibility measures, mainly because there was little perception of environmental or social problems associated with their activities.

There are two key reasons why seed companies have begun to adhere to voluntary corporate responsibility measures since the mid-1990s. First, as the environmental critique of genetically modified crops began to intensify following their commercial release, transnational seed companies felt the need to stress the environmental benefits of genetically modified seeds, and to downplay their potential risks. Pressure from activist groups, as well as a desire to protect their reputation as industry leaders, helped to push the seed industry in this direction. Second, beginning in the 1990s, there were a number of mergers and acquisitions in the agricultural biotechnology and agricultural chemical industries. The agricultural biotech seed companies became much larger and the industry much more concentrated, and in a number of cases it was chemical pesticide manufacturers that bought up the seed companies. For example, amongst the top ten seed companies globally are firms that initially started out as chemical manufacturers, such as Monsanto, Dupont, and Bayer CropScience. This marriage of the seeds and agro-chemicals industry is in large part due to the fact that much of the genetic modification of seeds is to make them tolerant of certain types of herbicides (Clapp 2003). As the large transnational seed companies merged with chemical companies, they adopted the voluntary corporate responsibility activities with which the chemical industry had already begun to engage.

Although the agro-food sector has adopted a range of types of voluntary corporate measures to promote sustainability, the effectiveness of such measures varies, depending partly on the place of the firm in the various stages along the global agro-food production chain. For firms that rely on safety and environmental performance to maintain their market—such as food safety standards, organic or fair trade products, and GMO-free products, there appear to be strong incentives for firms to voluntarily exercise precaution and minimize environmental costs. The reason is simple. Their market depends on them doing so. Customers who purchase products certified as organic, fair trade, GMO-free, or as adhering to 'good agricultural practices'— expect the firms selling those products to adhere to such standards which are built upon these broader environmental policy goals. But for those firms operating at a much further distance from the consumer, and where debate over the impacts are more prevalent and there is an asymmetry of information access, such as in the genetically engineered seed industry, there appears to be much less incentive for firms to take these broader policy goals seriously.

A key reason for this divergence in practice is that biotech seed companies can exploit the asymmetry in information access as a strategy to avoid accepting liability and accountability when something goes wrong. In other words, if challenged on the environmental impact of their products or practices, firms can easily produce volumes of reports to substantiate their own claim that the risks are minimal, and to argue that they should not be held liable. There are several reasons for this information asymmetry. The bulk of the research on agricultural biotechnology is funded by the industry itself, giving the biotech firms an upper hand in terms of access to research when they are challenged or when something goes wrong. Undertaking such research is expensive and time consuming, and much of the information on the genetic manipulations that firms undertake is done under intellectual property protection or in anticipation of an application for a patent, and thus are held by firms to be proprietary information. For these reasons, it is extremely difficult for independent researchers, or even government regulatory bodies, to independently verify the firms' research results. As a result, government regulatory bodies rely heavily on the studies carried out by firms in order to assess the safety of GMO crops.

These factors contribute to the agricultural biotechnology industry's failure to exercise precaution that would in turn have the effect of minimizing potential environmental costs of risky activities. Indeed, adherence to the precautionary principle established at the Earth Summit, and even alluded to in the UN Global Compact Principles, has been one of the weaker aspects of the contemporary CSR practice. Because they can use their privileged access to information to their advantage, there is a strong incentive for agricultural biotechnology firms to ignore potential environmental costs of the product they are marketing, which lowers their costs, and enables them to forge ahead with a potentially risky technology. But it is precisely in industries characterized by risk and uncertainty where environmental application of the precautionary principle is likely to be most useful.

III. Assessing Accountability and Responsibility in the Case of Accidental Releases of Unapproved GMOs

The behaviour of the agricultural biotechnology firms with respect to the accidental releases of unapproved GMOs illustrates the lack of corporate accountability with respect to the broader environmental policy goals of precaution in the face of uncertainty and environmental cost internalization. Accidental releases of GMOs have occurred with some regularity since these products first came onto the market. This chapter focuses on three of the most publicized cases, where unapproved seed varieties were released by mistake in the United States by major ag-biotech TNCs: StarLink (Aventis, discovered in 2000), Bt10 (Syngenta, discovered in 2005), and LLRICE601 (Bayer CropScience, discovered in 2006). In each of these cases, the unapproved GMOs made their way into the food and seed supply, and contaminated not just domestic supplies, but also made their way into exports, thus affecting numerous countries around the world. It should be noted that there have also been problems associated with accidental contamination of food crops by pharma-crops, as well as other incidents of seeds contaminated with GMOs and shipped internationally without the recipients' prior knowledge (see GeneWatch and Greenpeace 2005).

The debate over whether GMOs are safe in general is heated, and this debate has made its way into the debate over how to respond to accidental releases of unapproved GMOs. While some are confident of their safety and downplay their risks, others point out that there are valid concerns about the ecological, health, and economic ramifications of GMO contamination (on this debate, Dale 2002). Gene flow to wild plant relatives, for example, could transfer traits for herbicide tolerance or pest resistance and thus impact biodiversity (Ellstrand 2001, 2003a and 2003b; Pilson and Prendeville 2004). There are also concerns that genetically altered foods could spark allergic reactions or facilitate antibiotic resistance (Dauenhauer 2003). There are also economic impacts, as contaminated crops could be shut out of markets, causing economic losses for farmers (Pew Initiative on Food and Biotechnology 2002). At the same time, others argue that the risks are not as serious as critics claim, and that the level of risk depends very much on the particular crop and type of modification (Paarlberg 2002).

The accidental release of unapproved GMOs in a number of incidents in recent years has intensified the debate over the potential risks of GMOs more broadly. When unapproved GMOs are released into the environment, the concerns over their safety are amplified, because very little is known about the traits in unapproved varieties, and there is usually a reason why they were not approved. The transnational agricultural biotech companies responsible for these releases have tried to reassure the public that there is no serious harm that has resulted from the releases, while environmental groups have argued the opposite.

Regardless of the actual risks, and however controversial the question of GMO safety in general, the point remains that varieties of GMOs that have not been approved by any regulatory process have been released into the environment, thus making their release in effect illegal. The firms responsible for the accidental releases in the three most prominent cases had all signed onto one or more of the voluntary corporate responsibility measures outlined in the previous section. And in the US, where these illegal releases occurred, the regulatory bodies relied on self-policing as a key means by which to monitor and enforce the regulations. While in two of the cases it was the firm that reported the illegal release, the actions of the firms in the wake of the GMO releases have raised serious questions about the ability of voluntary measures to ensure that they implement the precautionary principle and pay for environmental costs associated with their activities. Failure to pick up the tab for the global costs of accidental GMO releases represents an externalization of the costs of agricultural biotechnology (see Belcher *et al.* 2005). And the weak procedures followed by the agricultural biotechnology industry, which enabled the incidents to occur in the first place, represent a failure to implement the precautionary principle.

StarLink

In 2000, environmental groups revealed that StarLink corn, a variety marketed by the agricultural biotech company Aventis (which was bought up by Bayer CropScience in 2002), had contaminated the food supply in the US. Because of concerns over allergenicity of the protein found in StarLink, Cry9C, this variety of corn was approved by the US EPA only for animal consumption, and not human consumption. This was referred to as a split registration, and strict procedures were to be followed to ensure that it would only be used for the approved use, as animal feed. When it was revealed that StarLink had made its way into the human food supply chain, there were widespread recalls of contaminated food products (Segarra and Rawson 2001; US FDA 2000).

It was the responsibility of the company marketing the seed to ensure that farmers were aware of the restrictions, and to supply them with a set of rules for its planting and handling. But it had become clear that Aventis had failed to make the restrictions on StarLink maize clear to farmers and grain handlers. The protein from the StarLink variety had contaminated the food supply in the US, and had been exported in the form of both bulk maize shipments and as processed foods. Traces of StarLink corn were found in imported corn and corn products in a number of countries, including Japan, Korea, Nicaragua, and Mexico. Five years later, Cry9C still turned up in the corn supply in the US and in other countries (FOEI 2005, p. 11). No one is certain whether the contamination occurred as a result of gene flow, or mixing of grains.

At the urging of the US Environmental Protection Agency (EPA), Aventis voluntarily cancelled its registration for StarLink shortly after the extent of the contamination was revealed (Taylor and Tick 2001).

But at the same time it petitioned for a temporary (four year) approval of the variety for human consumption (Flora 2001), citing that new evidence found diminished risk for allergenicity of StarLink. In this case, the US EPA refused to grant the exemption, because, although it agreed that the risk was small, there was still a potential for StarLink to be a serious allergen when ingested by humans. The US government took some measures to hold the company accountable, but only within the US. Aventis was required by the US government to pay for costs relating to the recall of StarLink maize in commodity form, as well as in processed foods. Farmers and suppliers were also awarded settlements for the costs they incurred as a result. But while the company was made to pay costs and legal fees for farmers in the US, there was no international accountability for the StarLink that made its way into other countries. StarLink has been found in farmers' fields in Mexico, in food aid shipments to Central America and Africa, and in shipments of processed food products to both Japan and Korea. There was special concern for the ecological impact of StarLink found in Mexican farmers' fields, as Mexico is a centre of origin of maize and gene flow from this variety had been documented, despite Mexico's ban on the planting of genetically modified varieties of maize (ETC Group 2003).

Aventis had, prior to this incident, undertaken some voluntary corporate responsibility measures, but critics argued that they made little difference with respect to preventing a recurrence of this type of incident. Aventis signed onto Global Compact in 1999, and the StarLink contamination was revealed in 2000. Environmental groups lobbied the UN in 2001 to have Aventis expelled from the Global Compact. It highlighted its failure to adhere to Principle 7 of the Global Compact, that business should support a precautionary approach to environmental challenges. The Global Compact website explains this principle and the concept of precaution for firms as including analysis of the potential environmental impact of their production processes and products; building in safety margins when setting standards where significant uncertainty still exists; banning or restricting activities whose impact on the environment is uncertain; and communicating with stakeholders.[3] According to the Institute for Agriculture and Trade Policy, on all counts Aventis failed to meet these criteria (see Flora 2001). Aventis was criticized for

[3] http://www.unglobalcompact.org/AboutTheGC/TheTenPrinciples/principle7.html

rushing the product into the market before adequate testing, not ensuring that safety controls were followed in planting and handling, pursuing a product that was inherently risky because of the potential for gene flow because corn is an open pollinating plant, and failing to fully inform farmers of the need to handle the corn variety with care. Moreover, Aventis was criticized further for its failure to locate and buy back all of the contaminated corn, as demanded by the US government. The UN was reluctant to eject the company from the Global Compact, on the grounds that there were no such conditions to be met by firms that are participants (Neuffer 2001). Aventis was purchased by Bayer CropScience in 2002.

Bt10 Maize

In early 2005, the Swiss TNC Syngenta announced that an experimental variety of genetically modified maize known as Bt10, not approved for commercial planting in any country, had accidentally been supplied by that company as seed in the US for four years without anyone being aware of it. When the release of Bt10 was revealed, Syngenta tried to allay fears by claiming that it was nearly identical to its Bt11 maize, which did have regulatory approval in the US and in the EU (Herrera 2005, p. 514). However, it soon emerged that Bt10 and Bt11 are not identical. The main concern over the Bt10 maize is that it contains an antibiotic resistant marker gene, which raised concerns about its health impacts, as it was feared that it could pass on resistance to the commonly used antibiotic, ampicillin (FOEI 2005, p. 12; Macilwain 2005). Before it was discovered in the seed supply, some 15,000 hectares had been planted with Bt10, and it made its way into the seed supply and into the food supply.

Syngenta discovered the mistake in December 2004 and notified the US government. No public announcement was made by either the US government or the company for several months (see GeneWatch UK and Greenpeace International 2005). In fact, it was the magazine *Nature*, which broke the story to the public in March 2005, only a few days after the EU had been officially notified of the release. By the time the story had become public, Bt10 maize ended up in maize shipments to Ireland and Japan, and likely to many other countries as well. It is unclear how many countries have been affected by imports of maize containing Bt10, as Syngenta declined to give a list of countries that had received it (Macilwain 2005).

Syngenta was fined US$ 375,000 by the US government for releasing an unapproved seed variety. The company was also required by the US government to hold a training conference on best practices in the agricultural biotechnology seed industry (APHIS/USDA 2005). Specifically, it was instructed to include as goals of the conference the development of a best management practice or technical guideline for preventing contamination of biotech genes in seed development; and also the development of a best management practices guide to identify and implement corrective measures when unintended releases occur (APHIS/USDA 2005). Syngenta was not under any legal obligation to provide details about the gene transformations that characterize Bt10, and it stalled on providing a testing method when the EU demanded that all imports of maize from the US be tested and certified as being free of Bt10 (Lezaun 2006, pp. 519–20). The company was reluctant to give out information on testing or on the genetic modifications that resulted in Bt10, because it was viewed as confidential business information (GeneWatch UK and Greenpeace 2005, p. 15). Syngenta eventually produced a test for Bt10 by mid-April 2005 (Kirwin 2005, p. 684). The exact extent to which the food system was contaminated with Bt10 will likely never be known.

Syngenta chose not to apply for approval of Bt10 maize for commercial purposes following the announcement that it had been accidentally released, and the existing seed stock known to contain Bt10 was destroyed. It is probable that Syngenta did not seek retroactive approval of Bt10 because it was unlikely that it would be approved due to the fact that it contained a marker gene that could potentially confer antibiotic resistance. However, the company has continued to stress the safety of Bt10.

Although not a participant in the UN Global Compact, Syngenta has been active in terms of CSR reporting and it funds a foundation for sustainable agriculture. Syngenta's 2005 CSR report identifies its breach of the law and briefly discusses the Bt10 release. The report states that there were no negative environmental or health impacts, and stresses that the amounts released were minimal. It points out the similarity between Bt10 and Bt11 in stressing its safety. The company concludes the section on Bt10 by noting: 'Since the misidentification, enhanced quality assurance and control procedures designed to prevent recurrence have been implemented.' (Syngenta 2005). While it may indeed be taking measures to improve its performance along these lines, critics argue that Syngenta did not apply stringent enough measures in the first place to prevent this release from happening, nor did it adequately explain how the accidental release of Bt10 happened in the first place (*Nature*, 14 April 2005, p. 807).

Liberty Link RICE 601

A more recent high-profile case of accidental release of a genetically modified seed variety was revealed in August 2006. Bayer CropSciene acknowledged that an unapproved variety of genetically modified rice, Liberty Link Rice 601 (LLRICE601), had been found in long-grain rice supplies in the US. The LL601 variety was tested by Bayer in small-scale field trials in the US years earlier. These trials ended in 2001 as Bayer had decided not to seek approval for the variety. This variety of rice contains a protein that gives it tolerance to Bayer's herbicide Liberty (*generic name*: glufosinate). It is not clear when Bayer CropScience became aware of the contamination, but Riceland, a US rice company, reported the presence of LLRICE 601. It is not clear how the contamination occurred, and the US government subsequently launched an inquiry into the case.

When the contamination was publicly announced, the EU, Japan, and South Korea immediately moved to ban shipments of long-grain rice from the US, as they could not be guaranteed that imports were free from unapproved GMOs. Within ten days of the announcement of the contamination with the unapproved variety, rice farmers in the US filed a class-action lawsuit against Bayer CropScience, as they lost export markets and the price of rice dropped significantly as a result of the contamination (Reuters 2006).

Bayer quickly moved to apply for retroactive regulatory approval of the variety for commercial planting. The US government immediately undertook a risk assessment, in which it concluded that the best option was to approve the variety because it saw no serious environmental or health concerns associated with it (APHIS/USDA 2006). The process for approval includes an opportunity for civil society groups to submit comments. A number of groups registered their protest of the approval application, and insisted instead that the GM rice variety should be strictly regulated. They noted, for example, that key components of the necessary information for an adequate risk assessment of the variety were missing from the documentation given to the public when the application for approval was posted for public comment. The Centre for Food Safety registered its concerns about the spread of the herbicide-tolerant variety of rice into US rice growing areas, as it could contribute to herbicide-tolerant 'superweeds', since rice grown in the southern US does have weedy relatives that could be affected by gene flow from the genetically modified variety (Center for Food Safety 2006). Further, GM rice poses serious problems for organic farmers as such weeds could cross pollinate with their fields, resulting in a loss of certification of their products as GMO-free. Because of disruptions that the incident caused to US exports of rice, the USA Rice Federation has endorsed deregulation, in order to calm market concerns. The EU stated publicly that LLRICE601 is likely safe for human consumption, but said there was insufficient information available to conduct a full-risk assessment on the variety (EFSA 2006).

By late fall 2006, the environmental group Greenpeace had conducted tests and revealed that LLRICE601 was found in shipments of imported rice in twenty-four countries, including a significant number of countries in the EU, the Middle East, West Africa, and Asia (GeneWatch and Greenpeace GM Contamination Register website). In late November 2006, the US granted regulatory approval to LLRICE601 on the grounds that it was similar to two other rice varieties that Bayer did have approval for, but which it never commercialized (Lee 2006).

Meanwhile, there are now fifteen class-action lawsuits, representing some 300 US rice farmers, filed against Bayer. In its response to one of the suits, Bayer claimed that the company is not to blame for the contamination, but rather it is the fault of farmers' negligence and carelessness, unavoidable circumstances, and 'an act of God'. Adam Levitt, a lawyer representing farmers in five of these lawsuits commented that 'It is unfortunate that Bayer, rather than accept responsibility for its actions, is instead trying to pin the blame on the American rice farmers, the very people most detrimentally affected by Bayer's conduct here' (quoted in Weiss 2006).

How can we assess this incident in terms of the Bayer CropScience's voluntary corporate social responsibility efforts? Bayer CropScience has participated in the UN Global Compact since this initiative began, and advertises on its Corporate Responsibility webpage that it adheres to the OECD Guidelines for Multinational Enterprises (albeit mistakenly referred to as 'OECD Principles for MNCs').[4] This incident appears to suggest that Bayer, like Aventis that it acquired in 2002,

---

[4] *http://www.bayercropscience.com/bayer/cropscience/cscms.nsf/id/HumanRights*

has not lived up to its pledge to implement the precautionary principle. Though it never intended to commercialize LLRICE601, and ceased to experiment with it in 2001, this seed variety still made its way into the food system. How this occurred is a mystery, as Bayer has emphasized. But this still raises serious questions about safety and handling procedures of this variety undertaken by the corporation. The fact that the unapproved variety was likely present for the past five years in the US rice supply, and was exported around the world without the company realizing it, represents a serious lack of testing and overall precaution with the development of GM varieties, and within the rice breeding operations of the corporation. By seeking regulatory approval of the variety after contamination was discovered appears to be a move by the firm to avoid liability for the costs it had externalized for the previous five years. Further, its claim that farmers and God are responsible, not the company, illustrates the company's efforts to escape liability in this instance (Weiss 2006).

But Bayer CropScience sees this case differently. Its main goals, as stated on its website, are to adhere to existing laws. Regarding this incident, the Bayer CropScience website states:

Bayer CropScience is cooperating closely with the authorities and others in the rice industry and continues to provide scientific and technical know-how. Farmers have filed lawsuits against our U.S.-affiliate Bayer CropScience LP in the meantime. Bayer CropScience believes that the company acted responsibly and in compliance with all applicable laws and regulations in this matter and will vigorously defend itself against these claims. Due to pending litigation, the company cannot comment further at this time.' (Bayer CropScience 2006)

IV. WHEN EXTERNAL GOVERNANCE MECHANISMS ARE NECESSARY

As the cases outlined above illustrate, the corporations involved in these accidental releases have not accepted that there is a risk or danger to the environment from these incidents, even though they were technically illegal. Although each claimed to adhere to one or more voluntary corporate responsibility governance mechanisms, there was very little effort to apply precaution or pay for the costs associated with the release of the unapproved GMOs. Their privileged access to the scientific information regarding the risks associated with GMOs, and the fact that other actors have not had the ability to independently verify industry studies, has enabled industry players to take the position that the risks are minimal. Industry has argued that there is no need to take responsibility in terms of paying damages to those affected by the illegal GMO releases, or to take more precautionary measures to prevent a recurrence of the problem. Further, they have argued that the seeds and crops produced using agricultural biotechnology are substantially similar or equivalent to other approved varieties, and as such they do not pose a serious risk.

It appears that where there is asymmetrical access to information on a new and potentially risky product, in this case where firms have access to information that other actors do not, that the firm has little incentive to pursue the precautionary principle and will likely seek to externalize environmental costs associated with the marketing of its product. The reason is that firms have a strong incentive to use their privileged access to information to build a case that the product is safe. This lowers their own costs, as they can deny any harm that may be caused by their product, and the lower costs encourage them to pursue the marketing of an inherently risky product. But where information on the production of the product is more easily available to other actors (that is, in this case products that are organic, fair-trade, or GMO-free), voluntary measures would seem to stand much more of a chance of changing a firm's behaviour with respect to precaution and cost internalization. They are much more likely to take such measures because their market for that product depends on them doing so. Thus, voluntary market-driven and corporate social responsibility measures to verify the safety and environmental claims of fair trade, organic, and GMO-free products, have much better odds of being effective because the impacts can be more easily verified by external actors. The important lesson from these cases is that the nature of the industry and the products it markets must be considered before concluding whether or not voluntary measures are likely to be effective in promoting corporate accountability and responsibility.

There are some signs of a tightening up of voluntary measures on the GMO release front, but because such measures are still voluntary, there is still a strong chance that such measures will remain weak. The Global Reporting Initiative revised its guidelines for CSR reports in 2006, including with respect to impacts on biodiversity (GRI 2006). These revisions have important implications for business practices related to agricultural biotechnology. Previously, the guidelines only asked for reporting, which provided a 'Description of significant impacts of activities on protected areas', but they now call for 'Description of significant impacts of activities, products, and services on biodiversity in protected areas and areas of high biodiversity value outside of protected areas' (GRI 2006). They also require more detail regarding not just programmes for managing impacts on biodiversity, but also on strategies, current actions, and future plans in this area. And they have shifted the reporting requirement from emphasis on initiatives to *manage* environmental impact of products, to initiatives to *mitigate* environmental impacts of products (GRI 2006).

In mid-2007, after the illegal GMO releases outlined in this paper, the Biotechnology Industry Organization (BIO), an industry association for firms in the biotech sector, announced plans to establish an industry-wide voluntary standard for the agricultural biotechnology sector, called the Excellence Through Stewardship Programme. This programme is based on 'quality management' and will set out guidelines on 'best practices' for the industry, and eventually will include third party auditing (Gillam 2007). It is expected that the programme will be adopted first in the US, and then globally, by 2010. These efforts to tighten up standards for corporate social responsibility in the agricultural biotechnology sector are laudable. But if the above analysis is accurate, it may not make much difference in terms of firms' actual behaviour in the agricultural biotechnology sector, as they have used privileged access to scientific studies on genetically modified varieties to consistently argue that they do not have a negative impact. Having more detailed information in CSR reports or a code of best practice for firms does not necessarily bridge the divide in terms of access to scientific information on the safety and environmental impact of a particular product marketed by a firm.

If the ultimate goal is to ensure that firms marketing products such as genetically engineered seeds pursue the precautionary principle to pick up the tab for environmental and other costs associated with the release of those seeds, more stringent government regulations and/ or external pressure is likely to have more impact in achieving that result. Surveys of TNCs in the early 1990s revealed that the most important motivating factor for firms to change their environmental practices are government environmental laws and regulations (UNCTAD 1993, p. 38). Whether that has changed with the growth of voluntary initiatives is not known. But the finding that external pressure in the form of laws and regulations is a strong motivator for environmental behaviour on the part of firms is still valid. In cases where voluntary measures do not seem to make a strong impact, it may well be prudent for states to re-enter the equation, and exert external authority, alongside voluntary codes.

One possibility for imposing external legal obligations on firms, particularly where government-level regulatory mechanisms are weak, is a global mechanism or treaty to hold firms liable and accountable for their activities. At a broad level, this idea of a corporate accountability treaty was raised in the run-up to WSSD by a number of environmental groups, including Friends of the Earth International, Greenpeace, the World Development Movement, Christian Aid, and the Alliance for a Corporate-Free UN (CEO 2001, p. 6). Friends of the Earth and Greenpeace put forward specific proposals, both of which call for liability to be squarely assigned to global firms when laws are breached, the rights of communities to seek redress, minimum environmental and social standards, as well as mechanisms to ensure that certain key principles articulated in the Rio Declaration are adhered to by firms, including those on liability, the precautionary principle and the polluter pays principle (the internalization of environmental costs) (FOEI 2001; Greenpeace International 2002a). The proposals for such a treaty were discussed at the WSSD, but were not adopted, in large part due to industry lobbying against the idea, and in favour of voluntary measures instead (Clapp 2005).

While efforts for a global mechanism have stalled, there are separate agreements on liability and redress with respect to a number of specific issue areas currently addressed by international environmental treaties. Specific to the case of accidental GMO releases, negotiations recently began to clarify issues of liability for such releases via a liability protocol to be attached to the Cartagena Biosafety Protocol (Falkner and Gupta 2004). The issue of how to handle liability for damage that results from transnational shipments of GMOs was discussed when the Biosafety Protocol was initially being negotiated (1995–2001). Considered too contentious at the time, negotiators left it to be negotiated at a later date. Work on this protocol on liability and redress began in 2005, but will likely take several years to complete.

The discussions on the liability protocol to the Cartagena Protocol on Biosafety are already mired in debate, and it is as yet unclear whether liability for illegal transfers of GMOs across borders will be assigned to states, exporters, or in the case of accidental releases, the firm responsible for the release. There are also debates over whether strict or other types of liability should be assigned. And there are debates over what constitutes harm, and what evidence will be required to trigger compensation mechanisms. Both industry and environmental groups are actively participating in the dialogue with parties to the Biosafety Protocol. Industry groups have argued against the assignment of liability for unintentional transfers of GMOs. Such a position is consistent with the behaviour of the firms outlined above with respect to the illegal GMO releases. CropLife international, for example, has stated that liability rules specific to biotechnology are '... neither legally nor scientifically justified ...' (CropLife International 2006). Environmental groups, on the other hand, are lobbying for a strong agreement that holds not just exporting states liable, but also the corporations that produce and market the GMOs (Greenpeace 2002b). The final outcome of the negotiations on this protocol on liability and redress with respect to transnational harm caused by GMOs remains to be seen.

CONCLUSION

Transnational corporations in the agricultural input industry have relied heavily on voluntary corporate measures as a means by which to self-govern and promote sustainability. By taking part in this self-regulation via CSR reporting, participation in the Global Compact and other mechanisms, these firms have played an important role in the way that they are governed with respect to GMOs. Furthermore, they have exerted significant influence over governance institutions.

The voluntary corporate efforts to promote sustainability have been relatively weak with respect to the issue of illegal releases of unapproved GMOs. In these cases, there was a lack of full accountability on the part of the corporations involved, despite their voluntary corporate responsibility initiatives. The corporation in each case downplayed the ecological, health, and economic risks associated with the accidental release of the GMO, and took moves to minimize its liability once the illegal release had been made public. The firms involved have done little on their own to compensate those affected. In the case of StarLink, the US government forced Aventis to compensate those negatively affected in the US, but this responsibility did not extend beyond the US border. In the case of Bt10 corn, Syngenta was fined a token amount and direct compensation was not paid by the company. In the case of LLRICE601, there has been no fine or compensation paid, and the firm has openly denied any responsibility in the face of class-action lawsuits filed on behalf of over 300 farmers.

As has been argued in this paper, it appears as though voluntary corporate responsibility measures are weak when firms have privileged access to information about the safety and impact of the product. In the case of accidental releases of unapproved GMOs, firms can easily work the available information and widely differing perceptions of risk associated with GMOs in general to their advantage when an illegal release occurs. If the firm fails to adopt a precautionary approach, or to pick up the tab for the environmental and other costs associated with GMO releases, the legal consequences can still be minimized by stressing the safety of the product, despite the illegal nature of the release when it is an unapproved variety. The principles of precaution and cost-internalization are thus set aside by firms precisely when they are most useful in promoting sustainability.

The tendency to ignore these principles in such cases points to the need for external regulation of some sort to achieve corporate responsibility and accountability with respect to this issue. There is an opportunity for exactly such an external governance mechanism with the protocol on liability and redress, which is currently being negotiated under the auspices of the Cartagena Protocol on Biosafety. It remains to be seen whether it will be firms or states who are held liable for compensating victims when illegal GMO releases that cross borders are discovered. Agricultural biotechnology firms and lobby groups are playing an active role in attempting to influence the negotiation of this liability protocol, and are arguing that they should not be the ones to be held liable. Given that firms are not likely to act responsibly regarding this issue, however, there is strong reason to push for holding firms directly liable, rather than putting that responsibility on the state. As the negotiations continue on the liability protocol, this is an important point to keep in mind.

REFERENCES

Action Aid International, *Power Hungry: Six Reasons to Regulate Global Food Corporations* (Johannesburg: Actionaid), 2005.

APHIS/USDA, 'What Are the Results of BRS' Fiscal Year 2005 Compliance Investigations', 2005, online at: *www.aphis.usda.gov/brs/compliance12.html*

APHIS/USDA, 'Draft Environmental Assessment: In Response to Bayer CropScience Petition 06–234–01P seeking Extension of Determination of Non-regulated Status for Glufosinate Resistant Rice, *Oryza Sativa*, Event LLRICE601', 2006, online at: *http://www.aphis.usda.gov/brs/aphisdocs/06_23401p_ea.pdf*

Bayer CropScience, Comments of Bayer CropScience on LLRICE601 as of September 19, 2006, 2006, available at: *http://www.bayercropscience.com/*

bayer/cropscience/cscms.nsf/id/D8B4D7C6D023DBD4C12571 FD004CDC35

Belcher, Ken, J. Nolan, and P. Phillips, 'Genetically Modified Crops and Agricultural Landscapes: Spatial Patterns of Contamination', *Ecological Economics.* 53, 2005, pp. 387–401.

Busch, Lawrence, 'The Moral Economy of Grades and Standards', *Journal of Rural Studies,* 16, 2000, 273–83.

Center for Food Safety. 'Legal Petition to Regulate LibertyLink Rice as a Plant Pest' (Executive Summary), 2006, Posted at: *www.centerforfoodsafety.org*

Clapp, Jennifer, 'Transnational corporate interests and global environmental governance: negotiating rules for agricultural biotechnology and chemicals', *Environmental Politics,* 12(4) 2003, pp. 1–23.

Clapp, Jennifer, 'Global Environmental Governance for Corporate Responsibility and Accountability', *Global Environmental Politics,* 5(3), 2005, pp. 23–34.

Corporate Europe Observer (CEO), 'Industry's Rio+10 Strategy: Banking on Feelgood PR', *The CEO Quarterly Newsletter,* 10, December, 2001.

CropLife International, 'Cartagena Protocol on Biosafety: Key Issues for the Liability and Redress Process', 2006, available at *http://www.croplife.org/ library/documents/Biotech/Biosafety%20Protocol/liability%20and%20redress/ CPB%20-%20liability%20and%20redress.pdf*

Dale, Philip J, 'The Environmental Impact of Genetically Modified (GM) Crops: A Review', *Journal of Agricultural Science,* 138, 2002, pp. 245–48.

Dauenhauer, Katrin, 'Health: Africans Challenge Bush Claim that GM food is Good for Them', *SUNS: South-North Monitor,* #5368, 2003. (23 June).

Ellstrand, Norman, *Dangerous Liaisons: When Crops Mate with their Wild Relatives,* Baltimore, MD: Johns Hopkins University Press, 2003a.

Ellstrand, Norman, 'Current Knowledge of Gene flow in Plants: Implications for Transgene Flow', *Philosophical Transactions of the Royal Society B: Biological Sciences,* 358, 2003b, pp. 1163–70.

Ellstrand, Norman. 2001, 'When Transgenes Wander, Should We Worry?' *Plant Physiology,* 125, 2001, pp. 1543–5.

ETC Group, 'Maize Rage in Mexico: GM Maize Contamination in Mexico—2 Years Later', 2003, Posted at: *www.etcgroup.org.*

European Food Safety Authority, 'Statement of the Scientific Panel on Genetically Modified Organisms in Response to the Request of the European Commission on Inadvertent Presence of Genetically Modified Rice LLRICE601', 2006 (September 14), available at: *www.efsa.europea.eu*

Falkner, Robert and Aarti Gupta, *Implementing the Biosafety Protocol: Key Challenges.* Chatham House Briefing Paper. Chatham House: London, 2004.

Flora, Gabriela, 'The Starlink Scandal: Aventis Violates Principle Seven of the United Nations Global Compact', Institute for Agriculture and Trade

Policy, 2001, Posted at: *www.gefoodalert.org/library/uploadedfiles/StarLink_Scandal_Aventis_violates_Principle_Se.htm.*

Friends of the Earth Netherlands (FOEN), *Using the OECD Guidelines for Multinational Enterprises: A Critical Starterkit for NGOs,* Amsterdam: FOE Netherlands, 2002.

Friends of the Earth International (FOEI), Tackling GMO Contamination: Making Segregation and Identity Preservation A Reality, Amsterdam: FOEI, 2005.

Friends of the Earth International (FOEI), *Towards Binding Corporate Accountability,* 2001, online at: *http://www.foei.org/publications/corporates/accountability.html.*

GeneWatch UK and Greenpeace International, *GM Contamination Report 2005,* 2005.

Gillam, Carey, 'Biotech Crop Sector Sets Standards, Seeks to Ease Fears'. Reuters News Service, July 25, 2007. Available at: *www.reuters.com/articlePrint?articleID=USN2535513320070725.*

Global Reporting Initiative (GRI), *Sustainability Reporting Guidelines,* Amsterdam: GRI, 2006.

Goodman, Michael, 'Reading Fair Trade: Political Ecological Imaginary and the Moral Economy of Fair Trade Foods', *Political Geography 23,* 2004, pp. 891–915.

Greenpeace International, *Corporate Crimes: The Need for an International Instrument on Corporate Accountability and Liability,* Amsterdam: Greenpeace, 2002a.

Greenpeace International, 'Liability and Redress in the Biosafety Protocol', 2002b, April, available at: *http://www.greenpeace.org/international/campaigns/genetic-engineering/biosafety-protocol.*

Hatanaka, Maki, Carmen Bain and Lawrence Busch, 2005, 'Third Party Certification in the Global Agrifood System', *Food Policy,* 30, pp. 354–69.

Herrera, Stephan, 2005, 'Syngenta's Gaff Embarrasses Industry and White House', *Nature Biotechnology,* 23(5), p. 514.

Kirwin, Joe, 'EC Experts OK Syngenta Test to Screen for Presence of Bt-10 GMO Corn Seeds', *International Trade Reporter,* 22(17), 2005, p. 684.

Konefal, Jason, Michael Mascarenhas, and Maki Hatanaka, 'Governance in the Global Agro-Food System: Backlighting the Role of Transnational Supermarket Chains', *Agriculture and Human Values,* 22, 2005, pp. 291–302.

Krut, Riva and Harris Gleckman, *ISO 14001: A Missed Opportunity for Global Sustainable Industrial Development,* London: Earthscan, 1998.

Lang, Tim and Michael Heasman *Food Wars: The Global Battle for Mouths, Minds and Markets,* London: Earthscan, 2004.

Lee, Christopher, 'Genetically Engineered Rice Wins USDA Approval', *Washington Post*, 25 November 2006, p. A06.

Lezaun, Javier, 'Creating a New Object of Government: Making Genetically Modified Organisms Traceable', *Social Studies of Science*, 36(4), 2006, pp. 499–531.

Macilwain, Colin, 'US Launches Probe into Sales of Unapproved Transgenic Corn', *Nature*, 23 March 2005, available at: *http://npg.nature.com/news/2005/050321/full/nature03570.html*.

McMichael, Philip, 'Global Development and the Corporate Food Regime', in *New Directions in the Sociology of Global Development*, F. Buttel and P. McMichael (eds), Amsterdam: Elsevier, 2005.

Murray, Douglas and Peter Taylor, 'Claim No Easy Victories: Evaluating the Pesticide Industry's Global Safe Use Campaign', *World Development*, 28(10), 2000, pp. 1735–49.

Nature, 'Don't Rely on Uncle Sam' (editorial), 434(7035), 14 April 2005, p. 807.

Neuffer, Elizabeth, 'Maker of Suspect Corn Seed Accused of Breaking UN Pact', *Boston Globe*, 15 June 2001, Posted at: *http://www.biotech-info.net/breaking_pact.html*.

Paarlberg, Robert, 'The Real Threat to GM Crops in Poor Countries: Consumer and Policy Resistance to GM Foods in Rich Countries', *Food Policy*, 27, 2002, pp. 247–50.

Pew Initiative on Food and Biotechnology, 'Is the World Embracing or Rejecting GM Foods?', *AgBiotech Buzz*, 2(9) 2002, Posted at: *http://pewagbiotech.org/buzz/display.php3?StoryID=78*.

Pilson, Diana and Holly Prendeville, 'Ecological Effects of Transgenic Crops and the Escape of Transgenes into Wild Populations', *Annual Review of Ecology, Evolution and Systematics*, 35, 2004, pp. 149–74.

Prakash, Aseem, 'Responsible Care: An Assessment', *Business & Society*, 39(2), 2000, pp. 183–209.

Raynolds, Laura, 'The Globalization of Organic Agro-Food Networks', *World Development*, 32(5), 2004, pp. 725–43.

Raynolds, Laura, 'Re-embedding Global Agriculture: The International Organic and Fair Trade Movements', *Agriculture and Human Values*, 17(1), 2000, pp. 297–309.

Reuters, 'US Farmers Sue Bayer CropScience over GM Rice', 2006, Posted at: *http://today.reuters.com/news/articleinvesting.aspx?view=CN&storyID=2006–08–28T224846Z_01_N8S372113_RTRIDST_0_FOOD-BAYER-UPDATE-1.XML&rpc=66&type=qcna*.

Segarra, Alejandro E. and Jean M. Rawson, *StarLink™ Corn Controversy: Background*, CRS Report for Congress, 2001, Posted at: *http://www.ncseonline.org/nle/crsreports/agriculture/ag-101.cfm*.

Syngenta, *Corporate Social Responsibility Report 2005*, 2005, Posted at: *www.syntenta.com/wn/responsilblity/intro_stewardship.aspx.*

Tallontire, Anne, 'CSR and Regulation: towards a framework for understanding private standards initiatives in the agri-food chain', *Third World Quarterly*, 28(4), 2007, pp. 775–791.

Taylor, Michael and Jody Tick, 'The StarLink Case: Issues for the Future', Washington, D.C.: Pew Initiative on Food and Biotechnology, 2001.

United Nations Conference on Trade and Development (UNCTAD) Program on Transnational Corporations, *Environmental Management in Transnational Corporations: Report on the Benchmark Corporate Environmental Survey*, Environment Series No. 4, New York: United Nations, 1993.

US FDA, 'StarLink Corn Investigation and Recall', at *http://www.cfsan.fda.gov/~dms/fdbioen2.html#starlink*, 2000.

Utting, Peter, *Business Responsibility for Sustainable Development*, Geneva: United National Research Institute for Social Development, 2000.

Utting, Peter, 'Corporate Responsibility and the Movement of Business', *Development in Practice*, 15(3/4), 2005, pp. 375–88.

Weiss, Rick, 'Firm Blames Farmers, 'Act of God' for Rice Contamination', *Washington Post*, 22 November 2006, p. A05.

6

Corporate Accountability in South Africa
An Evaluation of Sectoral Differences

Neil Eccles, Ralph Hamann, and Derick De Jongh[1]

INTRODUCTION

Since the 1992 Earth Summit in Rio de Janeiro, Brazil, terms such as corporate social responsibility (CSR) or corporate accountability have gained significant prominence. Companies (especially multinational corporations), business associations, governments, multilateral organizations, non-governmental organizations, trade unions, and academics have committed themselves to the notion that business should and can make contributions to sustainable development.

Some have seen a distinction between the voluntary approach to CSR commonly advocated by the business lobby and a greater emphasis on external, governmental control under the rubric of corporate accountability.[2] For the purpose of this article, we consider one of the core aspects of accountability that relates to 'answerability', as discussed in the introductory chapter to this volume, and defined as:

'To account for something is to explain or justify the acts, omissions, risks and dependencies for which one is responsible to people with a legitimate interest. To discharge its accountability, however, an organization has to go further than this and must demonstrate:
a) Transparency: the duty to account to those with a legitimate interest—the stakeholders—in the organization;
b) Responsiveness: the responsibility of the organization for its acts and omissions, including the processes of decision-making and the results of these decisions. Responsiveness entails a responsibility to develop

[1]We would like to thank Judith Njuguna, Steve Nicholls, and Sam Payne for their effort in evaluating the companies discussed. We would also like to thank Barloworld Ltd for providing financial support for this research.
[2]See Hamann *et al.* 2003; Utting 2005a; Christian Aid 2004.

the organization's processes and targets to support the continuous improvement of performance; and

c) Compliance: the duty to comply with agreed standards regarding organizational policies and practices and the reporting of policies and performance.' (Accountability 1999).

From this perspective, corporate accountability bears some resemblance to earlier definitions of corporate social responsiveness (Carroll 1999). The apparently increasing willingness of companies to adhere or aspire to such expectations of accountability is in contrast to the well-known argument that the only responsibility of a company should be to generate profits (Friedman 1970). The question of whether companies have responsibilities beyond generating profits seems to have been answered in the affirmative by the plethora of sustainability reports published by most large companies,[3] even though significant criticism is levelled at these efforts and doubts remain with regard to their actual impact on sustainable development (for instance, see Christian Aid 2004).

Perhaps a more crucial question that emerges is: What motivates companies to be more accountable? It is a question that has been the focus of intense discussion from both theoretical and empirical perspectives. From an analytical point of view, this question is motivated by a desire to explain the growing emphasis on various manifestations of the corporate responsibility movement among business (Utting 2005a), such as sustainability reporting. Beyond this, understanding what motivates companies will expose levers that can be used to encourage companies to help address material issues.

In this regard, there have been several discussions of the drivers of corporate responsibility that have yielded useful conceptual frameworks, many of which are embedded in institutional theory[4]. Three broad groupings of drivers have emerged (Bansal and Roth 2000; Hamann 2006):

a) Economic drivers;
b) Ethical drivers; and
c) Institutional drivers.

The first category focuses on the so-called business case for corporate responsibility, which maintains that it has positive impacts on profitability or competitiveness, at least in the medium and long

---

[3]See *www.globalreporting.org* for an overview of sustainability reporting.
[4]See Scott 1995; Hoffman 1999; Bansal and Roth 2000; Utting 2005b.

term (WBCSD 2002). The initial argument of this sort was the hypothesis that effective environmental management would increase the efficiency of the production process—in terms of less energy and material needs—and hence increase bottom line profits (Porter and van der Linde 1995).

However, the interaction between social issues and business success is in many instances more complex and uncertain. Margolis and Walsh (2003) surveyed 127 studies published between 1972 and 2002, which sought to establish a relationship between corporate social performance and economic performance. They conclude that all of this research effort fails to add up to a conclusive argument and, worse, that it misses the point by paying insufficient attention to the underlying tensions between the profit motive and social initiatives. It should also be noted that despite these manifold studies, the relationship between corporate responsibility and profitability has scarcely been investigated in developing country contexts, apart from a wide-ranging study by the International Finance Corporation (IFC) and others that relied primarily on anecdotal evidence (IFC *et al.* 2002).

The second approach to understanding the drivers of CSR focuses on ethical motives, often with an emphasis on why economic incentives are insufficient for circumscribing a social role for business. 'The standard model of simple profit maximization as the dominant (perhaps even exclusive) principle covering all economic activities fails to do justice both to the content of business principles which can be much broader, and to the domain of moral sentiments, which can be quite far-reaching' (Sen 1999, p. 16).

The third approach emphasizes the institutional dimension, directing 'attention towards forces that lie beyond the organizational boundary, in the realm of social processes' (Hoffman 1999, p. 351). It investigates how changes in companies' organizational field, constituted by government, business associations, funding organizations, NGOs, and other stakeholders, as well as more intangible cultural elements, influence these companies' behaviour. In particular, institutions— the 'rules of the game in a society' (North 1990, p. 3)—influence companies' behaviour because of the companies' need to establish and maintain legitimacy (Bansal and Roth 2000).

Rather than seeing economic, ethical, and institutional approaches to CSR as distinct, they can be characterized as being closely inter-related (Hoffman 1999), with an overarching role for the institutional dimension (Hamann 2004). Hence, institutional conditions, comprising cognitive, normative, and regulative structures (Scott 1995), provide the framework in which both the business case for corporate responsibility, as well as decision-makers' ethical perspectives are developed and implemented.

It can thus be postulated that a company's institutional context is a predominant factor in explaining the degree of corporate accountability among a company or sector. In this chapter, we assess the importance of institutional parameters in explaining the level of accountability among three key sectors—mining, finance, and retail—in the South African economy. We make use of an Accountability Rating™ analysis of the largest publicly listed South African companies. This allows us to add a quantitative, nomothetic dimension to this analysis, thus augmenting similar arguments—in the South African context— in Bezuidenhout *et al.* (2007). Our findings support our assumption that the 'strength' of the institutional drivers in each of the sectors is clearly related to that sector's apparent level of accountability. In particular, it points to a prominent role of the state in enhancing levels of accountability.

I. Methodology: The Accountability Rating™

As a general measure of accountability, we used the results from the 2006 Accountability Rating™ SA study (Accountability Rating 2006; Financial Mail 2006a) (Table 6.1). The Accountability Rating™ methodology was previously applied to the Fortune top 100 companies in both 2004 and 2005 (csrnetwork and AccountAbility 2004; Demos 2005). In 2006, the survey was expanded to include an evaluation of the top fifty-two listed companies on the Johannesburg Securities Exchange as reported in the *Financial Mail* (2006b) SA Giants List. The method uses documents made publicly available by companies to evaluate how well they account to their stakeholders for the socio-economic and environmental impacts of their core business activities. It considers all the major domains of a standard business architecture including strategy, governance, performance management, stakeholder engagement, public disclosure, and assurance (Accountability Rating 2006). This comprehensive approach, and particularly the consideration of assurance efforts that involve independent monitoring and verification, to some extent mitigates the potential risk that the method evaluates how accountable companies say they are rather than how accountable they actually are.

Table 6.1   Company, Sector, Ranking, and Scores

Full name	Sector	2006 Accountability Rating Rank	2006 Accountability Rating Score
BHP Billiton Plc	Mining	1	78.6
Anglo Platinum Ltd	Mining	2	70.1
Anglo American Plc	Mining	3	69.4
Nedbank Group Ltd	Financial Services	4	67.4
Anglogold Ashanti Ltd	Mining	7	54.9
Santam Ltd	Financial Services	8	54.7
Kumba Resources Ltd	Mining	10	53.8
Harmony Gold Mining Company Ltd	Mining	11	52.9
Massmart Holdings Ltd	Retail	12	51.3
Impala Platinum Holdings Ltd	Mining	15	48.4
Absa Group Ltd	Financial Services	17	46.6
Pick N Pay Stores Ltd	Retail	18	46.6
Standard Bank Group Ltd	Financial Services	19	45.7
Woolworths Holdings Ltd	Retail	20	45.1
Gold Fields Ltd	Mining	23	41.7
Metropolitan Holdings	Financial Services	24	41.1
Sanlam Ltd	Financial Services	25	40.1
Edgars Consolidated Stores Ltd	Retail	26	39.7
Investec Ltd	Financial Services	28	38.1
Firstrand Ltd	Financial Services	30	37.0
Liberty Group Ltd	Financial Services	33	34.8
JD Group Ltd	Retail	36	30.1
Old Mutual Plc	Financial Services	37	25.2
Shoprite Holdings Ltd	Retail	42	22.5
New Clicks Holdings Ltd	Retail	44	19.3
The Spar Group Limited	Retail	47	16.9
Remgro Ltd	Financial Services	49	13.0

Source: Financial Mail 2006a.

The evaluations were carried out by a team of four experienced local researchers. Consistency of evaluation was ensured by an initial calibration exercise, followed by quality checking of a third of all evaluations. Since the focus of this paper is on three specific sectors, we calculated the sector averages for the overall accountability scores (Table 6.3) as well as domain scores (Table 6.5). We also present the results for two specific Accountability Rating™ criteria which evaluate the performance of companies in recognizing and understanding: a) material socio-economic; and b) environmental issues (Table 6.4).

These criteria are useful in illustrating the scope of issues considered by the three sectors. In all cases, we present the standard deviations (SD) associated with these averages for completeness' sake, and comment on these where appropriate.

II. SECTORAL INSTITUTIONAL CHARACTERISTICS

The institutional 'rules of the game' are conferred via a number of mechanisms, each likely to be of varying efficacy, and indeed, each interacting with the others to together promote accountability (Utting 2005b). In this paper, we specifically focus on three categories:

a) Legal frameworks;
b) Sector-specific negotiated codes of conduct; and
c) Stakeholder perceptions and pressure.

Legal frameworks are managed via government bodies and usually provide both licensing criteria and explicit mechanisms for sanction which could ultimately involve revoking licences. Sector-specific codes of conduct on the other hand are frequently governed by industry, or in some cases, multi-stakeholder bodies. While the criteria are often clearly defined, the mechanisms for enforcing these are often more vague than in legal frameworks.

Finally, general stakeholder perceptions and pressures tend to be the least concrete or tangible of the three mechanisms. At a sector level, they usually do not provide a formal mechanism for enforcing corporate accountability, although both strikes and boycotts (which are usually associated with individual companies rather than sectors) have been used. In many respects however, stakeholder perceptions and pressures represent key precursors to the definition of either generally accepted codes of conduct or legal frameworks.

In summarizing the institutional frameworks for the sectors that we evaluate, we apply a basic three-level coding (strong / medium / weak) on the basis of the criteria described in Table 6.2. This codification is not meant to form a basis for rigorous statistical analysis but rather to provide a high level summary of each sector.

In doing this, we explicitly exclude generally applicable frameworks—frameworks that apply to all sectors. From a legal framework perspective, these would include amongst others, the following:

a) National Black Economic Empowerment (BEE) Act No. 53 of 2003: Sets out a national framework for the promotion of BEE; establishes the BEE Advisory Council; empowers the Minister

Table 6.2 Criteria Used for Coding the Sector Institutional Frameworks

	Strong	Medium	Weak
Legal frameworks	Laws and regulations exist with explicit reference to a broad range of socio-economic and/or environmental issues, and these include clear and enforceable sanctions.	Socio-economic and/or environmental issues are either considered only indirectly in existing laws and regulations or the enforcement of existing laws is relatively weak.	Socio-economic and/or environmental issues are not covered in laws or regulations.
Sector-specific codes	Codes or charters are formal, well established, and cover a comprehensive suite of socio-economic and/or environmental issues.	Codes and charters are formal, but are either very recently established or are restricted to a limited scope of socio-economic or environmental issues.	Codes or charters governing socio-economic or environmental issues are not established.
Stakeholder pressure	Significant stakeholder activism evident and cover a comprehensive suite of socio-economic and/or environmental issues.	Some degree of stakeholder activism emerging, or activism restricted to a limited scope of socio-economic or environmental issues.	Stakeholder activism not evident.

to issue codes of good practice on BEE, including a scorecard to measure achievement, and to promote sector-specific BEE charters that are deemed to be in accordance with the objectives of the Act. A strategy paper has so far been tabled, including a 'generic' scorecard;

b) Access to Information Act No. 2 of 2000: Promulgated to enforce the constitutional right to access to information that is pertinent to the Bill of Rights; it allows access to (almost) all information held by the state as well as to significant types of information held by private persons;

c) National Environmental Management Act No. 107 of 1998: Promotes development that is socially, environmentally, and economically sustainable; seeks environmental justice and equitable access to environmental resources; promotes public participation in environmental decision making; protects 'whistle-blowers'; allows for public interest litigation; provides for directors' liability and for duty of care and remediation responsibilities—particularly for employers;

d) Employment Equity Act No. 55 of 1998: Seeks to eliminate unfair discrimination in the workplace and implement affirmative action for 'designated groups': black people, women, or people with disabilities;

e) Constitution No. 108 of 1996: Contains the Bill of Rights, including the rights to equality, a clean and healthy environment, access to information, administrative justice, and others; significantly, constitutional provisions and case law suggests that key elements of the Bill of Rights are of horizontal application; that is, they bind individuals and corporations, as well as the state; and

f) Labour Relations Act No. 66 of 1995 and Basic Conditions of Employment Act No. 75 of 1997: Provide for basic conditions of employment, promotes collective bargaining at workplace and sector level, and promotes employee participation in company decision making through workplace forums.

As regards generally accepted codes of conduct, since all the companies in our sample are listed on the Johannesburg Securities Exchange (JSE), these would include the JSE listing requirements and in particular, the pressure from the JSE that companies should comply with the King II guidelines (King Committee on Corporate Governance 2002) on corporate governance. The King II guidelines have become the *de facto* standard for corporate governance practice in South African business. At a global level, we also exclude the United Nations Global Compact (UNGC), since this is technically not sector-specific. It is worth noting as an aside however, that the uptake of the UNGC across these three sectors has been much higher in the mining sector (four of the rated companies) than either the financial services companies (two participants) or retail (no participants).

It should be noted that South Africa provides an interesting case study of the role of institutional frameworks, with a particular role for the state, in motivating corporate accountability. This is especially pertinent in terms of the state-sponsored policy of Broad-Based Black Economic Empowerment (BBBEE). This is aimed at redressing the racial imbalances resulting from apartheid, including imperatives such as increased black ownership of the economy, employment equity, and rural development. The most significant force for BBBEE has been the state, which has promulgated a National BEE Act, as well as a number of other pertinent pieces of legislation, such as the Employment Equity Act. These legislative developments are based on the Constitution, which contains key clauses that explicitly refer to the need for social and economic transformation in the wake of Apartheid. The state has also facilitated a range of sector-specific charters and scorecards meant to assess companies' BBBEE performance. The most prominent elements of BBBEE are considered in Box 6.1.

Box 6.1: The Government Scorecard for Broad-Based Black Economic Empowerment

Direct empowerment and management

The extent to which Historically Disadvantaged South Africans (HDSA) own shares or access economic benefits, such as dividends or interest payments, and the proportion of HDSAs in senior levels of management.

Human resource development and employment equity

Enterprises are required to comply with employment equity and skills development legislation to bring about improved human resource development and an equitable representation of HDSAs at all levels of the organization.

Indirect empowerment

The creation and nurturing of new enterprises by HDSAs, with particular emphasis on preferential procurement and enterprise development, entailing targeted investment or joint ventures.

Miscellaneous or sector-specific issues

In order to allow sectors and enterprises to tailor the scorecard to their circumstances, a residual 10 per cent of the scorecard is left to sectors and enterprises to determine. For instance, such issues may pertain to community development initiatives or sector-specific issues such as the conversion of single-gender hostels to family accommodation for mine employees.

III. THE MINING SECTOR

The mining sector is traditionally viewed as a 'high-impact' sector from both a socio-economic and an environmental perspective. From a socio-economic perspective, besides the South Africa-specific BBBEE suite of issues discussed above, key sectoral issues include:

a) Bribery and corruption;
b) Community rights (including health and safety);
c) General poverty alleviation and employment opportunities;
d) HIV & AIDS;
e) Labour rights (including health and safety);
f) Skill development and training; and
g) Social planning for closure/decommissioning.

Key environmental issues include:

a) Energy and water usage;
b) Land rehabilitation/environmental decommissioning; and
c) Pollution and other site impacts.

The overall institutional landscape, both historical and present, of the south African mining sector has been reviewed by Hamann (2004). He argues that the cornerstone or guarantor of responsiveness in this sector is the state's sovereignty over mineral resources and the resultant power to formally withhold mining licences, as codified in the Minerals and Petroleum Resources Development Act, 2002. This, together with other powerful sector specific legislations dealing with a range of socio-economic and environmental issues (such as, Mines Health and Safety Act 1996), provides a basis for us to code the 'legal framework' pertaining to this sector as strong.

The Minerals and Petroleum Resources Development Act, 2002, requires the sector to establish a set of codes for the implementation of the far-reaching BBBEE requirements. This has led to the establishment of the Mining Sector Charter, which provides a scorecard for broad-based socio-economic empowerment in the sector. The Charter focuses on a broad range of issues including: human resource development, employment equity, migrant labour, mine community and rural development, procurement practices, beneficiation, and reporting among others. Based on this Charter, we would also score the sector-specific codes pertaining to this sector as strong with the caveat that environmental issues do not fall within the scope of the Charter. This is mitigated by the fact that environmental issues are covered in the legal frameworks governing the sector.

Finally, in terms of stakeholder perceptions and pressures, we would score the sector as a whole as strong. These perceptions and pressures have most frequently been voiced by labour unions, most notably the National Union of Mine Workers, and cover issues ranging from wages, occupational health and safety, and housing. In addition, the sector as a whole has received a significant amount of attention from NGOs and other civil society bodies both at a local (for instance, MMSD-SA 2002) and an international level (MMSD 2002; Leahy 2006).

IV. THE FINANCIAL SERVICES SECTOR

In contrast with the mining sector, the financial services sector has traditionally been viewed as a 'low-impact' sector. This view has, however, recently been challenged with the recognition of the profound impacts (both socio-economic and environmental) of lending and investment decisions in particular (Juniper 2000). Specific socio-economic issues that are key to the sector (besides BBBEE) include:

a) Cost and accessibility of banking services;
b) Socio-economic impacts of lending, investment, and insurance decisions;
c) Responsible marketing of products and services (especially credit); and
d) Positive impacts of channelling funds towards social agendas (such as, micro-credit schemes, entrepreneurialism).

The key environmental issues relevant today are largely associated with both the impacts and potential benefits that are associated with investment, lending, and insurance decisions. However, energy consumption and the contribution to greenhouse gas emissions particularly associated with extensive travel are also recognized.

From an institutional perspective, the most notable institutional framework defining licence-to-operate criteria is the Financial Sector Charter (National Treasury 2003), which falls into the 'sector-specific codes' category. This Charter emerged as a consensual response to proposed legislation in the form of the Community Reinvestment Bill, together with a campaign by civil society organizations called the Campaign for the Transformation of the Financial Sector (Moyo and Rohan 2006). As with the Mining Sector Charter described above, this Charter provides a set of transformation targets to which companies voluntarily subscribe. These targets relate to a broad range of transformation issues including human resource development, promotion of access to financial services in previously 'un-banked' sectors of the population, empowerment financing, ownership in the financial sector, shareholder activism, and corporate social investment (ibid.). Because of this, we would characterize the 'sector-specific codes' pertaining to this sector as being strong, again, with the caveat that environmental issues are not in any way covered by the Charter. Several sector-specific international codes of conduct such as the United Nations Environment Programme–Finance Initiative's (UNEP FI) Principles of Responsible Investment (UNEP FI 2006) and The Equator Principles (Equator Principles 2006) do include environmental issues. However subscription to these has been slow in South African financial services companies. To date, only a single South African bank has subscribed to the Equator Principles and a second is indirectly linked via a parent bank based in the United Kingdom.

Recently there has also been a significant amount of attention focused on the sector by stakeholders. Four issues in particular have received attention: service charges (Jara 2001; Rusconi 2004); competition (The Task Group for the National Treasury and South African Reserve Bank 2004.); early termination of pension schemes (Sanlam 2005); and accessibility to banking services by low-income sections of the population. Indeed, civil society activism was an important driver for the sector-specific negotiations leading towards the Finance Sector Charter mentioned above, whereby the so-called Financial Sector Campaign Coalition mobilized membership from a multitude of organizations including the ANC, COSATU, Treatment Action Campaign, and the Savings and Credit Co-operatives League. However, it may be argued that stakeholder pressure in the finance sector is not as consistent or focused as in the mining sector, whereby mines arguably face a more direct risk to their operations through community activism. As a result, we score the role of stakeholder perceptions and pressure in the finance sector as medium.

In terms of the role of legal frameworks and government pressure, we score this factor's significance in the finance sector as medium. For instance, in the case of early termination of pension schemes, the government adjudicator exerted significant pressure on the sector, culminating in a contractual agreement between the long-term insurance industry and the Minister of Finance (Ministry of Finance

2005). The Community Reinvestment Bill and the threat of possible government intervention—based on the Mining Charter Experience—played a crucial role in motivating the key finance companies to negotiate the Finance Sector Charter mentioned above. These various state-related pressures have, on the whole, not been as direct or significant as in the mining sector—hence the score of medium.

V. The Retail Sector

As with the financial services sector, the retail sector has traditionally been viewed as a 'low-impact' sector. However, again, this view has begun to be challenged principally due to the impacts that the sector has through its supply chain (Friends of the Earth 2005). Key socio-economic issues that are relevant to the sector include:
  a) Consumer credit practices;
  b) Diversity and equal rights for employees;
  c) Fair trade practices;
  d) HIV and AIDS;
  e) Labour rights (including health and safety); and
  f) Poverty alleviation and employment opportunities.
From an environmental perspective, major issues include:
  a) Products and packaging (waste and recycling);
  b) Product sourcing;
  c) Site impacts (of stores and distribution centres especially); and
  d) Transport impacts.
  Formal frameworks (legal or generally accepted codes of conduct) governing the management of socio-economic and environmental issues within the retail sector specifically, are noticeably absent. We would therefore score both of these dimensions as being weak. In terms of stakeholder perceptions and pressure, the sector has been receiving some attention recently. This pressure is currently focused on two specific issues: namely the import of cheap textiles from Asia (primarily China) (Barron 2006), and executive remuneration (Fin24 2006). In the case of textiles, this pressure has led to import restrictions on Chinese clothing being pursued by government (Department of Trade and Industry, South Africa 2006). Despite the relative success of this campaign, we would still only characterize the strength of stakeholder pressure as medium because of its very limited scope.

However, the fact that the supply chain has been recognized is promising since it sets a precedent for corporate responsibility amongst the retail sector beyond the company door.

VI. SECTOR SUMMARY

Thus in summary we would 'score' the three sectors that are investigated in this study as follows (Table 6.3):

Table 6.3   Relative 'strength' of licence-to-operate frameworks in selected sectors

Sector	Legal Frameworks	Codes of Conduct	Stakeholder Perceptions and Pressure
Mining	strong	strong	strong
Financial Services	medium	strong	medium
Retail/Consumer Services	weak	weak	medium

VII. RESULTS AND DISCUSSION

The results that emerge are interesting from a number of perspectives. Firstly, as expected, there is an apparent correlation between sectoral Accountability Rating™ averages and the relative 'strength' of the institutional frameworks that characterize the sectors. The mining sector with its strong legal frameworks, strong codes of conduct, and strong stakeholder perceptions and pressures was the most accountable sector (Table 6.4). This was followed by the financial services sector which is currently characterized by medium legal frameworks, a strong social code of conduct in the form of the Finance Sector Charter, and medium stakeholder perceptions and pressures. Bringing up the

Table 6.4   Sector-average Accountability Rating™ scores and standard deviations

Sector	Mean	SD
Financial Services	40.34	(14.24)
Mining	58.71	(12.59)
Retail/Consumer Services	33.94	(13.46)
Grand Total	43.89	(16.52)

rear was the retail sector characterized by an institutional framework restricted to medium stakeholder perceptions and pressures.

While this correlation is compelling, it is important to emphasize that our analysis is certainly not definitive. We would not unequivocally state that the drivers identified and discussed in this paper are the only drivers, or even the key drivers of corporate accountability. Several factors have not been included in the analysis that could theoretically account for a significant proportion of the variance in the sample. For example, the analysis does not consider the impact of listings on stock exchanges other than the JSE. Listings requirements for other exchanges may be more stringent than the JSE listing requirements, or may emphasize different socio-economic or environmental issues such that foreign listings might drive either higher quality accountability, or a broader scope of issues covered by accountability practices.

In terms of the overall score, the mining sector scored almost 20 per cent higher than the next best performing sector (Table 6.4) and this marked difference is worthy of particular focus. In this sector, more than any other, the state clearly retains the right to grant and revoke licence-to-operate through its retention of state sovereignty over mineral rights. Indeed in their annual reports, many mining companies made particular reference to the progress they were making towards reapplying for their mining licences. Hamann (2004) emphasized the importance of this driver in his case study on the South African mining industry. This situation is clearly contrasted with the situation in the next best performing sector, the financial services sector, where concern has been expressed regarding the ability of the self-regulated 'code of conduct' based model to drive responsiveness (Moyo and Rohan 2006).

In addition to the very obvious strength of the licence-to-operate mechanisms in the mining sector, the criteria that are considered in granting or revoking licences are comprehensive, covering both socio-economic (occupational health and safety, interactions with local communities, mine closure planning and so on) and environmental (pollution, mine closure, and rehabilitation etc.) impacts. This is again in marked contrast with the other two sectors, where, as a general rule, companies consider themselves to be 'low-impact'. While this is particularly from an environmental perspective, in some cases it does appear to overflow into socio-economic issues as well, as is indicated by the sentiment expressed by one of South Africa's largest

Table 6.5   Average Accountability Rating™ scores for the recognition
and understanding of material: (a) environmental and (b)
socio-economic issues

Sector	Environment		Socio-Economic	
	Mean	SD	Mean	SD
Financial Services	41.82	29.52	72.50	26.00
Mining	86.11	18.67	85.56	10.06
Retail/Consumer Services	50.63	43.38	73.75	19.41
Grand Total	58.57	36.05	77.05	20.34

financial services groups in their Annual Report that: 'as a knowledge-based financial services company, we have limited direct social and environmental impacts' (anon). The effect of this categorization into 'low-' and 'high-impact' is evident when considering the average performance of companies in recognizing and understanding material socio-economic and environmental issues (Table 6.5).

From an environmental perspective in particular, this notion of 'low-' and 'high-impact' sectors is largely premised on drawing a distinction between direct and indirect impacts. In the case of the financial services sector, indirect impacts would include the environmental impacts of lending decisions. Using an international example, several major international banks provided capital for the development of massive paper mills in Indonesia despite the lack of sustainable timber sources required to operate. In effect, the capital provided by these banks created a massive demand for timber, which was ultimately sourced by deforestation of tropical forests (Juniper 2000). In the retail sector, indirect impacts will generally involve the impacts of supply chains. These so-called indirect impacts are generally externalized by these sector players. The validity of this externalization, in South Africa at any rate, is questionable given that the primary environmental management legislation in the country (The National Environmental Management Act No. 107 of 1998) explicitly recognizes that liability can be attributed to parties that are both 'directly or indirectly' responsible for environmental infringements.

Further, this characterization of sectors as 'low-' and 'high-impact', and the apparent inverse relationship between the Accountability Rating™ scores and sector impacts (that is, 'high-impact' mining being most accountable vs. 'low-impact' other sectors being least accountable) has led a number of commentators to question the validity of the rating, and worse still to suggest that the rating might in fact let 'high-impact' companies off the hook. On one level this correlation is in fact explanatory. It seems intuitive that society as a whole will focus greater institutional pressure on sectors which are perceived to have the highest impact. And our thesis is that greater institutional pressure will result in greater accountability, which we postulate will lead eventually to greater responsibility.

Furthermore, we believe that some caution is required in accepting this common dogma that some sectors have such low socio-economic and environmental impacts as to justify a lack of accountability. Clearly, the socio-economic part of this caution is already widely recognized in that the gap between the mining sector and the other two sectors in terms of socio-economic issues is far narrower than the gap for environmental issues (Table 6.5). From an environmental perspective, we have already alluded to the distinction between the notion of direct and indirect environmental impacts above, which we believe is very material to this debate. At the end of the day, it is the intention of the rating method not to let anyone off the hook, whether they consider themselves 'low-impact' or not.

It is also interesting to note that when considering the average performance of companies in recognizing and understanding material socio-economic and environmental issues, the retail sector appears to be generally more aware of material environmental issues than the financial services sector, although this awareness is also more variable across the sector. One possible explanation for this is that a number of the retail companies (particularly the more exclusive ones) have begun to use environmental credentials as a differentiator. This points to economic or business case drivers (specifically through using niches to maximize revenue) being at work and would certainly explain the high variation. Despite this, and the fact that both sectors have a similar awareness of socio-economic issues (Table 6.5), it is clear that the financial services sector is far more organized and systematic in its response to these issues. This is particularly noticeable in the performance management domain of the Accountability Rating™, where the difference between the financial services sector and the retail sector was nearly 14 per cent (Table 6.6). This difference at the domain level can largely be attributed to the obvious performance management framework presented in the Financial Services Charter scorecard. This scorecard requires companies to define measurable targets and report annually on performance against these targets.

Table 6.6   Domain-average scores for all Accountability Rating™ domains

Domain	Mining Mean	Mining SD	Financial Services Mean	Financial Services SD	Retail Mean	Retail SD
Strategy	83	(12.1)	61	(17.7)	59	(20.2)
Governance	54	(12.9)	42	(16.0)	38	(14.5)
Performance Management	57	(14.6)	36	(19.0)	23	(17.6)
Stakeholder Engagement	57	(14.9)	44	(17.2)	37	(14.9)
Public Disclosure	67	(11.9)	46	(17.6)	36	(18.2)
Assurance	28	(22.2)	5	(9.1)	1	(3.5)

CONCLUSION

In the South African context, the relationships between each of the three sectors discussed above and broader society are governed by institutional frameworks of varying 'strength'. At one extreme is the mining sector where a strong legal framework is reinforced by a sector charter or code of conduct and clear penalties for non-participation. At the other extreme is the retail sector where there are no focused legal frameworks or formal sector-specific charters or codes. The financial services sector occupies the middle ground with a relatively new sector-specific charter which emerged out of the threat of legal interventions. This natural gradient correlates well with sector accountability scores. Particularly noticeable is the fact that the mining sector scores some 20 per cent higher than the next best sector, perhaps indicating the importance of strong legal frameworks. Besides strong legal frameworks, charters also appear to play a tangible role, particularly in informing company performance management systems. Finally, while ironic, it is almost inevitable that sectors that are generally considered to be 'low-impact' (financial services and retail) appear to be less accountable. This is unfortunate since the 'low-impact' status is generally the result of ignoring or externalizing significant indirect impacts.

In conclusion then, the results of this analysis present firstly, a compelling correlation between the breadth and strength of institutional drivers and observed accountability at a sector level in large South African companies from the mining, financial services, and retail sectors. In addition, in the sample of companies studied in this research at least, the existence of a strong legal framework seems to have a very large influence on accountability, as indicated by the mining sector (with such a framework) outperforming its nearest rival by nearly

20 per cent. Finally, the formulation of sector-specific charters, and in particular the associated performance scorecards, appear to provide companies with a very useful platform for developing their performance management systems.

REFERENCES

AccountAbility, *AA1000 Framework Overview*. London: AccountAbility, 1999.

Accountability Rating, 2006, available at: *http://www.accountabilityrating.com*, accessed on 23 November 2006.

Bansal, P. B. and Roth, K., 2000. 'Why companies go green: A model of ecological responsiveness' *Academy of Management Journal*. 43(4), 2000, pp. 717–36.

Barron, C., 'Perfectly happy with the cut of his cloth', *The Sunday Times*, 24 September 2006.

Bezuidenhout, A., D. Fig, R. Hamann, and R. Omar, 'Political economy', in *Corporate Social and Environmental Responsibility in South Africa*, D. Fig (ed), Durban: University of Kwa-Zulu Natal Press, 2007.

Carroll, A.B., 'Corporate social responsibility: evolution of a definitional construct', *Business & Society*, 38(3), 1999, pp. 268–95.

Christian Aid, *Behind the Mask: The Real Face of Corporate Social Responsibility*, London: Christian Aid, 2004.

csrnetwork and AccountAbility, *The Accountability Rating® 2004*, 2004.

Demos, T., 'Managing beyond the bottom line' *Fortune (Europe Edition)*. 17, 2005, pp. 68–73.

Department of Trade and Industry South Africa., *Import Restrictions of Chinese Clothing*, 2006, available at: *http://www.thedti.gov.za/article/articleview.asp ?current=1&arttypeid=1&artid=1206*, accessed on 4 October 2006.

Equator Principles. 2006. *The 'Equator Principles'. A financial industry benchmark for determining, assessing and managing social & environmental risk in project financing.* Available at: *http://www.equator-principles.com/documents/Equator_Principles.pdf*, accessed on 4 October 2006.

Fin24, *SA wage gap widening: Cosatu*, 2006, available at: *http://www.fin24.co.za/articles/print_article.asp?articleid=1518–1786_2000919*, accessed on 19 September 2006.

Financial Mail, 'Special Report: Accountability Rating', *Financial Mail*, 27 October 2006a, pp. 128–38.

Financial Mail, 'SA Giants', *The Financial Mail*, 30 June Edition, 2006b, pp. 29–52.

Friedman, M., 'The social responsibility of business is to increase its profits', *The New York Times Magazine*, 13 September 1970.

Friends of the Earth, *Checking out the Environment. Environmental Impacts of Supermarkets*, London: Friends of the Earth, 2005.

Hamann, R., 'Can business make decisive contributions to development? Towards a research agenda on corporate citizenship and beyond', *Development Southern Africa*, 23(2), 2006, pp. 175–95.

Hamann, R., 'Corporate social responsibility, partnerships, and institutional change: The case of mining companies in South Africa', *Natural Resources Forum*, 28(4), 2004, pp. 278–90.

Hamann, R., N. Acutt, and P. Kapelus, 'Responsibility vs. Accountability? Interpreting the World Summit on Sustainable Development for a Synthesis Model of Corporate Citizenship', *Journal of Corporate Citizenship*, 9, 2003, pp. 20–36.

Hoffman, A.J., 'Institutional evolution and change: Environmentalism and the US chemical industry' *Academy of Management Journal*, 42(2), 1999, pp. 351–71.

IFC (International Finance Corporation), Sustainability, and Instituto Ethos, *The Business Case in Emerging Economies*, Washington: International Finance Corporation, 2002.

Jara, M., 'Make banks serve the people!', *The Shopsteward*, 10 (4), 2001.

Juniper, T., *Investing In a Better Future—Your Money and the Global Environment*, London: Friends of the Earth, 2000.

King Committee on Corporate Governance, *King Report on Corporate Governance in South Africa 2002*, Johannesburg: Institute of Directors, 2002.

Leahy, S.,*Activists push for sustainable mining*, 2006,a vailable at: *http:// www.corpwatch.org/article.php?id=14150*, accessed on 30 October 2006.

Margolis, J.D and Walsh, J.P., 'Misery Loves Companies: Rethinking Social Initiatives by Business', *Administrative Science Quarterly*, 48, 2003, pp. 268–305.

Ministry of Finance, *Media Statement: Agreement between the Minister of Finance and long-terms insurance industry on minimum standards applicable to insurance industry savings products*, Pretoria, Republic of South Africa: Ministry of Finance, 2005.

MMSD (Mining, Minerals, and Sustainable Development), *Breaking new ground: the report of the mining, minerals, and sustainable development project*. London: Earthscan, 2002.

MMSD-SA (Mining, Minerals, and Sustainable Development: Southern Africa), *Mining, Minerals and Sustainable Development in Southern Africa; the Report of the Regional MMSD process*. Johannesburg: MMSD Southern Africa, 2002.

Moyo, T. and S. Rohan, 'Corporate citizenship in the context of the financial services sector: what lessons from the Financial Sector Charter?', *Development Southern Africa*. 23(2), 2006, pp. 289–303.

National Treasury. 2003. *Financial Sector Charter*. Pretoria: The National Treasury, 2003.

North, D., *Institutions, Institutional Change, and Economic Performance*, Cambridge, MA: Harvard University Press, 1990.

Porter, M. and C. Van Der Linde, Green and Competitive: Ending the Stalemate', *Harvard Business Review*, 73(5), 1995, pp. 120–34.

Rusconi, R., 'Cost savings for retirement. Options for South Africa', 2004, paper presented at the Convention of the Actuarial Society of South Africa, October 2004, Cape Town, South Africa.

Sanlam, *2005 Annual Report*, 2005.

Scott, W.R., *Institutions and Organizations*. London: Sage Publications, 1995.

Sen, A., 'Economics, Business Principles, and Moral Sentiments' in *International Business Ethics: Challenges and Approaches*, G. Enderle (ed), Notre Dame: The University of Notre Dame Press, 1999.

The Task Group for the National Treasury and South African Reserve Bank., *Competition in South African Banking*. Pretoria: The National Treasury, 2004.

Utting, P. 'Corporate responsibility and the movement of business', *Development in Practice*. 15(3–4) 2005a, pp. 75–583.

Utting, P., *Rethinking Business Regulation: From self-regulation to Social Control*, Geneva: UNRISD, 2005b.

UNEP FI. (United Nations Environment Programme—Finance Initiative), *Principles for Responsible Investment*, 2006, available at: *http://www.unpri.org/files/pri.pdf*, accessed on 4 October 2006.

WBCSD (World Business Council for Sustainable Development), *Corporate Social Responsibility: The WBCSD's journey*, Geneva: World Business Council for Sustainable Development, 2002.

7

Corporate Environmental Behaviour
A Comparative Study of Firms in the Indian Steel and Paper Industry

RUNA SARKAR

INTRODUCTION

Corporate environmental behaviour (CEB) refers to the set of strategies deployed by a firm to manage its business–environment (ecological) interface, whether as a response to external pressures such as legislation or stakeholder dissatisfaction or as a proactive measure to mitigate the environmental impact of its activities because of enlightened self-interest or both. As CEB has evolved from externally induced behaviour through regulatory means to taking on a strategic dimension for the firm, responsible environmental behaviour could give a firm the much needed competitive edge. Hence, there is a need for clarity with respect to explaining a manager's rationale for adopting corporate sustainable strategies (Salzmann *et al.* 2005). According to Clark, 'CEB research will be most effective if it can explain conditions under which each of the approaches (traditional or alternate) works and suggest new approaches to environmental protection, including integrated strategies that make synergistic use of multiple tools.' (Clark 2005, p. 423) For this objective to be attained, there is a need for descriptive empirical work on CEB.

To address this particular need, this chapter analyses and compares the CEB of four firms that are top players in the Indian steel and paper industries. The firms studied include J K Paper Mills (JKPM), Rayagada; Tamil Nadu Newsprints and Papers Limited (TNPL), Kagithapuram; Tata Steel (TS), Jamshedpur; and Bhilai Steel Plant (BSP), Bhilai. Of these, JKPM and TS are private sector firms while BSP is part of a larger steel conglomerate owned by the central government and TNPL is owned by the state government of Tamil Nadu. The chapter identifies relevant external pressures on firm behaviour and assesses their relative effect through a qualitative assessment of the evolution of environmental management practices and subsequent outcomes. The purpose of the study is to understand the types of responses elicited by these different pressures so as to evaluate the relative efficacy of the different drivers of environmental behaviour. In this context, it examines the particularities of public and private sector firms while also looking at external pressures from activists and other stakeholders such as employees, customers, the community at large, and regulators for socially responsible economic activity. Although responsible CEB that results from enlightened self-interest is desirable, our study of these leading firms indicates that this is rather rare. In addition, the research validates the observation that while regulators have many opportunities to shape CEB, their capacity to 'command and control' are limited. Hence, rather than policing, a better role for a regulator is that of an administrator: encouraging, cajoling, and threatening various parties to move towards behaviour that meets societal expectations. We also focus on this aspect of coerced environmental behaviour.

The rest of the chapter is organized as follows. First, the research methodology followed for the study is explained. This is followed by a description of anecdotal evidence in Sections 3 and 4, describing the paper and steel industry respectively. The sections are predominantly descriptive, summarizing the CEB of the four firms. They start with a very brief overview of the paper industry and selected firms within it. The environmental behaviour of the chosen firms is then summarized. The forces and factors that cause the firms to change their behaviour from business-as-usual are identified as the determinants of environmental performance. The responses to these stimuli are classified as environmental strategies, with their impact on the environment categorized as environmental outcomes. It is demonstrated that the nature of a firm's response is a result of the interaction of external stimuli coupled with inherent firm characteristics. Similarities and differences in the two firm's approaches are also highlighted, demonstrating the impact of firm characteristics. Section 5 concludes with a comparison of all four firms, generalizing key differences between types and intensities of pressures felt by the public and private sector.

I. RESEARCH METHODOLOGY

The firms selected for study filled theoretical categories and constituted examples of polar types. Thus, the chosen industry had to be polluting in nature so that their environmental behaviour provided stark measures that were easily observable. To ensure that profitability concerns did not overshadow all other non-market decisions of the firms, they had to be making consistently high profits for a period of five years prior to this study. The firms chosen were relatively large firms so that activist threats such as dissemination of information on socially unfriendly behaviour were credible, and to ensure that firms had a reasonable amount of market power. For ease of data collection relating to environmental practices, we also ensured that the firms were ISO 14001 certified companies. One firm from the public sector and one from the private sector were chosen to represent the polar opposite in each industry. Thus, we shortlisted the paper and steel industry, and the firms studied included JKPM, TNPL, TS, and BSP.

Table 1.1 provides a comparative overview of these firms, although their profile and environmental behaviour is discussed in somewhat

Table 7.1 Summary of Select Firm Characteristics

Industry	Firm	Ownership	Market Share (%)	Remarks
Steel	Tata Steel (TS)	Private (Tata Group)	11.43	Based on data from firms that contribute to 93% of total market share
	Bhilai Steel Plant (BSP)	Public—Steel Authority of India (Central/Federal Government)	27.81	Refers to Steel Authority of India's (SAIL) share. BSP's contribution to SAIL is approximately 20%
Paper	JK Paper Mills Ltd, (JKPM)	Private (JK Group)	4.27	Based on data from firms that contribute to 60% of total market share
	Tamil Nadu Newsprint and Paper Limited (TNPL)	Public (state Government)	3.14	

greater detail below. Categorizing coerced environmental behaviour, which was taken to be environmental responses because of some external pressure, and separating it out from environmental behaviour as a result of enlightened self-interest (as a result of internal pressures) and then identifying the drivers required several personal interviews as well as participant observations of day-to-day environmental activities of the firms.

II. THE INDIAN PAPER INDUSTRY, JKPM AND TNPL

The paper industry in India has a long history, with the first mill being commissioned in 1832 (Cleantechindia 2001). It is characterized by several uncompetitive resource- and energy-intensive small and medium scale fragmented paper making units with a poor record of capacity utilization. Less than 10 per cent of paper mills are in the large scale sector. The combined capacity of the larger mills equal or exceed the combined capacity of the rest of the small and medium scale mills (Centre for Science and Environment 1999). With trade liberalization in India, larger mills have continued to expand driven by the need for economies of scale arising from having to generate their own power, chemical recovery units and cost-related pressures. The Indian paper industry is very price-sensitive, partly due to supply side flexibility since the smaller players can change their product mix with short lead times. From the demand side, demand for printing and writing paper is highly price-elastic; and softening prices boost demand considerably. Even though India has among the lowest per capita consumption for paper among developing countries, domestic paper demand outstrips supply.

JKPM is one of the two integrated pulp and paper plants of JK Paper Ltd., a member of the JK Organization, a leading multi-product, multi-business group of India. Located in an industrially backward area in the eastern part of India, it is the largest manufacturer of copier paper in the country. It was commissioned in October, 1962 with a single paper machine of installed capacity of 18,000 tonnes per annum (tpa). Periodic expansions and modification of the paper machines coupled with the installation of other equipment for balancing of capacities, between 1970 and 1995, resulted in quintupling the installed capacity to 90,000 tpa. Further, a state-of-the-art fibre line of 127,000 tpa capacity was installed at the turn of the century using a low energy batch cooking system for digestion of pulp before conversion to paper.

TNPL is the largest bagasse-based paper unit in India (and the world), presently having an installed capacity of 230,000 tpa of newsprint and printing and writing paper in various combinations. At present, however, demand side economics coupled with lower costs of imported newsprint has resulted in TNPL producing only printing and writing paper. It is a Government of Tamil Nadu (a state government) enterprise commissioned in 1985 with a World Bank loan of US$100 million with technical assistance from Beloit Corporation Research Centre, USA, with a capacity of 90,000 tpa. It doubled its capacity in 1996, with another World Bank loan. In 2003, it increased its capacity through rebuilding its paper machines and has the potential of expanding further to 0.35 million tonnes in its existing location, although the availability of water is a binding constraint. In addition to producing paper, TNPL is self-sufficient in meeting its own power requirement and has also invested in wind farms to generate electricity that is directly sold to the electricity grid. Table 7.2 summarizes relevant parameters comparing JKPM and TNPL.

Table 7.2   JKPM and TNPL—A Comparison of Select Parameters

Particulars	Status of JKPM	Status of TNPL
Year of commissioning	1962	1985
Current Production Capacity	127,000 tonnes per annum (tpa)	230,000 tpa
Raw Material	Wood	Bagasse and wood, fraction of wood in raw material mix increasing
A. CREP Requirements		
(i) To reduce AOX discharge to 1kg/T in five years	0.5–1 kg/T already achieved	0.6–0.8 kg/T achieved, further reduction measures being considered to reach international norms
(ii) Install lime kilns by 2007	To be installed	Already achieved
(iii) To reduce waste-water discharge to less than 120m3/T paper	Less than 100m3/ T paper already achieved	60 m3/T already achieved
Installing odour control systems by 2007	Odour lower compared to other plants, H2S emissions within norms	TNPL's odour control systems in place

(contd...)

Table 7.2 (contd...)

Particulars	Status of JKPM	Status of TNPL
Colour removal by effluent	600–700 Pt Co, JKPM waiting for appropriate technology from CPPRI	Alum dosing has resulted in reducing colour to 150–200 Pt Co
B. *Water Consumption (m3/T) (data for 2001–02)*	110	70
C. *Gross Profit as a percentage of total turnover (data for 1999)*	14% (margins have increased since stabilization of RDH system)	33%

D. *Trade Links: Export Performance*

	Status of JKPM		Status of TNPL	
Year	2003–2004	2002–2003	2002–2003	2001–2002
Qty of paper exported (T)	1,722.8	10,316	25,871	27,780
Exports as a fraction of total production (%)	9.4	5.75	15.4	15.07
Earnings from exports (Rs millions)	476.88	295.88	768.8	802.1

Source: Data collated from Company Documents, Data submitted to governmental authorities, Annual Reports and Personal Interviews with Company Personnel.

Corporate Environmental Behaviour of JKPM

At JKPM, the responsibility to meet environmental obligations rests with the CEO. A General Manager oversees the activities of the environment and quality cell, which is headed by a Manager (Environment), responsible for planning expansion projects. Repetitive and day-to-day environment-related activities are taken care of by an Assistant Manager, who has twenty-one workmen and four chemists for his assistance. While the environment cell takes care of production-related environmental issues, the forest organization, an independent department, ensures sustainable supply of raw material. Its mandate includes developing high quality seedlings and clones, distributing them to farmers for farm forestry, and buying back the wood. Such programmes are currently running in farmlands covering an area of over 27,000 hectares. JKPM's thrust on farm forestry and its well-developed Environment Management System (EMS) led to it being recognized as India's greenest paper mill by the Centre for Science and Environment (CSE), New Delhi in 1999.[1]

Modernization of the mill resulted in pollution prevention as a desirable side effect. Along with the installation of a rapid displacement heating (RDH) system[2] and new fibre line, JKPM has upgraded or modified various systems to curb emissions and has initiated recycling of process water. In 2002, the effluent treatment plant (ETP) at JKPM was retrofitted with a cooling tower[3] and a new activated sludge-based system to handle a greater effluent load, which would be required after an expansion of the plant planned in 2008. Although its treated effluent is well within the compliance norms, JKPM does not discharge it during the day because there is a concern that the characteristic brown colour of the discharge could create unrest among the local population. Although a proposal to provide treated effluent (high nutrient content) for agriculture through a lift irrigation scheme was mooted as early as 1963, it has yet to take off. Table 7.3 summarizes key environmental activities and achievements of JKPM since inception.

While regulations have been the prime driver of JKPM's environmental response, there are other factors as well. As the government's forest policy, which restricted using trees from natural and protected forests as sources of wood, became more stringent, JKPM emerged as a leader in initiating farm forestry. It leveraged its strength as a major wood and bamboo distributing agent to have the first mover advantage in identifying plots of land close to the mill for farm

[1]Supported by the United Nations Development Programme (UNDP) and the Ministry of Environment and Forests, the green rating project by CSE was an attempt to rate paper mills in India for environment-friendly processes and policies. Although none of the 28 industries surveyed could cross the half-way mark set by CSE, JKPM got the highest weighted score of 42.75 per cent, making it eligible to receive three green leaves out of a maximum of five. One of the major criticisms of the CSE rating project is that it has relied heavily on voluntary disclosure. Also, since it was evaluating mills using norms for 'standard' paper-making processes, adjustments for 'different' processes were not adequately carried out.

[2]The RDH or rapid displacement heating system is a low-energy batch cooking system for wood pulp that minimizes emission of foul-smelling gases.

[3]The cooling tower is expected to lower the temperature of effluent, facilitating better biological degradation.

Table 7.3   Historical Milestones in Environmental Management at JKPM

1930s	Started as Straw Products Ltd. supplying bamboo to Orient Paper Mills.
1962	JK Paper Mill set up with a capacity of 18,000 tpa, which was raised by 5,000 tpa every five years (till 1972) through process optimisation measures.
1977	Paper machine 2 added, environmental issues not considered
1985	Hydrogen Peroxide bleaching introduced in addition to chlorine & hypochlorite. Certificate of Merit for Pollution Control Measures, National Productivity Council of India.
1988	First modernisation phase—capacity enhanced; no environmental improvements.
1990	Plantation wing set up in response to the 1988 Forest Policy.
1995	Environment & quality cell formed to obtain ISO 9001 & ISO 14001 certification. ClO2 plant set up, resulting in reduced hypochlorite consumption. Paper machine added.
1997	Certificate of Appreciation for undertaking cleaner production assessment by Network for Industrial Environmental Management.
1998	ISO 14001 Certification. RDH pulping and fibre line (Rs. 300 Crores) installed. Original plan was for 400 tpd capacity. Installed capacity only 240 tpd, perhaps because of the sudden downturn in the paper market following liberalization. Drastic reduction in water, steam, and power consumption as a result. Best Environment Management Award from Orissa state Government.
1999	Drive to implement TPM launched. Use of hypochlorite eliminated leading to elimination of direct chlorine bleaching to the tune of 75 per cent. Awarded three green leaves by CSE for being the greenest paper mill in its first ever green rating project of Pulp and Paper Industry.
2001	Pulp Drying Plant set up to eliminate wastage of pulp as a result of the mismatch between pulping and papermaking capacity. Greentech Environment Excellence Award, Greentech Foundation, New Delhi.
2002	Ecovision, an in-house journal on environment, health, and safety released. Effluent Treatment Plant modified at a cost of Rs. 6 Crores to handle larger effluent volumes from future plant expansions and improve effluent quality by reducing its temperature for optimal reaction in the Activated Sludge Basin.
2003	Dry Fog system installed in boiler plant improving work area environment.
2005	Coating Plant installed to increase fraction of value added products in product mix—no adverse impacts as it is 'zero discharge' by design. Environmental clearances for plant obtained in 1995, after conducting an EIA.

forestry. When the government clamped down on use of wood from forest areas, the high prices and shortage of pulp affected the paper industry adversely; JKPM, however, was able to weather this disruption through its links with farmers, to whom they provided seeds and extension services to grow trees for the paper industry.

JKPM is located in an industrially backward region, at the border of two states. There are some perceptions that JKPM's location is strategic, to exploit loopholes in regulations, through which a State Pollution Control Board (SPCB) can do little to curb the polluting activities of a firm located in another state, especially if effluents are released at night. While it was difficult to gauge the validity of such assertions, we noted that pressures from local communities are low at JKPM. That JKPM has found it difficult to find approved buyers for disposing of hazardous materials as legally mandated, demonstrates the low level of development of the region where JKPM is situated. This in turn means that stakeholders living in and around Rayagada derive their livelihood from the plant and would not want to jeopardize their relations with the plant management. Other community members are predominantly involved in subsistence agriculture and have not asserted their right to a clean environment. Hence, judicial activism is not a concern for JKPM. Owing to their preoccupation with backward mills in the small-scale sector, industry associations such as Indian Paper Manufacturers Association and the Indian Pulp & Paper Technical Association, of which JKPM is a member, also fail to put pressure on JKPM to improve its CEB. Competition, from the likes of TNPL and other large firms, however, acts as an incentive to proactively improve environmental behaviour.[4]

It is intriguing that a cost-conscious company like JKPM has invested over Rs 60 million in a higher capacity effluent treatment plant (ETP) to exceed legal norms, keeping in mind a mill expansion that is yet to take off (Ecovision 2003). Moreover, several other people in the paper industry doubted the efficacy of the ETP's much hyped cooling tower and aeration system in the bio-degradation process. Although power-intensive, a cooling tower is necessary to lower the temperature of the effluent for better bio-degradation. Similarly, large mixers, called aerators, catalyze the bio-degradation process. There were concerns that not operating the cooling tower, aerators and so on

---

[4]It is common for personnel at JKPM to continuously compare many aspects of its process with TNPL, often with regret, as they consider TNPL far more progressive in its processes as well as its attitude towards the environment.

could result in substantial power saving for JKPM, while hood-winking enforcement agents who were impressed with the large capital investment. The lax implementation and monitoring by regulatory authorities and their susceptibility to rent seeking was evident with respect to disposing of lime sludge as landfill, when JKPM personnel showed a clear preference to incur transaction costs in continuing with land filling activities rather than invest in a lime kiln, which is part of the Ministry of Environment and Forest's (MoEF) Charter on Corporate Responsibility for Environmental Protection (CREP).[5]

JKPM is among the highest profit making firms in the Indian paper industry. Pressure from Indian customers with respect to environmental or social responsibility is non-existent, nor is JKPM making any efforts to educate them. Nevertheless, investing in ISO 14001 was essential for the firm to meet the needs of its international customers, primarily those of Fiji and New Zealand. Unfortunately, its links with the developed world appear to be only through the sales of its products, with JKPM personnel unaware of developments related to resource-efficient production or optimal pollution prevention measures. Even participation in CSE's green rating project was because CSE actively sought out firms rather than JKPM volunteering to be rated. In a follow-up rating conducted in 2004, although its score has improved, JKPM has not been able to maintain its position.

JKPM's vision to be a 'dynamic benchmark and leader in the Indian paper industry' is one of the reasons why it reacts to environmental initiatives of its Indian competitors (Ecovision 2003). For example, in its quest for leadership, the firm aims to be the first paper mill in Asia to obtain Total Productive Maintenance (TPM) Certification[6] from the Japan Institute of Productive Maintenance. The positive fall out of this is a better ecological environment as a result of better housekeeping and lower resource use intensity.

While the implementation of an EMS and ISO 14001 certification in 1998 was an attempt to go beyond legislation, it would at best qualify as a strategic response by the firm to reduce its environmental

[5]CREP is a voluntary initiative mooted by the MoEF to improve environmental standards in industry. Specific guidelines have been drawn up for different industries.

[6]Total Productive Maintenance, a critical adjunct to lean manufacturing, is a proactive approach that develops a system of productive maintenance for the life of an equipment involving all the workforce that come in contact with the equipment for maximizing its effectivenes. Thus, its aims are to prevent equipment deterioration and reduce maintenance for it.

risk. Environmental issues were not viewed as a means of gaining access to newer markets, but as a means of retaining old export markets which had started to make newer demands. In JKPM, there is no evidence of any steps towards rainwater harvesting, a practice encouraged by the Ministry of Environment and Forests (MoEF) as a means of conserving precious water resources. The company's efforts to address state government concerns that effluents from the mill should be used in a more eco-friendly manner for irrigation rather than released into the river have also been weak. There has been little follow up by JKPM with the state government on a two-decade old plan to use the mill's effluent for irrigation in neighbouring farm land.

Corporate Environmental Behaviour of TNPL

From inception, the Utilities Division of TNPL took care of environment-related issues with an environmental wing (part of the R&D division) being set up only in the mid 1990s. Table 7.4 presents a historical overview of the evolution of environmental management at TNPL. The focus of its environmental policy is sustainable development. Daily walk through audits by responsible personnel is an optimally used environment management tool at TNPL. Intermittent water and energy audits are also conducted. Rather than direct disposal into the Cauvery River, TNPL's effluent is used for irrigation of nearby fields, reducing use of fertilizer and farmer dependence on the monsoon. However, the effluent colour is brownish, and research efforts are underway to reduce the colouration in a cost-effective manner.

Coordinated teamwork of upper management and floor executives coupled with a dedicated in-house R&D team has led to several successful environmental initiatives at TNPL. These include operating a lime re-burning kiln to recycle lime, installing multi-fuel burners to use pith and biosludge, installing an energy-efficient falling film evaporator and adopting a four-stage washing sequence. In 2001, it experimented (successfully) with the possibility of utilizing its high biological and chemical oxygen demand (BOD/COD) effluent to recover biogas. By 2003, a large scale bio-methanation plant was set up which resulted in multiple benefits of generating fuel, reducing methane emissions, and improving effluent quality. Using government research funding, TNPL experimented with composting

Table 7.4   Historical Milestones in Environmental Management at TNPL

1985	Plant Set up with 90,000 tpa capacity with World Bank assistance, resulting in them having state-of-the-art environmental control technologies including ESPs. TNPL is the first paper mill in the country to have ESPs.
1991	Rapid Environmental Impact Assessment performed by NEERI as TNPL was considering doubling its capacity.
1992	Wind farm commissioned for energy generation.
1994	TEWLIS started operation.
1994–6	Activated Sludge Basin commissioned, lime kiln commissioned.
1996	Public Interest Litigation against TNPL (politically motivated?) TNPL was cleared in 1997; however the judiciary had several recommendations for TNPL to improve its environmental behaviour. Plant capacity doubled to 180,000 tpa with the assistance of the World Bank, again.
1997	Environment Division regrouped from Utilities Division. Lime kiln set up to use lime sludge (reduced solid waste generation).
1998	The Green Rating Project evaluated TNPL as 7th overall among all Indian paper mills with respect to its environmental responsibility, and awarded it two leaves on a scale of one to five leaves, with five indicating a highly environmentally responsible company. Winner of annual CAPEXIL award every year from 1997 onwards, for export performance.
1999	TG set of 22MW capacity installed for captive power consumption.
2001	Wind energy capacity expanded.
2001–2	Paper Mill of the Year (IPMA), CEIRA by NEERI.
2002	Paper Machines modernized at the cost of Rs 140 crores. ISO 14000 Certification.
2003	Mill capacity expands to 205,000 tpa by reconfiguring the paper machines, resulting in lower specific consumption of water and steam LCA work commenced, Bio-methanation plant commissioned.
2004	Working towards OHS 18001 certification.

mixed liquor suspended solids (MLSS),[7] to find that the resultant compressed organic waste was excellent manure and resulted in reduction of residual AOX[8] in sludge by over 50 per cent. It has experimented

[7]MLSS, the secondary sludge from activated sludge process and bagasse pith from the bagasse clarifier underflow is used as landfill by all other Indian paper mills.

[8]AOX measures adsorbable organic chlorines in effluent from pulp mills using chlorine in the bleaching process, which have deleterious ecological impacts.

extensively with TCF and ECF[9] technology also. Currently, TNPL is concentrating on improvement of its work area environment through commencing activities which would finally lead to an OHSAS 18001[10] certification.

Since TNPL was commissioned in 1985 when Indian environmental legislation was already in place, the role of regulations in influencing its environmental behaviour was limited. It had the opportunity to comply with many of the standards at the time of inception using pollution control equipment, which was synchronous with the prevalent end of pipe mindset. Of late, compliance with TSS norms[11] in effluent is a problem for TNPL in the summer months, primarily because the input water quality does not even meet effluent quality norms. This is due to the poorer regeneration capacity of the river Cauvery, which serves as TNPL's water source, after the release of untreated or poorly treated effluent by upstream industries. During the time that there was a fiscal benefit for using bagasse, the quantum of bagasse use in TNPL was over 75 per cent. Now the ratio is reversed. Since pulp wood imparts better strength and quality to paper, it is an economically sound but ecologically unsound decision.

Since a large fraction of TNPL's products are exported, TNPL is sensitive to the needs of international customers. Personnel at TNPL's environment division are in constant touch with developments in paper production process in India and abroad, and are aware of public disclosure and voluntary schemes to project a green company image. With a bagasse-based production system, it acquired the WWF panda logo and can use Planet Ark's Ecofriendly tag to describe its paper. While TNPL's decision to acquire ISO 14001 certification was a logical extension of obtaining ISO 9001, its trade links and demand factors played an enabling role in the decision. Although TNPL concedes that domestic customers are not very demanding with respect to green production, it has persisted in trying to obtain the eco-mark[12] for over two years, overcoming several layers of bureaucracy and

[9]TCF and ECF stand for total chlorine free and elemental chlorine free technology respectively.

[10]OHSAS 18000 is an internationally accepted occupational health and safety management system standard specification.

[11]TSS stands for total suspended solids in effluent.

[12]The ecomark is an eco-labelling scheme launched in 1991 to educate Indian consumers and as a means for easy identification of environment friendly products and packaging.

red tape. It plays a dominant role in educating the customer about environment friendly ways of producing paper; strategic philanthropy, perhaps as it can reap the advantages of being a first mover in creating a niche domestic market for ecofriendly paper.

The reputation incentive of the Green Rating Project by CSE was well understood by TNPL; it improved its standing to three green leaves with a rank of 4 in 2004 from two leaves and a rank of 7 in 1998. Pressure from domestic competition is minimal for TNPL. As a state-owned enterprise, it is beyond industry association pressure, but works through industry associations to communicate with the government, as it did with respect to BIS eco-mark standards. It also cooperates with industry associations, being one of the five paper mills nominated by the Indian Agro Recycled Paper Mill Association, to conduct a life cycle analysis study. Energy conservation (and subsequent cost savings) has also been the driving force for many process changes, with a reduced ecological footprint as a secondary outcome.[13]

Despite the fact that production levels are affected by scarcity of water in the summers, TNPL maintains a high profit margin giving shareholders, including the Tamil Nadu Government, little to complain about. However, public interest litigation (PIL) filed against TNPL in 1996 for its environmentally unsound practices made several of its stakeholders uncomfortable. While the PIL was quashed and TNPL absolved of all charges by 1997, the impact of this judicial move is still visible at TNPL. Despite there being no legal norms for effluent colour, TNPL has followed a non-binding court recommendation following the PIL to use alum to reduce colour at a cost of Rs 25,000 per day. Moreover, an independent body, the Tamil Nadu Agricultural University monitors ground water contamination as a result of using TNPL's effluent for irrigation.

III. THE INDIAN STEEL INDUSTRY, TS AND BSP

India has the advantage of a very early start in steel making at the beginning of the 20th century when Tata Steel (TS) commenced production. After the country achieved independence, special efforts were made by the state to systematically develop the steel industry

---

[13]The fact that energy costs comprise 19.5–22.5 per cent of manufacturing costs at TNPL (despite higher power and fuel costs in India) compared to the international best practice figure of 20 per cent corroborates TNPL's energy consciousness (TNPL 2003; Schumacher and Sathaye 1999).

as a part of the overall economic development planning effort. The industry grew in a highly protected and controlled environment with raw materials allocated through a centrally planned process, administered prices, and large import tariffs. Tata Steel remained the only private integrated steel plant in a steel industry where large integrated plants were the close preserve of the public sector. Until the 1960s, the Indian steel industry maintained a distinct cost advantage over their overseas competitors. Its cost advantages subsequently eroded over the next two decades due to old and inefficient technologies and very low per capita productivity (Sengupta 1994). The decade of the 1990s witnessed interesting events in the global steel industry which resulted in overcapacity and destructive price competition. Thus, the emphasis of the steel industry quickly shifted to competitive pricing, improved quality, and customer satisfaction. Despite past downturns, the current outlook for the steel industry is very bright. With a burgeoning demand and high finished product prices, plans are in place that will double India's steel production capacity within a decade.

Tata Steel was established in 1907 at Jamshedpur, in the eastern part of India. While the plant had an installed capacity of 0.1 million tonnes per annum (mtpa) of crude steel when it commenced operation, its current installed capacity is 4.0 mtpa of crude steel. It has undergone four phases of modernization, which have witnessed the phasing out of old, energy-intensive, inefficient and pollution prone technologies, installation of pollution control equipment, and an increase in installed plant capacity. Having successfully commissioned (in record time) and operated a new cold rolling mill complex in its works, the company is among the lowest cost steel producers in the world, and has been identified as the only world-class steel plant in India (Tata Steel 2003). With its progressive outlook, strong domestic demand, and increased exports, TS has performed well economically in recent years, with record production, sales, and profitability.

Bhilai Steel Plant (BSP) was one of the first three integrated steel plants set up by the Government of India in 1959. With an original capacity of 1 mtpa, the plant has gone through two major expansions, one an increase to 2.5 million mtpa in 1967 and onward to 4 million tonnes of steel a year in 1988. It is managed and operated by the Steel Authority of India Limited (SAIL), which is the umbrella organization for four other integrated steel plants, four special steel

Table 7.5   TS and BSP—A Comparison of Select Parameters

Parameter	Tata Steel	Bhilai Steel Plant
Net Income from Operation (2003), Rs Million	87213.2	68716.4
Total Profit before Tax (2003) Rs Million	14920.7	10885.2
Capital Employed (Rs Million)	81540	24759
Implementing ISO 14001 (year)	by 2000	by 2005
CDM Project	Under way	Under consideration by MoEF
Implementing OSHAS 18001 (year)	2004	Under consideration
Specific Water Consumption (m3/T saleable steel)	25.9 (1990–1) 7.31 (2002–3)	8.1 (1990–1) 3.52 (2002–3)
Specific Particulate Emission (kg/T crude steel)	6 (1991–2) 1.6 (2002–3)	7.22 (1991–2) 0.57 (2002–3)
Specific Energy Consumption (GCal/T crude steel)	9.565 (1989–90) 6.975 (2002–3)	8.86 (1989–90) 6.84 (2002–3)

plants, and associated raw materials and services. Bhilai is the only steel plant in the country to have been awarded the Prime Minister's Trophy for the best integrated steel plant five times in seven years, starting 1992–3. The first Indian integrated plant to surpass the four mpta mark, Bhilai was also the first in the country to receive the ISO 9002 quality certification. Table 7.5 presents a quick comparison between the two steel plants.

Corporate Environmental Behaviour of Tata Steel

Tata Steel established its Environment Management Division (EMD) in 1986, as a response to the spate of legislation introduced by the government. The primary duty of this division at that time was to monitor and report pollution levels. In line with the Tata culture,[14] other activities of the division included imparting training and increasing awareness, as well as tree planting, land reclamation, and rehabilitation. Considering that annual generation of solid wastes was

[14]The Tata philosophy is to uphold and exceed the tradition and standards of honest and fair management, product quality, congenial labour relations, and philanthropy set by its founder.

over 1.2 tonnes per tonne of crude steel, which made disposal difficult, this was also an area of attention.

Tata Steel started introducing newer, more efficient, and cleaner steel making technology in a phased manner in the 1980s and 1990s, ushering in a cleaner environment as a by-product. Since its inception, the EMD was actively involved in formulating modernization projects, as well as with the research and development division of TS in conducting laboratory and pilot investigations on use of wastes. These include, for example, tar injection in blast furnaces, using oily material as supplementary fuel in the power plants.

Tools used for environment management by TS include performance audits of existing pollution control systems, characterizing its waste streams and quantifying the extent of pollution, environment impact assessments, assessment of carrying capacity of the Jamshedpur region, reporting environmental parameters to all stakeholders, benchmarking with global best practices and so on. Gaining a competitive edge through environment management, inventorying resources, and tracking specific resource use was taken up seriously with respect to water, power, and solid wastes. Solid waste management has been a thrust area for the firm with the goal of getting wealth from waste.

A watershed event in the efforts to internalize environmental management into mainstream operations has been the implementation of a structured EMS, in line with the internationally accepted environmental standard, ISO 14001. Specific to the cause of social and environmental issues, the Tata Group has initiated a group environment network, of which TS is a committed partner. As the flagship company of the Tata group, it has a leadership role to play in this group environment network. Currently, the EMD has obtained the OHSAS certification for its steel plant at Jamshedpur. Table 7.6 summarizes major environmental initiatives of TS.

Despite several initiatives, solid waste utilization hovered around the 40 per cent mark at TS, till in 1997, a task force for solid waste management identified better solid waste management practices through benchmarking. This included novel approaches like injecting coal tar in blast furnaces as fuel, utilizing oily and tarry wastes in blast furnaces, using slag in place of fluorspar in ladle furnaces and so on, which resulted in large cost savings. Certification for ISO 14001 at TS was driven by a need to keep up with global trends. Even the production of the Corporate Sustainability Report, which follows the guidelines of the Global Reporting Initiative (GRI), and obtaining

Table 7.6 Historical Milestones in Environmental Management at TS

1911	First Blast Furnace blown in.
1944	Four MGD Sewage Treatment Plant installed in India for the first time.
1959	A sintering plant was installed in the works to 'to not only utilize the hitherto wasted iron ore fines' but also materially improve blast furnace efficiency. (Chatterjee 2000).
1971	Pelletising plant set up in iron ore mines to utilize blue fine dust (Lonial, 2000).
1973	Coal washeries constructed at collieries.
1980	Modernization programme launched to include state-of-the-art technologies for environment control.
1989	End of Modernization Phase 2—Bar and rod mill installed with closed circuit water recirculation, raw material bedding and blending yard set up for servicing the sinter plant (consistent quality, better use of fines), second sinter plant commissioned to use up to 50 per cent of 'blue dust' and other solid wastes, coal injection in blast furnaces introduced stamp-charged coke oven batteries to use low grade coal.
1986	Environment Management Division established.
1991	Environment Manual released in August.
1993	40 per cent utilization of solid waste.
1994	Modernization Phase 3 completed. More efficient blast furnace with state-of-the-art environmental control facilities installed, LD converters installed to replace open hearth furnaces, semi continuous hot strip mill with close circuit water system.
1994	First Environmental Policy Released. Secondary Products Profit Centre set up.
1995	Five Open Hearth Furnaces shut down, last two connected to an existing gas cleaning plant.
1997	On 5th June, Green Millennium countdown launched to plant 1000 trees per day for the next 1000 days. October—top management in Tata Steel decide to implement EMS based on the ISO 14001 standard.
1998	Initiatives to implement Environment Management systems as per ISO 14001 begin.
1999	Some units granted ISO 14001.
2001	The entire works granted ISO 14001. Waste utilization is at 70 per cent.
2002	Cold rolling mill and continuous galvanising line operational.
2003	Environmental, Occupational Health & Safety Policy Issued—integrating environment with health and safety, to obtain ISO 18001.

OHSAS 18001 certification, were viewed as necessary steps to be a world class steel plant.

Corporate Environmental Behaviour of Bhilai Steel Plant

The EMD at Bhilai Steel Plant came into being in 1983 as a response to the spate of environmental regulations in the late 1970s and early 1980s. The process of setting up an EMD was hastened due to pressure from the Workers' Union, as around this time, the Union leaders and management were coming to a broad-based agreement on several issues including environment. The intense stakeholder pressure is evident from an internal document of BSP's: 'Bhilai Steel Plant constituted its environment management division in 1983, exclusively dedicated to meet the legal requirements, social demands, and commitments made in the memorandum of settlements with the National Joint Committee for Steel (NJCS) with respect to environment. It became necessary due to notification of the Water Act 1974 and Air Act 1981.' (Bhilai Steel Plant 1998, p. 229). Setting up an EMD was also one of the recommendations in a memorandum of agreement dated 25 May 1983 between top management and union leaders under the aegis of the Committee for the steel industry. Initiation of pollution control measures was one of the aspects covered in addition to recommendations on wages, housing, allowances, education facilities, and skill development of workers.

The newly formed department entrusted BHPE-Kinhill, an Australian consulting company, to conduct a study of the steel works to suggest ways to bring the plant in compliance with existing environmental regulations. In addition, the National Environmental Engineering and Research Institute (NEERI) was contracted to conduct a regional environment impact assessment of the area around Bhilai. By 1991, a comprehensive report identifying pollution areas with suitable recommendations was submitted by BHPE-Kinhill, which served as a blueprint for activities related to the EMD. In addition to routine monitoring activities as prescribed by regulation, the EMD worked towards implementing 28 identified pollution control and prevention measures. Meanwhile, a Corporate Environment Management Division (CEMD) was set up in 1988, with headquarters in Calcutta, and the EMD at Bhilai took up its role as a supporting department (EMD 1998).

The EMD at Bhilai comprises a fairly large group, with around twelve to thirteen executives and fifteen non-executive staff. These include a General Manager, who is responsible for Power and Energy in addition to Environment and three Assistant General Managers responsible for environment laboratory activities, routine plant activities and planning, procurement and project activities respectively. Legal issues and ISO 14000 activities are dealt with by a Senior Manager and Manager respectively, who report to the General Manager. A Senior Manager, Manager, and Junior Manager are responsible for routine activities such as inspection and monitoring of pollution control equipment and ensuring compliance in association with other production units of the plant. Some of the achievements of Bhilai on the environment front are presented in Table 7.7.

In Bhilai, fresh water consumption was as high as 50 m3/ tonne steel in the 1950s. Now, it has been brought down to 3.54 m3/tonne crude steel in 2002–3, the lowest figures in India and comparable with the best worldwide. This is mainly because in addition to water cess, a token tax charged on quantum of water consumption, and other statutory fees related to water and water pollution, it has to pay the Government Irrigation Department for the water withdrawn as it operates in a water-scarce region. In 1996, SAIL released its environment policy, which was also adopted by Bhilai. By this time most units of the latter were ISO 9000 certified, and the EMD started working towards an ISO 14000 certification. The Plate Mill and Environmental Monitoring Laboratory were certified as ISO 14001 by 1999. Other divisions were certified in a phased manner with the entire plant getting certified by 2005.

On the social front, the EMD has performed commendably in 'greening' the steel plant and the entire township and in creating a deep awareness for the environment through programmes such as the eco-clubs. 'Being part of a public sector undertaking, community development initiatives of all types have become a matter of habit and faith.' (EMD 2002). The fear of public interest litigation is a potent driver of risk limiting environmental endeavours, with concerns related to judicial activism cropping up at every level, including meetings of the Board of Directors at SAIL.

Interestingly, the use of innovative approaches[15] is not encouraged in Bhilai. Concerns over unwarranted probes by the Indian Vigilance Commission are so high that the EMD prefers to adopt an approach

[15]These would refer to trying out unconventional approaches to eliminating environmental problems which have not been tried by Indian firms so far.

Table 7.7   Historical Milestones in Environmental Management at BSP

1983	Environmental Management Division established primarily due to regulatory requirements and internal pressure from blue collar (non executive) workers in the plant.
1988	Environment Management Division set up at the Corporate Level.
1991	BHPE—Kinhill, Australia conducted environmental study of BSP and made recommendations.
1992	An Action Plan was initiated on the basis of the recommendations. Environmental Laboratory set up inside the plant.
1996	Coke oven 10 commissioned, with significantly higher resource efficiency in comparison to the other coke batteries. Environmental Policy for SAIL released. Environmental Audits as a tool for environmental management were introduced.
1997	100 per cent Compliance for all Stacks obtained.
1998	All recommendations of BHPE-Kinhill finally implemented.
1999	Plate Mill and Environmental Monitoring Laboratory awarded ISO 14001 certification. BSP EnMD produces a brochure on marketable solid by-products of BSP, including specifications of each by product and, where established, their suggested end uses.
2001	Environmental Policy for Bhilai Steel Plant released.
2002	Rail and Structural Mill, BSP awarded ISO 14001 certification. Initiation of efforts for ODS substitutes.
2003	Formulation of Action Pan under CREP.
2005	Entire BSP ISO 14001 Certified.

of 'waiting and watching'. A project is considered only after it has been implemented by other SAIL plants, or it is a suggestion from the corporate EMD as a result of successful implementation in other Indian steel plants such as Tata Steel. An alternate catalyst for change is monetary aid, equipment supply or technical advice from foreign organizations, so that the technical and financial uncertainty factor is minimized.

CONCLUSION: RESPONSES TO EXTERNAL PRESSURES BY THE PUBLIC AND PRIVATE SECTOR

The empirical observations above suggest that the causal forces that drive the public and private sectors' environmental behaviour differ in their intensity and impact. At the private firms, JKPM and TS, most responses have been due to decisions emanating from the top. At JKPM, these were primarily concerned with the objective of achieving cost reductions; at TS, environmental actions have generally been initiated to meet the objective of becoming world class, whether with respect to cost, quality or market leadership. For the public sector enterprises TNPL and BSP, environmental policy and activist pressures in the form of threatened public interest litigation, have been key drivers for environmental activity. Interviews with environmental managers at the different firms revealed that concern for judicial activism and its impact is much higher for the public sector firms when compared to firms in the private sector. Since both the private sector organizations studied (TS and JKPM) had significant economic (and social) clout among their stakeholders, enlightened stakeholders expressed that they were always hesitant to raise their voice in public protest against the firms. In contrast, in relation to the public sector firms, the protesters had the option of taking a different approach: they could influence their local political representative to take the matter up with the offending firm. If this approach did not yield results, the politician could take the matter a step further to the respective government ministry responsible for the public sector organization. The CEO of the organization would then be compelled to react to the protester. The costs of the protest and activism for the CEO include both personal humiliation and harassment and loss of face, as well as a significant dent in the reputation of the public sector firm. Another difference related to social responsibility that could be gleaned from the evidence is that the public sector has some social responsibilities built into its operating mandate, which is not necessarily true of the private sector. This was reflected in the development of the Bhilai township in the case of BSP, and demonstrating an eco-friendly way of producing paper in case of TNPL.

In general, for the four firms studied, it is seen that while strategic environmental initiatives dominate environmental behaviour for the private sector, coerced environmental behaviour best explains public sector environmental outcomes. Altruistic environmental behaviour is hard to detect, except when it is mandated in the firms' operational principles, hints of which are seen in the environmental responses of the public sector firms, TNPL and JKPM. Table 7.8 below summarizes the anecdotal evidence with respect to coerced environmental initiatives.

Table 7.8   Coerced Environmentally Responsible Initiatives for four Indian Firms

Firm	Examples of Coerced Environmentally Responsible Initiatives	Concerns about activism	Stakeholder opinions
JKPM	None	None	Not collected
TNPL (Public)	Irrigation with effluent Adding alum to reduce effluent colour Research on: - reducing effluent colour - MLSS - TCF and ECF production Installing Limekiln	The negative publicity, and loss of CEO time as a result of past litigation rankles Very wary of activist pressures, especially if any politics is involved	Not collected
TS	Release of Environment Performance Report	Minimal concerns, although it is important to keep activists apprised of the firms activities for maintaining a good firm image	Firm is becoming less socially responsible in its quest for becoming world class.
	Having a social development wing of its own		Activist groups feels they are too small to challenge such a large organization
BSP (Public)	Comply with Coke Oven Work Area Norms	Concern and fear with respect to judicial activism very high	In general, firm is meeting its social obligation
	Discussion of Social and Environmental expectations of stake-holders regular feature in board meetings		Activist groups will not hesitate to complain to state regulatory authorities or local politicians if there are any social or environmental concerns
	Sponsoring and deve-loping Eco-clubs in neighbouring schools		

Such observations could lead us to draw interesting maps of stakeholder pressures on public and private firms, demonstrating the relative intensity of pressures depending on the nature of firm ownership. This could lead to useful inputs for policy formulation, suggesting that the potency of different policy instruments could vary depending on the nature of firm ownership.

Despite some similarities between public and private sector firms, we also found that although all the four firms have highly profitable businesses, their approach towards managing the business-environment interface was different. Through our analysis we tried to identify reasons for these differences. It is quite clear that firms, when faced with changing environmental scenarios, react in different ways depending on their commercial motivations, decision-making procedures, organizational structure, and other external factors, such as activist pressures and environmental policy. The analysis of the inner workings of the firm helped us infer that while regulatory pressure usually elicits a reactive response, social pressures tend to elicit innovative responses. Thus, even in a situation of stringent environmental regulations with lax implementation, factors like judicial activism, competitive market conditions, and appropriate resource pricing can provide firms the right incentives to behave in an environment friendly manner. By investigating the many challenges faced by firms seeking to implement strategies because of environmental pressures, this study is an attempt to inform environmental policy makers for better design and implementation to lead to sustainable growth.

REFERENCES

Bhilai Steel Plant, *Works Visit Notes*, Training and Management Development Department, Bhilai, 1998.

CSE (Centre for Science and Environment), *Issues Paper on Pulp and Paper Sector, Part I*, The Green Rating Project, New Delhi, 1999.

Chatterjee, A., *Evolution of Technical Facilities and Technologies at Tata Steel*, Jamshedpur, Sec.SC2: Tata Search, 2000.

Clark, M., 'Corporate Environmental Behaviour Research: Informing Environmental Policy', *Structural Change and Economic Dynamics*, 16, 2005, pp. 422–31.

Cleantechindia, *Report on Pulp and Paper Industry: Survey of Industrial Environment, Environmental Information Centre*, Sectoral Papers and Reports, 2001, available at *http://www.cleantechindia.com/eicnew/bhupindex.htm* accessed January 2005.

Ecovision, A., *Journal on Environment Safety and Health*, Rayagada: JK Paper Ltd., Unit—JK Paper Mills, 2003.

EMD (Environment Management Division), *Annual Report 1997–98*, Kolkata: Steel Authority of India Limited, 1998.

EMD (Environment Management Division), *Annual Report 2001–02*, Kolkata: Steel Authority of India Limited, 2002.

Lonial, S.K., *Evolution of Raw Materials at Tata Steel, Jamshedpur*, Sec. SC1: Tata Search, 2000.

Salzmann *et al.*, 'The Business Case for Corporate Sustainability: Literature Review and Research Options', *European Management Journal*, 23(1), 2005, pp. 27–36.

Schumacher, K., and J. Sathaye, 'India's Pulp and Paper Industry: Productivity and Energy Efficiency', LBNL-41843, Lawrence Berkeley National Laboratory, 1999, available at *http://eetd.lbl.gov/ea/IES/iespubs/ 41843.pdf*, last accessed June 2007.

Sengupta, R., *The Indian Steel Industry: Investment Issues and Prospects, Part I: Market Demand and Cost Competitiveness*, ICRA Sector Focus Series No. 2, New Delhi: Investment Information and Credit Rating Agency of India Limited, 1994.

Tata Steel, Tata Steel, An Organizational Profile, 2003, available at *http:// www.tatasteel.com/corporateprofile/organization.htm*, accessed June 2004.

TNPL—Tamil Nadu Newsprints and Papers Limited, 23rd Annual Report 2002–2003, Chennai, available at *http://www.tnpl.co.in.*

8

Patterns of Pollution Compliance
A Cross-State Analysis of Industrial Pollution Compliance in India

PRABHA PANTH AND RAHUL A. SHASTRI

INTRODUCTION

Industrialization, while contributing to economic development, is also a prime contributor to environmental degradation. Industrial pollution can be controlled either through direct government regulation (often referred to as command and control), or through market forces by manipulating prices through taxes and/or subsidies. However, since many less industrialized and newly industrializing countries have a weak market structure, it is usually necessary to depend on command and control methods to ensure compliance with environmental regulations such as pollution targets.

In India, the Ministry of Environment and Forest (MoEF) and its subsidiaries—the Central and State Pollution Control Boards (CPCB and SPCB), enforce environmental regulation. Various methods have been used over the past three decades to ensure that polluters are made responsible for their pollution. However, the track record of industrial compliance with environmental regulation is still very poor in the country. Industrial pollution regulation is dogged by various problems. These include a shortage of trained staff in the State and Central Pollution Control Boards, corruption, evasion of regulations on the part of certain industrial firms, and the overriding authority of other departments and ministries (World Bank 2003). Despite these drawbacks, the CPCB assumed that that there is substantial improvement in the levels of industrial pollution compliance, and that its measures to ensure industrial pollution control have been largely successful[1] (CPCB Annual Report 2004). Moreover, the level of compliance is not uniform over different states and industries within India; while some states have been more successful in enforcing pollution control regulations on industries; others have lagged behind (Gupta and Saxena 2002).

In this chapter, we measure and examine the patterns of industrial pollution compliance across different states in India, and explore the relationship between compliance rates and the average share and growth of highly polluting or 'red' firms. We have devised an index called the FCI (Final Compliance Index), which shows the relative rate of compliant to non-compliant units of the states to the all-India ratio. We find that the number and composition of states that have an FCI>1 has changed over the period of study (2002–4), with some highly compliant states in 2002 (such as, Tamil Nadu) sliding down to lower levels of compliance in 2004, while others have improved their positions. Hence, we cannot accept the CPCB's assurance that the total level of industrial compliance in the country has improved. We cross-check this by running regressions of compliant rates on the growth and share of compliant units of different states. We also check if compliant rates are related to the levels of profitability across different states.

Bivariate regressions reveal that: a) level of compliance is not related to the levels of profitability in different states, b) states with a greater concentration of highly polluting industries report a somewhat higher proportion of compliance in the polluting industries, c) growth of polluting industries is significantly higher in states with higher reported compliance rates, and d) growth of polluting industries is significantly lower in states that have a higher rate of closure of polluting industries. These findings lead us to infer that compliance reports do not reflect the cost of compliance, since growth of polluting industries goes up with the reported compliance. In contrast to compliance reports, closures that impose a direct cost for pollution seem to deter the growth of polluting industries. Hence, it appears that pollution compliance reports are being issued to promote investments as an instrument of state patronage, and may bear little relation to actual compliance in the field.

[1]The CPCB itself claims that it has achieved a high level of compliance based on its data that showed the share of compliant units rising from 62 per cent of all highly polluting units in 1993, to 83.75 per cent in 2004 (CPCB Annual Report 2004). See section III A 1.

I. INDUSTRIAL POLLUTION AND REGULATION IN INDIA

India has had environmental legislations dealing with water pollution since pre-independence times (British rule). The earliest government act concerning control of water pollution in India was the Shore Nuisance (Bombay and Kolaba) Act of 1853 (Iyer 1984). The Indian Penal Code 1872, recommended prosecution of those who pollute the environment—Section 277 dealt with water pollution, Section 278 with air pollution, Section 269 with punishment for negligent acts likely to spread infection of diseases dangerous to life, and Section 290 with public nuisance. Similarly, the Indian Forest Act 1927 made the poisoning of the water of a forest area, a punishable act.

After Independence, the Factories Act was enacted in 1948, and one of its stipulations was prohibiting factories from discharging their effluent into water bodies. Section 12 of the Factories Act made it mandatory for all factories to make effective arrangements for the safe disposal of their wastes and effluents (Iyer 1984).

However, it was only after the United Nations Conference on the Human Environment, also known as the Stockholm Conference 1972, that environmental regulation in India was enforced in a regulated manner with the establishment of a proper Department of Environment. India was also the first country to provide for environmental protection explicitly in the Constitution[2] (Sangal 1996).

In 1974, the Water (Prevention and Control of Pollution) Act was passed, which identified water quality as an environmental issue. This Act provided for:

- The prevention and control of water pollution and maintaining the wholesomeness of water, in streams, wells, sewer, or on land,
- The establishment of Central and State Pollution Control Boards with a view to carrying out the above, and
- The prohibition of persons from discharging sewage or trade

[2]The 42nd Amendment (1976) made it a fundamental duty for the state, as well as the citizens to protect and improve the natural environment. According to Art.48 A. in the Directive Principles of State Policy of the Indian Constitution, 'The state shall endeavour to protect and improve the environment and to safeguard forests and wild life of the country.' Art.51-A (g) of the Constitution states, 'It shall be the duty of every citizen of India to protect and improve the natural environment including forests, lakes, rivers and wild life, and to have compassion for living creatures' (Sangal 1996, p. 106).

effluent into streams without the consent of the Board. Standards for effluents and tolerable water pollution were also set up. Contra-violation of these could earn imprisonment not less than six months, which could be extended to six years, and fines.

This Act was followed by the *Water (Prevention and Control of Pollution) Cess Act* of 1977, directed to collect cess taxes on water consumption from polluting industries, basically to help meet the expenses of the Central and State Water Boards. Through this Act, the government hoped to create some economic incentives for pollution control through a differential tax structure on water consumption by different types and levels of industrial activities—such as on process water, cooling water, and so on. (MoEF website).

In 1985, the Ministry of Environment replaced the Department of Environment. In 1986, the Environment Protection Act (EPA)[3] was passed; it is an *Umbrella Act* under which large and sweeping powers were given to the MoEF and CPCB. These included: the responsibility of deciding pollution standards, restricting industrial sites, laying down procedures and safeguards for accident prevention and handling of hazardous waste, investigations and research on pollution issues, on-site inspections, establishment of laboratories, and collection and dissemination of information. It empowered the CPCB to coordinate and maintain ambient water standards, to demand information from polluting sources regarding effluent emissions, to shut down firms with excessive polluting activities, and to prevent new discharges of effluent and sewage (Sangal 1996).

With these various regulatory bodies and environmental acts, the government plays a key role in determining pollution standards, co-ordinating between domestic and international environmental agencies, and between industry and the local population. The CPCB also uses regulatory instruments (like no-objection certificates, consents, standards, and so on), as well as various fiscal instruments (such as fines, subsidies) to control and prevent industrial pollution. Also, the SPCBs and the public are allowed to sue polluting units in a Court of Law.

But despite the large number of environmental regulations adopted

---

[3]These Environmental Acts are periodically upgraded to include the most recent environmental problems. See CPCB and MoEF Websites.

by the Indian government, the levels of industrial pollution have been rising in the country.

According to World Bank data, industrial pollution in India, as measured by BOD emissions per industrial worker, increased from 1422 kgs per day in 1980 to 1582 kgs per day in 2000. The BOD levels fell in the early 1980s, but started rising from 1985 onwards, peaking in 1997 when it was a high 1702 kgs. After that it took a slight dip in 1998, but started rising up again, up to 2000. Overall, it shows a U-shaped trend in pollution levels over the 21-year period, as shown in Fig. 8.1.

The rising level of industrial effluents shows that environmental regulations and laws have not been very successful. It is especially surprising that the impact of the Environmental Protection Act of 1986, and the Central Action Plans of 1991 (discussed below), did not have any perceptible impact on reducing industrial effluent emissions, as can be see in Fig. 8.1. Further, regional concentration of pollution hotspots in various industrial belts of the country—such as in the Ankleshwar region of Gujarat and the Patencheru region of Hyderabad since the 1980s, highlights the worsening environmental impacts because of industrial water pollution in different parts of the country.

There are many reasons for the ineffectiveness of the environmental acts on industrial pollution emissions in India. Pargal *et al.* (1997) have found that there is minimal impact of governmental inspections on

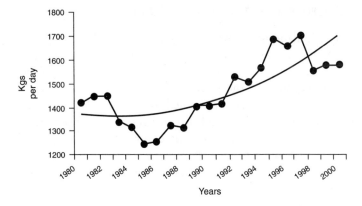

Fig. 8.1   Industrial BOD emissions—India (1980–2000)

polluting industries. Similarly, Mani, *et al.* (1996) find that so-called 'strict' environmental laws in various states of India do not affect the location of polluting industries. They attribute this to the low probability of enforcement as well as the low penalties for non-compliance. Their paper draws attention to shortcomings in the working of the formal regulatory system in India, with inspections having no significant impact on emissions. A number of other studies (Kathuria and Haripriya 2000, World Bank 2003) have also shown that government regulations are not effective in controlling industrial pollution.

Some authors like Murthy *et al.* (1999), have pointed out that bargaining with local residents has a greater impact on industrial pollution control, than mere command and control methods. Others feel that judicial intervention is an important source of enforcement of environmental regulations on industry (Venkatachalam, L. 2005). But it should not be forgotten that even here the standards are set by the MoEF, which is also the final reporting authority. Therefore, the ultimate responsibility of regulating industrial pollution lies with the government.

However, no study so far has taken up a cross-state analysis of environmental compliance by highly polluting red industrial units in India, nor tried to link the levels of compliance with the growth of polluting (red) units. This chapter aims to fill this gap, by analyzing the pattern and the relationship of industrial compliance to growth of red units, in various states of the country.

II. THE CENTRAL ACTION PLAN—1991

Since the stipulations of the Water Pollution Control Acts (1974 and 1977) and the Environmental Protection Act of 1986 were ineffective in reducing industrial pollution, the MoEF felt that stricter regulations had to be imposed on the polluting industrial sector. It therefore took up a 15-point programme called the 'Central Action Plan for Pollution Control' in 1991. This plan stressed the importance of priority action for industrial pollution control. Under this plan, the CPCB was first asked to identify seventeen categories of polluting industries under the Red or 'most polluting' category.[4] The CPCB

---

[4]Another category of industries, the Orange category, consists of less polluting industries, and a third—the Green category, consists of least polluting or no pollution creating industries.

in turn directed the SPCBs to identify all large and medium scale industrial firms in these seventeen categories in their respective states, so that action could be taken against those factories or units that were flouting environmental laws. The exercise was carried out from 1991–2002, and again in 2003 and 2004. The factories under 'red' or most polluting category of industries were then classified under compliant, defaulting, and closed units.

The present analysis of state-wise industrial compliance is based on this data, collected from the CPCB's and MoEF's (Annual Reports of 2002, 2003, and 2004), published online on their respective websites. The data include large and medium scale units belonging to these seventeen categories of 'red' industries in the states and Union Territories of India.

Compliant and Non-Compliant Units

The First Round (1991–2002)

Data collected by the CPCB in 1991 showed that there were 1551 medium and large scale firms in the seventeen categories of the most polluting or red category. These firms were set up on or before December 31, 1991. The data included industrial units that had installed the necessary air and water pollution control measures (compliant), and those that had not done so (defaulters).

Based on the extent of compliance by the industrial units, the SPCBs were asked by the CPCB, to modify the industrial consents already issued to these factories.[5] According to the CPCB ruling issued in 1991, the SPCBs had to ensure that a time-bound programme for installing pollution control facilities was implemented

[5]Under the Air and Water Pollution Control Acts, established industrial units should obtain an annual Consent to Operate, (which is a form of 'green clearance') from their SPCBs, which are granted only if the latter is satisfied with their compliance status. New units get environmental clearance from the SPCBs before starting production, only by showing that they have installed the necessary pollution treatment facilities. This is called the 'Consent to Establish'. Consent is required after the completion of the industrial project, but before commissioning of the industrial process. Without such consent, the factory cannot start its operation. The consent has to be renewed every year and is renewed only if pollution standards are complied with. This is known as the 'Consent to Operate'. It can be conditional or unconditional; it may be refused or withdrawn if measures to control pollution are found to be inadequate (Kathuria *et al.* 2000).

by all the industrial units in the seventeen categories. The schedule given to the polluting units to install the required pollution treatment facilities was as follows: those industrial units set up between 1981–91 had to comply with the above regulations (of installing pollution treatment equipment) by December 31, 1991, while those set up before 1981 were given until December 1993 to do so. In 1994, the SPCBs were directed by the CPCB to grant renewal licences only to those units that had the requisite pollution treatment facilities installed, and to take the following actions with respect to the defaulting units:

a) to verify if the defaulters had taken any steps to install adequate pollution control facilities,

b) to examine bonafide cases[6] and determine the time required by each of the units to complete the pollution control programme,

c) those units that had started the process of pollution control were given more time—not exceeding a maximum of six months (that is, up to June 30, 1994), to come into compliance, and

d) to initiate legal action against the identified wilful defaulters. (CPCB Annual Report 2002).

In 1994, the MoEF delegated power under Section 5 of the Environmental Protection Act of 1986 to the Chairman of CPCB to enable initiation of direct action against defaulting firms. Show cause[7] notices were issued in 1996 to the those firms that were defaulting. Affidavits were issued to those units that had claimed to have provided effluent/emission control facilities, and to others to complete the procedure by the specific target dates issued. Those units that had not installed the required pollution control measures by the specified dates were forcibly closed down.

The initial impact of these measures was encouraging. Table 8.1 shows that the share of compliant units out of the 1551 units identified earlier, increased from 62 per cent in 1993 to 85.4 per cent in 2000, while the defaulting ones fell from 35 per cent to 4 per cent. At the

---

[6]Units that had genuine reasons for wanting more time to implement pollution control measures.

[7]In accordance with the principles of Natural Justice, a show cause notice has to be issued if any department/court/employer etc. contemplates any action prejudicial to any party. The show cause notice details the provisions of law allegedly violated and asks the concerned party to 'show cause' why action should not be initiated against him. Thus, a show cause notice gives the accused an opportunity to present his case.

Table 8.1   Year-on-Year Status of Highly Polluting Industrial Units—
1993–2000. [Total units = 1551]

Year-wise Status	Closed	% of closed units	Compliant*	% of compiling units	Defaulters+	% of defaulters
March 1993	51	3.29	960	61.90	540	34.82
March 1994	74	4.77	1154	74.40	319	20.57
March 1995	121	7.80	1178	75.95	252	16.25
March 1996	111	7.16	1237	79.75	203	13.09
March 1997	125	8.06	1260	81.24	166	10.70
March 1998	125	8.06	1261	81.30	165	10.64
March 1999	135	8.70	1269	81.82	147	9.48
March 2000	164	10.57	1320	85.11	67	4.32
June 2000	165	10.57	1324	85.36	62	4.00
Annual average growth rate %	7.68		3.05		−85.66	

* Having adequate facilities to comply with the standards. +Not having adequate facilities
to comply with the standards
Source: CPCB. Annual Report 1997–98.

same time, firms that refused to install pollution control equipment
were closed down by the government. Although from 1993 to 2000,
the number of units complying with pollution control standards
increased by some 85 per cent, it did so at a very slow rate of about
roughly 3 per cent on a yearly average. The number of defaulting
units decreased dramatically from 540 units in 1993, to 65 in 2000,
or an annual average decrease of 85.66 per cent.

At the same time, the number of non-compliant units also grew
in this period. Non-compliant units include 'defaulters'—those who
have not installed adequate pollution control measures, and 'closed'
units that have failed to implement any type of pollution control,
and were therefore forcibly closed down by the Pollution Control
Board authorities. The total number of these recalcitrant units
increased from 51 in 1991, to 165 units in 2000, largely because of
an increase in closed units. The share of closed units increased from
3.3 per cent of the total in 1993 to 10.6 per cent in 2000. The
average annual rate of growth of closed units was more than double
that of compliant units over this time period (7.68 per cent p.a. of
the former as compared to 3.05 per cent of the latter).

This trend is cause for concern, since it shows that many units
prefer to close down rather than to install the requisite pollution control

measures.[8] It has been reported by Deily and Gray (1991) that even in the United States, in case of a declining industry like steel, the firms preferred to close down, rather than enforce environmental regulations. This further imposes economic costs on the community and economy.

The Second Round (2003 and 2004)

An inventory of highly polluting firms was again completed in 2003. A further 604 red units established on or after January 1, 1992 were identified, and the total number of highly polluting units now increased to 2155 units in 2003. In June 2004, another survey gave the latest position—a total of 2301 units in the red category in the country (MoEF Annual Report, 2003–04), that is, a growth of 48.36 per cent over the three years, or an average of 16.12 per cent per annum.

This new data also showed that the number of compliant units had increased over the years from 1351 in 2002, to 1927 in the year 2004. This seemed entirely satisfactory to MoEF[9] that the Central Action Plan was largely successful in reducing industrial effluents, since the number of compliant units had increased.

The closure of defaulting red units increased from 178 in the year 2002 to 235 units in 2004. This was also taken as a sign of success of the SPCBs in identifying and bringing unruly firms to book, and reducing their pollution to zero. Thus, closure and compliance were regarded as two methods of ensuring reduction in industrial pollution. However, it is doubtful if we can include 'closed units' as an indicator of environmental compliance. Closure shows the recalcitrant attitude of firms, which prefer to close down rather than take up pollution control. To that extent, it spells failure of the environmental authorities in enforcing pollution control in industrial units. This

---

[8]While the SPCBs have been successful in closing down such factories, it should also be kept in mind that while closure reduces their pollution to zero, it works against the interests of the economy by reducing output and employment. In the long run, the closure of industrial units is not the solution to industrial pollution control.

[9]A study, conducted by the World Bank states: 'Recent evaluation shows that the situation has improved with respect to compliance with the Action Plan recommendations'. *India: Strengthening Institutions for Sustainable Growth: Country Environmental Analysis*. South Asia Environment and Social Development Unit, World Bank Study, 2003. This study was conducted with the collaboration of MoEF.

is the interpretation that will be taken up in this paper, and non-compliance will include both closed and defaulting firms.

The number of defaulting units also rose—from 22 units in 2002 to 139 in 2004. If we take the shares of the compliant, closed, and defaulting units over this period, we can see from Table 8.2 that the share of compliant units fell from 87 per cent in 2002 to 84 per cent in 2004. The rate of growth of compliant units was 42.64 per cent over the same period. This indicates that along with the growth of compliant units, there is also growth of non-compliant ones.

The share of closed units fell from 11.48 per cent to 10.21 per cent in the three years, while the share of defaulting units increased from 1.42 per cent to 6 per cent. Also, the rate of growth of the latter category of firms is an enormous 531.8 per cent over the three years, highly surpassing the growth rate of the other two groups.

If industrial pollution compliance is really rising, then the rate of compliance should exceed the rate of non-compliance (defaulting and closed firms). This is possible only if the rate of compliance rises at a faster rate than the rate of non-compliance, as it eliminates the degree of non-compliance. Only then can the latter slowly peter out, achieving 100 per cent compliance.

A glance at the data in Table 8.2 shows that such a scenario of rising compliance has not emerged. While the number of compliant units is larger than non-compliant ones, there is no possibility of judging if the overall 'compliance performance' is improving or not. Merely depending on the number of compliant units and their increase, does not ensure that there is greater compliance, since the number of non-compliant units is also rising. Also, we cannot ascertain the position of the states in terms of their compliance and their relative positions over the two-year period. A different method of analysis must be adopted, and is attempted below.

III. A CROSS-STATE ANALYSIS OF COMPLIANCE

There are a number of difficulties associated with attempting a cross-state analysis of industrial pollution compliance. For example, it is not possible to say offhand whether a state with large numbers of pollution compliant units is a better 'environmental performer' than a state with a smaller number, because this does not take into account either the levels of non-compliance, or their share in total units in the country. Further, the size of the state in question also needs to be

Table 8.2 Share and Growth of Total Compliant, Closed and Defaulting Red Units (2002–2004) (in percentage)

	Total 2002	Total 2003	Total 2004	Total Closed 2002	Total Closed 2003	Total Closed 2004	Total Compliant 2002	Total Compliant 2003	Total Compliant 2004	Total Defaulting 2002	Total Defaulting 2003	Total Defaulting 2004
Total Red Units	1551	2155	2301	178	225	235	1351	1877	1927	22	53	139
% Share of Total Units*:				11.48	10.44	10.21	87.11	87.10	83.75	1.42	2.46	6.04
% Rate of Growth (200 to 2004):			48.36			32.02			42.64			531.82
Average Annual Rate of Growth % (2002 to 2004)*			16.12			10.67			14.21			177.27

Source: CPCB and MoEF Annual Reports—2002, 2003 and 2004. *Estimated from above data.

taken into account. A state may have only a single firm, which may
be compliant such that there is 100 per cent compliance. Can we
then say that this state has a better environmental record than a large
state with 200 out of 300 units in compliance, or only 66 per cent
compliance? Another problem is that the number of defaulting units
may not increase over the years in the case of some states. How
would that affect their environmental performance or record?

Due to such discrepancies, we construct a 'Final Compliance
Index', which will take into account both the compliance and the
non-compliance ratios of various states, as compared with the all-
India levels. Such an index will show the relative position of a state
in terms of the rate of compliant to non-compliant units, compared
to the all-India level. A Final Compliance Index is constructed for
different years to ascertain if a state is improving its environmental
performance or not. The actual construction of such an index and
its findings will be discussed in section IV.

Cross-State Compliance Performance

Cross-state data in terms of total, compliant, and non-compliant
large and medium industrial units in the seventeen categories of red
industries is available for three years—2002, 2003, and 2004 in the
Annual Reports of CPCB. The data includes the number of compliant,
defaulting, and closed units in the twenty-eight states and seven
Union Territories of India in different industrial categories. As indicated
in the data, eight states and union territories[10] had no polluting units,
and three states had only one each. Nine states can be classified as
more industrialized states, as the number of red units in these states
is greater than the average for India as a whole for the said year.[11]
Naturally the focus of attention with regard to pollution compliance
will be greater in these more industrially oriented states, as the extent
of their industrial pollution will be higher than in other states of India.

[10]In India there are seven Union Territories (UTs); these are small states, some
merely cities like Chandigarh, that are ruled directly by the Central government.
These include the Andaman and Nicobar Islands, Dadra and Nagar Haveli,
Lakshadweep, Pondicherry, Chandigarh, Daman and Diu, and Delhi. Some of
these UTs were formerly the colonies of other European states, such as Pondicherry,
which was ruled by the French.

[11]Of course, a better indicator would be the state's relative share of industrial
income, or employment, or investment in total.

The composition of the more industrialized states changed from 2002 to 2004. Although only thirty-four states and union territories are included in the CPCB Annual Reports of 2002 and 2004, seven of these had no polluting units, and were therefore dropped from the analysis. The remaining twenty-seven have been included, but even amongst these there were a few (like Tripura) with zero units in the initial or subsequent years. Their role in both pollution generation and in compliance is therefore very marginal.

Let us now look at the broad picture of compliance in the different states of India. The analysis will take note of the shares and growth of total, compliant, and non-compliant units in the Red category of industries from 2002 to 2004.

Total Red Units 2002–04

We now examine the total number of highly polluting (red) units in India as a whole, as well as the break-down across states over the 2002–4 period. The total number of polluting (red) units in India increased from 1551 units in 2002 to 2301 units in 2004—an increase of 750 units, or an average annual growth rate of 16.12 per cent per year between 2002 and 2004. Of these, the highest increase in numbers took place in the states of Gujarat (108 units), Tamil Nadu (97 units), and Andhra Pradesh (96 units). In terms of ranking of red units, Maharasthra stood at first place both in 2002 and 2004, with 335 and 392 red units respectively. But in 2004, Gujarat and Andhra Pradesh moved up to second and third positions compared to 2002, pushing Uttar Pradesh from its earlier second position to fourth. Punjab and Haryana, which were not in the initial top nine industrial states in 2002, now entered this group in 2004. Smaller states such as Uttaranchal and Kerala also showed substantial increase in their total number of red units over these two years (2002–4). In fact, the number of red units increased in 22 states, except in Goa— where it seems to have fallen from 16 to 8 from 2002 to 2004. Four states and union territories showed no increase in the number of red units in 2004, as compared to their status in 2002.

Share and Growth of Total Red Units Across States

From Fig. 8.2 it can be seen that Maharasthra had the largest number of total red units both in 2002 and 2004, although its share fell from 21 per cent to 17 per cent over that period. This was due to the rise in the shares of a number of other states—such as Gujarat,

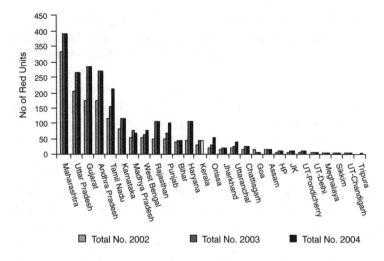

Fig. 8.2   Statewise Number of Red Units

Tamil Nadu, and Andhra Pradesh, which increased their shares by one per cent each, while Rajasthan, Punjab, and Haryana increased their shares by two per cent each in 2004. In terms of average annual growth rates over the last two years, Haryana showed the highest growth of total red units, followed by Rajasthan and Punjab. All other states registered positive growth in red units except Goa, which had a negative growth for such firms in 2004.

Total Compliant Red Units in 2002 and 2004

At the all-India level, the number of compliant red units increased from 1351 units in 2002 to 1927 units in 2004, an annual average rate of growth of 14.21 per cent. However, this rate of growth is lower than the average annual rate of growth of total red units (which was 16.12 per cent. See Table 8.2). This denotes that the rate of compliance is not rising on par with that of *total* red units in the country. We had seen earlier that in the year 2000, there was a substantial backlog of non-compliant units. Therefore, if the level of compliance has to reach 100 per cent, then it becomes necessary for the backlog of non-compliant units to also achieve compliance. At the same time, the number of new red units is also rising—so that the rate of compliance has to rise faster, to accommodate both the backlog of non-compliant and the new red units, to achieve full compliance of all units. In other words, it is necessary for the rate of growth of compliance to exceed that of the growth rate of total polluting units. Only then can the stock of old non-compliant units, plus those of the additional red units, be reduced. But this has not taken place—whereas the average annual growth of all red units was 16.12 per cent between the years 2002–04, the average annual rate of growth of compliant units in this time period was only 14.21 per cent. Therefore, since the growth of compliant units has lagged behind the growth of total red units, it means that the growth of non-compliant units has increased.

Share and Growth of Compliant Red Units Across States

Maharashtra had the highest number of compliant red units both in 2002 and 2004, but its share fell from 22.65 per cent to 18.47 per cent within this time period. The shares of Gujarat and Andhra Pradesh rose to the second and third position respectively in 2004, as they pushed Uttar Pradesh to the fourth rank. The shares of all other states in total compliant red units increased in 2004, except those of thirteen states such as West Bengal and Bihar, and so on, which fell. (See Fig. 8.3)

Looking at the rate of growth of compliant red industries, Orissa and Rajasthan recorded the highest average growth rate per annum over the two years; all states also experienced a rise in their compliant units, except West Bengal which showed a negative growth of 3.51 per cent in this time period.

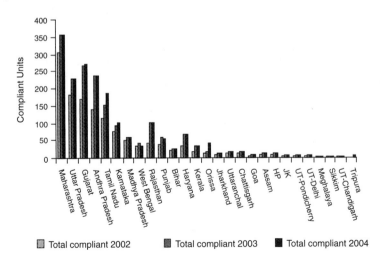

Fig. 8.3   Statewise Compliant Red Units

As mentioned above, non-compliant units consist of defaulting and closed units—the former do not have adequate pollution control facilities or are being sued in courts, and the latter are those units that have refused to install pollution control measures, and hence have been forcibly closed by the SPCBs. Both defaulting and closed units have also grown over these two years, as explained below.

Closed Red Units

The red units that showed a recalcitrant attitude towards the adoption of pollution control measures were closed down by their respective SPCBs. The total number of closed red units across India increased from 178 in 2002 to 285 in 2004, a rise of about 32 per cent in the three years, or an average annual growth of 10.6 per cent (though lower than the growth of total red units in operation). Therefore, this shows a positive growth of closed units over the years, as many units preferred to close down rather than undertake environmental controls.

Share and Growth of Closed Red Units Across States

Andhra Pradesh ranked first in both years in terms of closed units, though its share fell from 16.39 per cent in 2002 to 12.34 per cent in 2004. It was followed by Maharashtra, Uttar Pradesh, and Bihar in 2002. (Fig. 8.4) But in 2004, Uttar Pradesh replaced Maharasthra

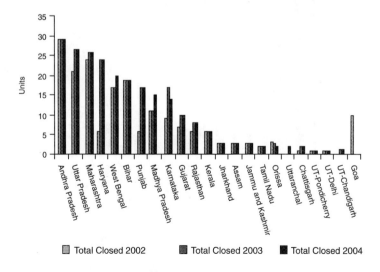

Fig. 8.4   Statewise Closed Red Units

in the second position, pushing the latter to the third rank. The state was followed by Haryana and West Bengal, pushing Bihar to fifth place from its earlier fourth place. Four states did not have any closed units during this time period, but these are small states with just one or two red units in operation.

The highest growth of closed red units between 2002–04 was in Haryana, with 100 per cent of such firms being closed down, followed by Punjab with a 61 per cent annual average growth in closed units. Two states—Goa and Orissa—saw negative growth of closed units, showing that the earlier non-compliant units may have joined the ranks of the compliant units. Thirteen states had zero growth in the number of closed units, showing that their numbers had remained constant over these years.

Defaulting Red Units

The total number of defaulting red units in India also showed an increase over the two years—from 22 units in 2002, to 139 in 2004. 19 states had no defaulting red units in 2002, but by 2004 this had reduced to 14 states—in other words five more states had firms that had joined the ranks of defaulters (See Fig. 8.5).

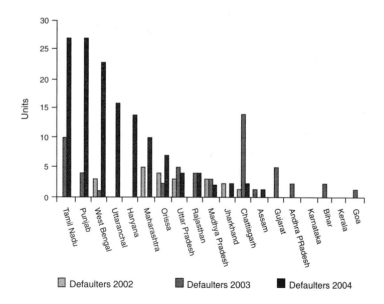

Fig. 8.5 Statewise Number of Defaulting Units

Share and Growth of Defaulting Red Units Across States

Maharasthra, which had the highest share of defaulting units in 2002 (22.7 per cent share of total defaulters), fell to seventh place (with only 7.2 per cent) in 2004. Surprisingly, four states that had zero defaulting units in 2002, jumped to within the top five numbers of defaulters in 2004. Tamil Nadu and Punjab stood first, each with a share of 19.42 per cent, followed by West Bengal (16.55 per cent), Uttaranchal (11.5 per cent), and Haryana (10 per cent) in 2004. This shows that new factories set up in these states after 2002 were all non-compliant.

The overall annual average rate of growth of defaulting units turned out to be about 177 per cent per year over these years or an annual average growth of 59 per cent. This rate of growth of defaulting units is much higher than the growth of total red units (16 per cent) and denotes the failure of the government authorities in enforcing strict industrial pollution regulations. The problem with defaulting units, unlike closed units, is that they continue to pollute, while defying the authorities and the public. Hence, they create environmental problems while at the same time defying governmental regulations.

To summarize

- From Table 8.2 it can be seen that the total number of compliant units rose from 1351 to 1927 while the share of compliant firms in the total fell from 87.11 per cent in 2002 to 83.75 per cent in 2004. But the average annual rate of growth of compliant units was less than that of the total red units over the two years (14.21 per cent against 16.12 per cent respectively).
- The total number of closed units increased, but the share of closed firms also fell marginally from 11.48 per cent in 2002 to 10.21 per cent in 2004. The average annual rate of growth of closed units was less than that of total red units (10.67 per cent against 16.12 per cent respectively).
- The reason for this fall in the shares of the compliant and closed units is the increase in the share of defaulters from 1.42 per cent in 2002 to 6.04 per cent in 2004. The average annual rate of growth of defaulting units was much higher than the growth of total red units (177.27 per cent against 16.12 per cent respectively).

However, the above analysis does not give a clear picture about the level and pattern of pollution compliance. While the total number of compliant units has increased, the average annual growth rate over the two years is lower than that of non-compliant units (closed and defaulting). Nor does it show which states are in the forefront of compliance and which are lagging behind. To determine these trends, further analysis has to be done. These aspects will now be taken up below.

IV. THE FINAL COMPLIANCE INDEX

As the level of industrialization is different across states, it is to be expected that the compliance ratios will also differ. Different states have reacted differently to the Central Action Plan, and we now look at their compliance performance by constructing an index of compliance.

At the state level, while some states have improved their pollution compliance, others have not. In some states, the share and rate of growth of non-compliant firms has overtaken that of compliant units, but it is the reverse for other states. The relative position of states is also not uniform. Some states have slid down the ladder of compliance as compared to non-compliance, others have climbed up. Different states have different environmental records—more industrial states have a large number of polluting (red) units, but also have a larger number of compliant, defaulting and closed units.

In terms of size, large states typically will have a larger number of polluting units. They cannot easily be compared with small and less industrialized states, which may have only one or two polluting units. For instance, we cannot say that a large industrial state like Maharasthra with 306 compliant units in 2002, is more/less compliant compared to Sikkim with only one compliant unit. Such problems also arise in locational and agglomeration theories of industrial concentration (Panth 2006)

Another problem noticed earlier is that the numbers of non-compliant units are also growing. Therefore, to know whether a state is turning more compliant requires that we have to study its rate of compliance with that of non-compliance. If its rate of compliance is greater than its rate of non-compliance, then its level of 'compliance performance' is better than that of other states. This will help environmental authorities to judge which states are serious about the implementation of the Central Action Plan, and the extent to which they have succeeded.

Since it is not possible to compare small states with large ones, it is necessary to construct an index which takes into account not just a state's compliance ratio, but also its position *vis-à-vis* the all-India ratios. This will give a picture of the relative position of the state with respect to the country's standard.

An index of compliance performance called the 'Final Compliance Index' or FCI is suggested here to measure states' ratios with the all-India ratio. Such an index will show whether a state has a disproportionately larger share of non-compliant units to compliant ones, compared with the Indian average. At the same time, comparing the indices for the two years 2002 and 2004 will show if the states have improved or worsened their position over time.

Method of Construction of the Index

The Final Compliance Index is somewhat like the Location Quotient Index, familiar to students of Regional Economics and Location Theory of Industries (Gartner 2001). This index has been modified to measure the relative rate of compliance/non-compliance by different states. Put simply, it measures the share of compliance to non-compliance rates of a given state, to the all-India ratio of compliance to non-compliance rates.

The Compliance Rate: measures the ratio of compliant units to total red units within a state.

The Compliance Rate or CI =

$$\frac{Number\ of\ Compliant\ Red\ Units\ of\ a\ state}{Total\ Number\ of\ Red\ Units}$$

The Closed Rate: measures the ratio of closed units to total red units within a state.

The Closed Rate or CLI =

$$\frac{Number\ of\ Closed\ Units\ of\ a\ state}{Total\ Number\ of\ Red\ Units}$$

The Defaulting Rate: measures the ratio of defaulting units to total red units within a state.

The Defaulting Rate or DI =

$$\frac{Number\ of\ Defaulting\ Units\ of\ a\ state}{Total\ Number\ of\ Red\ Units}$$

These rates have been worked out for the different states, and are given in Table 8.3.

The Compliance ratio: The Final Compliance Index shows the ratio of compliance to non-compliance: We estimate FCI at both the states and the all-India level.

$$\text{The Compliance Ratio or } C = \frac{Compliance\ Rate}{1-Compliance\ Rate} = \frac{CI}{(1 - CI)}$$

The Final Compliance Index (FCI): The FCI is the ratio of state Compliance Ratio to all-India Compliance Ratio. It shows the relative position of a state with reference to the all-India level.

Here we are taking both closed and defaulting units as being non-compliant, for as explained earlier, closed units are also non-compliant, and have therefore been closed down.[12]

$$\text{FCI} = \frac{State's\ Compliance\ Ratio\ Cs}{All\ India\ Compliance\ Ratio\ Ci}$$

If FCI > 1, it shows that the state's compliance ratio is greater than the all-India level.

If FCI < 1, then the state's compliance indices are lower than the all-India level.

If FCI = 1, then the state's compliance ratio equals that of the all-India level.

Results of the Final Compliance Index

The FCI was estimated for twenty-seven states. Of these, three states had just one industrial unit each, which were compliant. Tripura had five units—all compliant. These four states were therefore not included in the analysis,[13] and the FCI was estimated for the remaining twenty-three states.

The results of the FCI estimates gave some surprising results.

In 2002, seven states had an FCI > 1; these were Tamil Nadu, Gujarat, Maharashtra, Karnataka, Uttar Pradesh, Rajasthan, and Chattisgarh. Tamil Nadu had an FCI nearly 9 times the all-India level. Fourteen states had FCI < 1, with Punjab and Haryana close to 1. (See Table 8.3, Col. 10). Four states had just one red unit each,

---

[12]The closed factories are those closed by the respective SPCBs for non-compliance, and not those closed for other reasons—such as sickness.

[13]Since the non-compliance ratio for these four states would be zero, it creates the problem of dividing by zero.

Table 8.3   Estimation of FCI

1	2	3	4	5	6	7	8	9	10	11
State/UT	Share of closed units (CLI) to total units (2002)	Share of closed units (CLI) to total units (2004)	Share of compliant units (CI) to total units (2002)	Share of compliant units (CI) to total units (2004)	Share of defaulting units (DI) to total units (2002)	Share of defaulting units (DI) to total units (2004)	C_s^+ (2002)	C_s^+ (2004)	FCI* (2002)	FCI* (2004)
1. Tamil Nadu	1.68	0.93	98.32	86.57	0.00	12.50	58.52	6.45	8.66	1.25
2. Gujarat	3.95	3.53	96.05	96.47	0.00	0.00	24.32	27.33	3.60	5.30
3. Maharashtra	7.16	6.63	91.34	90.82	1.49	2.55	10.55	9.89	1.56	1.92
4. Karnataka	10.59	12.07	89.41	87.93	0.00	0.00	8.44	7.29	1.25	1.41
5. U P	10.14	10.27	88.41	88.21	1.45	1.52	7.63	7.48	1.13	1.4
6. Rajasthan	12.24	7.41	87.76	88.89	0.00	3.70	7.17	8.00	1.06	1.55
7. Chattisgarh	6.25	8.00	87.50	84.00	6.25	8.00	6.97	5.25	1.04	1.02
8. Punjab	13.33	16.67	86.67	56.86	0.00	26.47	6.50	1.32	0.96	0.26
9. Haryana	13.95	22.43	86.05	64.49	0.00	13.08	6.17	1.82	0.91	0.35
10. A.P.	16.76	10.78	83.24	89.22	0.00	0.00	4.97	58.52	0.74	1.61
11. Pondicherry	16.67	12.50	83.33	87.50	0.00	0.00	5.00	7.00	0.74	1.36
12. UT-Delhi	20.00	20.00	80.00	80.00	0.00	0.00	4.00	4.00	0.59	0.78
13. Kerala	21.43	13.95	78.57	86.05	0.00	0.00	3.67	6.17	0.54	1.20
14. M.P.	17.74	21.13	77.42	85.92	4.84	2.82	3.43	6.10	0.51	0.70
15. Assam	20.00	18.75	73.33	75.00	6.67	6.25	2.75	3.00	0.41	0.5

(contd...)

Table 8.3 (contd...)

1 State/UT	2 Share of closed units (CLI) to total units (2002)	3 Share of closed units (CLI) to total units (2004)	4 Share of compliant units (CI) to total units (2002)	5 Share of compliant units (CI) to total units (2004)	6 Share of defaulting units (DI) to total units (2002)	7 Share of defaulting units (DI) to total units (2004)	8 C_s^+ (2002)	9 C_s^+ (2004)	10 FCI* (2002)	11 FCI* (2004)
16. Jharkhand	16.67	14.29	72.22	76.19	11.11	9.52	2.60	3.20	0.38	0.62
17. Orissa	13.04	3.92	69.57	82.35	17.39	13.73	2.29	4.67	0.34	0.91
18. W. Bengal	29.31	25.97	65.52	44.16	5.17	29.87	1.90	0.79	0.28	0.15
19. J & K	37.50	30.00	62.50	70.00	0.00	0.00	1.67	2.33	0.25	0.45
20. Bihar	43.18	41.30	56.82	58.70	0.00	0.00	1.32	1.42	0.19	0.28
21. Goa	62.50	0.00	37.50	100.00	0.00	0.00	0.60	0.00	0.09	
22. Uttaranchal	0.00	5.26	100.00	52.63	0.00	42.11	0.00	1.11	0.00	0.22
All India	11.48	10.21	87.11	83.75	1.42	6.04	6.76	5.15	6.76	5.15

$^+C_s = CI/(1 - CI)$, *FCI = $(C_s) + (C_I)$ Estimated from CPCB Annual Reports 2002, 2003, 2004.

which was compliant, and so these four states were dropped, to avoid the problem of division with zero.

In 2004, although the number of states with FCI >1 increased to ten, (with Pondicherry, Andhra Pradesh, and Kerala joining the ranks), the record of many compliant states of 2002, fell to much lower levels—that of Tamil Nadu fell from a record 8.66 to 1.25. Similarly Maharashtra, Karnataka, Uttar Pradesh, and Chattisgarh—all had a lower FCI in 2004 compared with 2002—though they were all above the benchmark, that is, the all-India Ratio. Gujarat improved its position, and had the highest FCI in 2004.

Three states—Punjab, Haryana, and West Bengal—fared even worse, with their FCI sliding down to much lower levels than their position in 2002; while Madhya Pradesh, Jharkand, Bihar, Orissa, and Jammu & Kashmir, improved their positions marginally, though they were still below the benchmark. (See Table 8.3, Col. 11, Fig. 8.6).

From the analysis of FCI, the pattern of compliance levels of all states does not emerge very clearly, as the states' FCIs tend to fluctuate over the two years.

We next try to determine if there is any relationship between compliance and growth of red firms in the different states over the two years—2002–04.

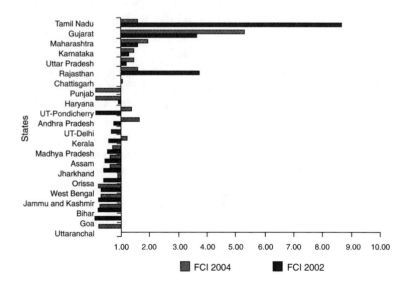

Fig. 8.6   The Final Compliance Index

V. ANALYSIS OF COMPLIANCE RATES

As seen above, the rate of compliance to pollution laws varies widely across states. If we exclude three states that had only one red unit[14] in the year 2002, we find that the reported compliance ranges from 37.5 per cent in Goa to 100 per cent in Uttaranchal. On an average, states reported that 80 per cent of the red units had complied with pollution laws.

Pollution Compliance and Profitability

Why do some states have a higher compliance rate while others have a low compliance rate? It might be suggested that profitability of red units is higher in some states when compared to others, so that it is worthwhile for a larger proportion of the red units to comply in such states than in others that have a lower profitability.

But why should some states offer higher profitability? It can be supposed that this may be due to better and cheaper infrastructure, better work culture, more efficient and skilled labour force and so on, in such states when compared to others. These factors affect all industries generally, and not just the highly polluting industries. Hence, we can assume that the profitability of industries in general will be higher in states that are favoured by the above conditions. If the reasoning in the previous paragraph is valid, we can expect a positive correlation between average profitability of industries across states with their reported rates of compliance.

Data on the average profitability of investments across states is given by the Annual Survey of Industries,[15] which provides summary statistics of organized manufacturing across states. Using this data, we now measure average profitability of investment by the ratio of the gross operating surplus in each state to total capital in the factory sector of that state (see Table 8.4). Three different measures of capital were used: Fixed Capital, Total Productive Capital, and Total Invested Capital.

The correlation of compliance rates to the average profitability of investments across states was estimated and found to be insignificant and close to zero (see Box 8.1 below). Thus, there seems

---

[14]Inclusion of such states tends to distort the analysis since compliance can only be zero or 100 per cent in such states. Also, any growth of red units would be in multiples of 100 per cent. This distorts analysis.

[15]Annual Survey of Industries (2001–02), Central Statistical Organization, Government of India, *www.mospi.nic.in*.

Table 8.4   Rate of Compliance of Red Units across States and Profitability
of Investment (in per cent)

	Gross Operating Surplus on Invested Capital	Gross op. Surplus on Productive Capital	Gross op. Surplus on Fixed Capital	Rate of Compliance in 2002 (CI)
Maharashtra	18.9	23.6	28.7	91.3
UttarPradesh	17.8	20.7	26.0	88.4
Gujarat	15.4	16.5	19.6	96.0
Andhra Pradesh	16.1	18.6	22.7	83.2
Tamil Nadu	17.7	20.1	25.6	98.3
Karnataka	16.6	19.9	22.2	89.4
Madhya Pradesh	27.5	29.8	38.8	77.4
West Bengal	5.0	6.4	6.5	65.5
Rajasthan	21.3	22.6	28.4	87.8
Punjab	24.2	26.3	43.0	86.7
Bihar	8.5	10.7	16.1	56.8
Haryana	22.9	26.7	34.4	86.0
Kerala	14.1	15.3	21.0	78.6
Orissa	8.3	8.9	10.2	69.6
Jharkhand	6.3	7.2	7.8	72.2
Uttaranchal	9.8	13.4	18.5	100.0
Chattisgarh	8.6	9.4	11.9	87.5
Goa	35.0	40.4	49.4	37.5
Assam	10.5	12.2	14.7	73.3
Himachal Pradesh	24.4	23.1	30.7	100.0
Jammu & Kashmir	3.8	4.3	6.5	62.5
Pondicherry	52.2	52.9	76.7	83.3
Delhi	27.5	23.1	54.2	80.0

Source: Annual Survey of Industries (2001–2), Central Statistical Organization, Government
of India, *www.mospi.nic.in* Rate of compliance estimated from MoEF and CPCB Annual
Reports, 2002. See Table 8.3 above.

Box 8.1: Correlation of Compliance Rates with Average
Profitability of Investments across States in 2002

	Gross Op. Surplus on Fixed Capital	Gross Op. Surplus on Productive Capital	Gross Op. Surplus on Invested Capital
Pearson Correlation	0.048	0.033	0.056
Sig. (2–tailed)	0.827	0.880	0.799
N	23	23	23

to be no link between profits and compliance, that is, it is not possible to say that compliance rates are higher in states in which investments are more profitable in the factory sector.

This finding is in line with a study by Mani *et al.* (1997) who used a conditional logit model to estimate the impact of different variables on firm profits as reflected in firm location decisions. After controlling for the impact of factor price differentials, infrastructure, and agglomeration, they found that the number of proposed new plants in different states of India did not appear to be adversely affected by the stringency of environmental enforcement at the state level.

Thus, higher compliance rates reported by states cannot be ascribed to higher profitability of investments in those states. Can they be related to the concentration of the polluting units in those states? Indeed, the correlation between compliance rate and the share of a state in the total red units of the country was found to be positive and somewhat significant. This is analysed in the next section.

Compliance Ratio and a State's Share of Red Units

Next, the relationship between a state's share of red units, to its compliance rate (that is, compliant units/total red units of a state), was examined, to see if the share of a state in polluting units has any relation with its rate of compliance. A regression was run on the data on compliance rates for 2002, and states' average share of red units of 2002 and 2004.

Removing the outliers, it was found that there was a very slight positive relationship between its size (in terms of average share in red units) to compliance rate (See Fig. 8.7).

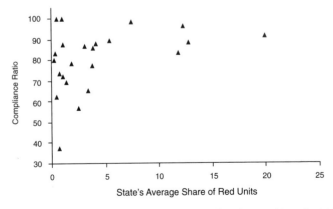

Fig. 8.7 Compliance Ratio to Average Share of Red Units (States) 2002–04

The regression results are as follows:

Box 8.2: Linear Regression Statistics of Compliance Rate
on Average Shares of Red Units

Multiple R	0.37344			
R Square	0.139458			
	Coefficients	Std Error	t Stat	P-value
Intercept	75.74881	3.937393	19.23832	8.14E-15
Average Shares %	1.091262	0.59154	1.84478	0.079222

It can be seen that there is a positive relationship, that is, states in which the share of highly polluting units is one per cent higher, tend to have one per cent higher compliance rate. However, the estimate is of very weak significance (that is, at 10 per cent). Therefore, it cannot be firmly concluded that compliance rate is higher for states which have higher share in the red units. Nevertheless, the possibility that states with greater reported compliance rate also have a larger concentration of polluting units is suggestive and merits a closer look. Is higher compliance associated with higher growth of polluting units? Do states that report a higher compliance rate in one year attract a higher *growth* of polluting units in the subsequent years?

Pollution Compliance—Real or Reported

Although the numbers and shares of reported compliant units are quite high, the levels of industrial pollution in India are also rising (Fig. 8.1). There is some contradiction here which needs to be examined, as it raises doubt about the actual vs. the reported compliance rates, especially since higher compliance was not found to be correlated with higher average profitability of investments in states, as discussed above.

If the compliance is mainly factual (on the ground), then it should impose costs of compliance on the industrial units. It may be assumed therefore that in states that have a higher compliance rate, red industrial units have a higher cost, and as a result, the growth of red units in such states should be lower than in states with a lower compliance rate *ceteris paribus*. That is, a negative relation between the compliance rate and growth of red units is to be expected on this premise. So, if compliance rates are factual, then states with higher compliance rates should have a lower growth of red units *ceteris paribus*.

On the other hand, if compliance is mainly fiction, being a product of reports by dishonest officials, the compliance rate should bear no relation to the growth of red industry units across the states. There should be no statistically significant relation between compliance rate and growth of red units across states on this premise. For example, as mentioned earlier, the study by Mani *et al.* found no relationship between location of new plants in different states of India and the stringency of their environmental regulations.

There is a third possibility. Fictional compliance reports can be taken as evidence of a congenial industrial climate in a given state. In such a case, states with a higher rate of reported compliance ought to experience a higher growth of red industrial units. That is, a positive relation between compliance rate and growth of red units across states is to be expected on these premises. But so far no studies have been conducted which show the link between growth of red units and their rate of compliance, across the states of India.

Compliance Rates and Growth of Red Units

We had mentioned earlier that the cost of higher compliance might discourage the growth of red units. Hence, we should expect a negative relationship between rate of compliance and growth of red units over the states between the years 2002–04.

To determine the relationship between rate of compliance and rate of growth of red units, a regression was run on the biennial growth[16] of red industrial units between 2002 and 2004, (taking 2002 as the base) across states, on the compliance rates of different states in 2002.

The following results were obtained:

Box 8.3: Linear Regression Statistics of Compliance Rate on Growth of Red Units

a Dependent Variable: gr2yr04	B	Std. Error	t	Sig.
(Constant)	–88.277	50.859	–1.736	.097
cmprate2	1.709	.621	2.750	.012
Rsq = 0.265				

[16]In percentage.

The results of the regression show that there is a positive relation between growth of red units and compliance rates that is statistically significant. That is, states that report a higher compliance rate of polluting industries in a given year, experience a higher growth of such units in subsequent years, when compared to states that report a lower rate of compliance.

The results suggest that states which reported a compliance rate that is higher by ten percentage points, tended to have a growth of red units that was 17 percentage points higher than others.

The positive relation leads us to infer that the reported rates of compliance are largely fictional, and only serve as indicators of a positive industrial climate in a state to the industrial sector, rather than being indicators of actual compliance. For instance, Modak (not dated) points out that while industrial units claim to have set up the required pollution treatment facilities, the actual usage of these is highly suspect. A study by Pargal *et al.* (1997) finds that while higher emissions lead to more inspections by the pollution control boards in various industries across India, there is little or no impact of more inspections on the levels of emissions.

Reported cases and studies on non-compliance by units have become quite common all over the country, and instances of pollution violation abound in different industrial estates in India. A study by Greenpeace (2004), showed that industrial effluents are still being discharged indiscriminately into water bodies and agricultural land in Patencheru, Bollaram, Kazipally, and other regions of Medak District of Andhra Pradesh, creating an environmentalist's nightmare (Basu 2005).[17]

The Centre for Science and Environment, an NGO of Delhi, states in one of its reports: 'Drive down the Mumbai-Pune highway and you will witness the horrible truth of industrialization. Hundreds

[17]The article states: 'The Patencheru industrial belt is an industrialist's dream but an environmentalist's nightmare. Local villagers suffer the ill-effects of violation of environmental norms.Villagers in Kazipally, Bollaram, and Patencheru in Medak district of Andhra Pradesh are dying a slow death due to severe health problems like arthritis and bone deformities, skin cancer and tumours, visual and neural disorders, premature deliveries and abortions. This is the result of blatant violation of all environmental norms by pharmaceutical and industrial units.' Yet in the same year (2005) when we spoke to some officials from the Andhra Pradesh PCB, they said that all operating units in the state were compliant with its environmental regulations!

of industrial units dealing with chemicals and fertilisers dump their sludge along the roadside. Chimneys emit gases that make breathing difficult. As per the CPCB Action Plan for Vapi (an industrial estate in Maharashtra), factories cannot dump effluent in the rivulet Bhil Khadi but have to send it to a common effluent treatment plant (CETP). But it is seen that hundreds of industrial units do not treat their wastes as per the inlet parameters of the CETP, and are releasing untreated effluents into Bhil Khadi, which ultimately meets and pollutes the Kolak River and the Arabian Sea [CSE 2000].[18]

Growth of Red Units and Closure of Polluting Firms

Recalcitrant firms are forcibly closed down by the state's respective pollution control boards. Unlike paper-based compliance reports[19] (which are subject to doubt), closure is a physical action involving penalties. Hence logically, closure rate should be negatively correlated with the growth rate of red units.

This presumption is borne out by the data. Regression analysis of closed rate of 2002 to growth of red units was carried out.

Box 8.4: Regression of Closed Rate to Growth of Red Units

Rsq= .301	Un-standardized Coefficients			
	B	Std. Error	T	Sig.
(Constant)	81.425	13.903	5.857	.000
clsrate2	–1.874	.623	–3.009	.007
a Dependent Variable: gr2yr04				

The results show that states that had a higher ratio of closed units to total polluting units in 2002 also experienced a lower growth of polluting units over the next two years. Specifically, if the closure rate is one per cent more in a state compared to another, the biennial

[18]For other horrific stories on the high level of non-compliance in various industrial estates, visit the following sites: *www.leadpoison.net*, 'Exporting cures, importing misery,' Stan Cox, January 19th, 2005 *www.alternet.org*, *http://www.corpwatch.org/print_article.php?&id=11798*, DTE (Down to Earth), 'Not a non-issue', *http://www.cseindia.org/dte-supplement/industry20040215/non-issue.htm*, 15 February 2004.

[19]It is well documented that PCBs do not monitor the *working* of pollution control equipment, but are satisfied if the firms report as having them. [Modak]

growth of polluting units in that state is likely to be 1.87 percentage points lower than the other. Thus, states that have a higher rate of closure of polluting units in a given year, experience a substantially lower rate of growth of polluting units in the subsequent years. These results contrast with those of the previous section. It was seen there that states that reported a higher rate of compliance in polluting industries in 2002, also experienced a higher growth of polluting industries in subsequent years. In contrast to this, it has been shown here that states that have a higher closure rate of polluting industries in 2002 (compared to other states), have experienced a lower growth of polluting industries in subsequent years.

Conclusion

The chapter seeks to examine the relative rates of industrial pollution compliance of red units within states of India, as well as to trace the impact of various factors on compliance ratios, over the time period 2002–04.

1. First the FCI was estimated, which shows the relative rate of compliant to non-compliant units of states to that of the all-India ratio. Taking the all-India ratio as unity, the relative positions of the states was estimated. It was found that only seven states had an FCI >1 in 2002, and this rose to ten states in 2004. However, the composition of the states changed, with some states (like Tamil Nadu, which had a very high initial FCI) taking a backward trend in 2004.

2. The study found a negligible correlation between average profitability of industries across states, and their reported rate of compliance by highly polluting industries. This suggested that greater reported compliance in those states could not be ascribed to higher average profitability of industries in those states.

3. This raised the question whether the higher compliance ratios were influenced by the share of red units in the states. In other words, is the higher compliance due to more compliance in states with larger average share of red units, or is there no relationship between the two? Regression analysis of the compliance ratio (share of compliant red units/total red units in a state) on average share of red units over the two years showed that although there was a positive relation between size and compliance rates, it was very insignificant. Hence, we cannot conclude that the size of a state (in terms of its share of red units) influences its rate of compliance.

4. Another question that was examined was the impact of the compliance rate with growth of red units—that is, does higher compliance have a negative influence on growth of red units in states, due to stricter environmental regulations? A regression was therefore run on the growth rate of red units and compliant rates. The results of the regression showed a positive relation between growth of red units and compliance rates. That is, states with a higher reported compliant rate had a higher growth rate of red units. The results suggested that states that reported a compliance rate that is higher by ten percentage points, tended to have a growth of red units that was 17 percentage points higher than others.

It was argued that there is no good reason to believe that greater compliance with pollution norms should encourage red units to growth faster. Hence, the positive relation can only lead us to infer that the reported rates of compliance are largely fictional, and only serve as indicators of a positive industrial climate in a state to the industry, rather than being indicators of actual compliance.

5. This inference also seems to be supported by the negative relation between the rate of closure of polluting units in a given year to the growth of polluting units in that state in subsequent years. Regression analysis revealed that states that had one percentage point higher rate of closure of red units in 2002, than other states, also experienced a 1.9 percentage point lower biennial growth rate of red units between 2002 and 2004. Thus, whereas states that report a higher compliance rate in polluting units experience subsequently, a higher growth of polluting units when compared to other states; and states that have a higher rate of *closure* of polluting units experience subsequently, a lower growth of polluting units. Closure of violators appears to have a clear deterrent effect on future growth of polluting units in a state, whereas higher reported compliance does not. Thus, in contrast to the reported compliance rate which seems to bear positive relation to growth of red units, closures are clearly treated as a cost of pollution, and deter the growth of red units.

While there have been no previous studies of the relation between rates of compliance and closure of polluting industries and their growth, numerous studies testify to the ineffectiveness of environmental regulations on industrial pollution. For instance, Pargal *et al.* (1997) find that growing inspections have failed to check the growth of emissions. There is widespread observation of growing pollution in industrial estates (for instance, Basu, 2005, CSE 2000), while at least one authority suspects that the pollution treatment facilities by industries may not be actually used. This suggests that industries tend to avoid or reduce the costs of compliance to pollution laws. This renders the rates of compliance reported by states suspect. Our analysis shows that higher compliance rates declared by the states not only do not deter the subsequent growth of red industries in such states, but are positively correlated with them.

It appears from our analysis that compliance rates of states are more reported than real, more fictional than fact, and the positive relation seems to suggest that they seem to be used by some state governments as a device to encourage industrial investments in red industries in their state, rather than to discourage pollution by red units. In contrast, closures are physical, unambiguous, and impose a clear cost on industrial pollution by red units, thereby discouraging their growth. Hence, the correct yardstick for evaluating administrative performance of states in regulating pollution by red units appears to be the closure rate in states, rather than their reported compliance rates.

REFERENCES

ASI (Annual Survey of Industries), (2001–2), Central Statistical Organization, Government of India, *www.mospi.nic.in.*

Basu, Soma, 'The Price of Pollution', *The Hindu*, December 17, 2005, available at: *http://www.thehindu.com/thehindu/mag/2005/07/17/stories/2005071700290400.htm.*

CPCB (Central Pollution Control Board), 1997–98, 2002, 2003, 2004. *www.cpcb.nic.in.*

CPCB (Central Pollution Control Board), 'National Inventory of Large and Medium Industry and Status of Effluent Treatment and Emission Control System'. CPCB, Nov. 1997, *www.cpcb.nic.in.*

CSE (Centre for Science and Environment), 'Industry at any cost,' *Down to Earth*, April 15, 2000, available at: \l 'river' *http://www.rainwaterharvesting.org/Crisis/Industrial-pollution.htm#river.*

Gartner, S., 'Clusters, Growth poles and Industrial districts', Regional Studies Association, Aalborg, 2001.

Greenpeace, *State of Community Health at Medak District*, Greenpeace publication, Mumbai October 2004.

Gupta, S and S. Saxena, 'Enforcement of pollution control laws and firm level compliance: a study of Punjab, India', 2002, available at: *http:// weber.ucsd.edu/ ~carsonvs/papers/1011.pdf.*

Iyer, Justice V.R. Krishna, *Environmental Pollution and Law*, Vedpal Law House, Bhopal, 1984.

Kathuria, Vinish and G.S. Haripriya: 'Industrial Pollution Control— Choosing the Right Option', *Economic and Political Weekly*, October 28, 2000.

Mani, M. Sheoli Pargal and Mainul Huq, 'Does environmental regulation matter? Determinants of the location of new manufacturing plants in India in 1994', *World Bank Papers*, November, 1997.

Modak, P., *Waste Minimisation: A Practical Guide to Cleaner Production and Enhanced Profitability*, Centre for Environment Education, Ahmedabad (date not given).

MoEF (Ministry of Environment and Forest), *Annual Report*, 2003–04, 2005–06. *www.enfor.nic.in/annual.*

MoEF (Ministry of Environment and Forest), website, available at: *www.enfor.nic.in/laws.*

Murthy, M.N., A.J. James and S. Misra, *Economics of Water Pollution*, New Delhi: Oxford India Paperbacks, 1999.

Panth, Prabha, 'Regional Concentration of Polluting Industries, A Study of Andhra Pradesh', *Indian Economic Journal*, July–September, 2006.

Pargal, Sheoli and Mani, 'Inspections and Emissions in India—Puzzling Survey Evidence on Industrial Water Pollution', *Policy Research Working Paper Series* 1810, World Bank, Aug. 26, 1997.

Sangal, P.S., 'Law as a tool for Environmental conservation and management in India' in R.B. Singh and Suresh Misra (eds), *Environmental Law in India, Issues and Responses*, Concept Publishing Company, New Delhi, 1996. *www.enfor.nic.in/laws.*

Venkatachalam, L. 'Damage Assessment and Compensation to Farmers, Lessons from Verdict of Loss of Ecology Authority in Tamil Nadu', *Economic and Political Weekly*, April 9, 2005.

World Bank, Development Data Group, World Development Indicators, available at: *http://www.worldbank.org/data/*, Washington: World Bank, 2004.

World Bank, *India: Strengthening Institutions for Sustainable Growth: Country Environmental Analysis*, 2003, available at: *http://siteresources.worldbank.org /INDIAEXTN/Resources/295583-1176163782791/ch1.pdf.*

9

The Effect of International Conventions on Oil Spills

MARIA L. LOUREIRO[1]

Oil spills are very serious natural hazards that have been affecting the coasts worldwide for many decades (see Map 9.1). Although oil spills from tankers are highly publicized, very little is known about the role played by the incentives and the regulatory instruments in place to prevent them.

Most countries are members of the specialized agency of the United Nations dealing with marine affairs and pollution, the International Marine Organization (IMO). Over the years, the IMO has set multiple conventions and restrictions in order to increase marine safety and reduce pollution. These safety standards, however, are voluntary at international level for each nation, given that the IMO has no enforcement capacity over the signing states. The states that sign the conventions internalize them in national law which make them binding. Consequently, the responsibility for implementing the standards agreed and adopted by the IMO rests with the Member states themselves (IMO 2006). States should ensure that ships flying their flag comply with provisions of the IMO Conventions that they have ratified. Many of the states choose to delegate the survey and inspection of vessels to so-called 'recognized organizations' such as classification societies. In order to overview the fulfilment of the signed conventions and protocols, IMO has adopted a voluntary audit scheme that will help flag states to assess how effectively they are complying with their obligations under the various IMO conventions. The first audits took place in 2006, and public information related to compliance is not yet available. This chapter

[1]The author wishes to thank, without implication, *Fundación Arao* for funding support for this project.

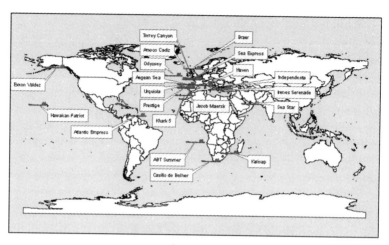

Map 9.1   Biggest Oil Spills by Location

Source: *http://www.itopf.com/stats.html.*

examines the performance of these IMO regulations on the reduction of pollution at sea caused by oil spills.

The United States is considered nowadays the country with the most stringent legislation regarding oil spills and oil pollution protection. This is the consequence of the ecological and political impact of the Exxon Valdez oil spill, which provided the impetus for the U.S. Congress to pass the Oil Pollution Act in 1990 (OPA-90), which went well beyond IMO's conventions in terms of stringency. The OPA-90 strengthened accountability for vessel oil spills in U.S. waters, and as such the compensation paid by Exxon was an example of stringency at the international level.[2] Under the OPA-90, the strict liability of the vessel owner is limited to US$ 1200 per vessel gross ton or US$ 10 million per vessel over 3000 gross tons, whichever is greater. However, if the vessel owner is found guilty of gross negligence in violation of laws, liability is unlimited, and liable parties are subject to both criminal and civil sanctions (Wayne and Kite-Powell 2005). Furthermore, the OPA-90 also requires vessels utilizing U.S. waters to carry certificates of financial responsibilities, proving that the owners

---

[2]The settlement between the State of Alaska, the United States government, and Exxon was approved by a U.S. District Court on October 9, 1991. Exxon had to pay 1.15 billion US dollars as compensation, while claims by private parties are still being litigated (Wendel 2003).

have funds or insurance to cover the maximum liability limits under the law. In addition to all those financial requirements, the OPA-90 also mandates double-hulls for ships and tank barges travelling US waters by the year 2015. The OPA-90 also requires interim structural and operational measures to reduce the spill of oil in the event of an accident (Wayne and Kite-Powell 2005).

Some of these OPA-90 measures, such as the double-hull requirement, have been recently adopted in 2003 by the IMO, banning single-hull tank ships by the year 2015. However, recent spills such as the Erika (1999) and Prestige (2002) oil spills have accelerated the schedule of adoption in Europe. In addition, the EU is also pushing forward for a set of stricter regulations, more consistent with OPA-90. The large oil spills caused by the Erika and the Prestige caused much public concern about the safety of marine transport in European Union (EU) waters (see Table 9.1). After the Erika spill, the EU Commission prepared urgent measures to increase marine safety off the EU coasts. These were adopted three months later, on

Table 9.1   List of Important Oil Spills

Ship	Year	Country	Oilspill–Tonnes
Torrey Canyon	1967	UK	119000
Sea Star	1972	Oman	120000
Jakob Maersk	1975	Portugal	84000
Urquiola	1976	Spain	101000
Hawaiian Patriot	1977	USA	90000–99000
Amoco Cadiz	1978	France	227000
Atlantic Empress	1979	Trinidad & Tobago	276000
Independenta	1979	Turkey	95000
Irenes Serenade	1980	Greece	100000
Castillo de Bellver	1983	South Africa	250000
Odiseey	1988	Canada	132000
Exxon Valdez	1989	USA	40000
Khark 5	1989	Spain	75000
ABT Summer	1991	Angola	260000
Haven	1991	Italy	133000
Katina P	1992	Mozambique	66000
Aegean Sea	1992	Spain	66800
Braer	1993	Shetland Islands	85000
Sea Empress	1996	UK	73000
Erika	1999	France	19500
Prestige	2002	Spain	77000

21 March 2000, known as the Erika I package, which was quickly followed in December 2000 by a second set of measures, the Erika package II, designed to provide answers to pending questions from the previous package. The Erika I legislative package entered into force on 22 July 2003. These maritime safety regulations, proposed in the wake of the shipping disaster and adopted on 19 December 2001, have been in force since 22 January 2002. Member states had until 22 July 2003 to apply the Erika I package by adopting the requisite laws, regulations, and administrative provisions, and were required to notify the EU Commission of the transposition of these acts into national law as soon as they enter into force. Only Denmark, France, Germany, Spain, and the United Kingdom have complied with this. Other states (such as Greece) have openly shown their discontent with such measures. In addition, the Commission, pursuant to the Directive on Port State Control, has published a list of ships to be denied access to EU ports if they are detained again after 22 July 2003.

Nevertheless, and up to now, the IMO countries have been applying International Liability Conventions, which have been criticized for not being able to deter oil spills. The relationship between this body of international conventions and oil spills has not received much attention in the economic literature. In order to fill this void, this chapter assesses the role of the main international conventions and liability limits in place to deter oil spills.

The analysis is based on data collected on large oil spills from multiple databases, and merges these with regulation records from the IMO countries, which indicate the adoption of international conventions and compensation funds by each member country. Summary results indicate that International Liability Conventions, with their corresponding compensation funds, were for many years unsuccessful in deterring the occurrence of oil spills worldwide. In the recent years, more stringent conventions (in terms of liability) have decreased the incidence of oil spills worldwide.

The rest of the chapter is divided into the following sections. First, a review of the main international agreements and their evolution, as well as an international outlook regarding oil spills and volumes of transport of oil, are provided. In this introductory section, special attention is given to understand the relationship between tightening national and international laws, after recent incidents occurred in European waters such as the Erika and Prestige oil spills. The chapter continues with a description of the data set used in the analysis, the empirical methods employed, and results. It concludes with some policy implications derived from the current results.

I. INTERNATIONAL LIABILITY CONVENTIONS AND COMPENSATION FUNDS

There are mainly three types of international conventions: a) major international marine pollution prevention and response conventions, b) conventions related to liability for response and funding of response costs, and c) conventions which promote regional cooperation (Steen *et al.* 2003). The IMO is the United Nations specialized agency with responsibility for all safety and security of shipping and the prevention of marine pollution by ships. Member governments use IMO to draw up internationally agreed standards to be applied to all ships (IMO 2006). The International Marine Organization's main international conventions and agreements are reported in Table 9.2. The application of such conventions related to liability and marine pollution has not been uniform around the world. As can be observed in Map 9.2, the ratification of such conventions has been very uneven

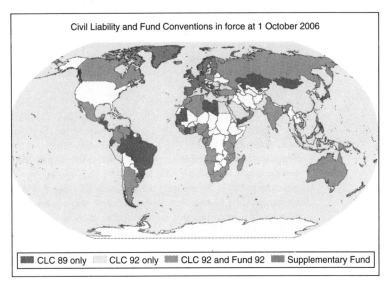

Civil Liability and Fund Conventions in force at 1 October 2006

CLC 89 only   CLC 92 only   CLC 92 and Fund 92   Supplementary Fund

Map 9.2   Regions of Application of International Conventions and Civil Liability

Source: The International Tanker Owners Pollution Federation Limited (ITOPF).

Table 9.2   List of Main International IMO Conventions

MARPOL 73/78	International Convention for the Prevention of Pollution from ships was adopted on 2 November 1972, although it did not enter into force, the 1978 Convention has entered into force on the 2 October 1983 (Annexes I and II). States parties must accept Annexes I and II, but the others (Anex III, IV,V, and VI) are voluntary. After the Erika accident, this Convention has been emended in order to speed up the adoption of the double hull requirement.
OPCR/90	International Convention on Oil Pollution Preparedness, Response and Cooperation, 1990: requires ships to carry a shipboard oil pollution emergency plan, to be developed by the IMO. Operators of offshore units are also required to have oil pollution emergency plans or similar arrangements which must be coordinated with national systems for responding promptly and effectively to oil pollution incidents. Ships are required to report incidents of pollution to coastal authorities and the Convention details the actions that are then to be taken.
OPRC HNS, 2000	Protocol on Preparedness, Response, and Co-operation to pollution Incidents by Hazardous and Noxious Substances, 2000 (HNS Protocol) ensures that ships carrying hazardous and noxious liquid substances are covered, or will be covered, by regimes similar to those already in existence for oil incidents. In 1996, the IMO adopted the International Convention on Liability and Compensation for Damage in connection with the carriage of Hazardous and Noxious Substances (HNS) by sea, which provides for a compensation and liability regime for incidents involving these substances (it has not yet entered into force).
CLC69	The International Convention on Civil Liability for Oil Pollution Damage (CLC69) regulates liability and compensation regimes for oil pollution incidents, which was reformed by the 1992 CLC Protocol. The CLC69 was adopted to ensure that compensation is available to persons who suffer oil pollution damage. The Convention places liability for such damage on the owner of the ship, from which the polluting oil escaped or was discharged. The Convention covers pollution damage resulting from spills of persistent oils suffered in the territory (including the territorial sea) of a State Party to the Convention. It is applicable to ships which actually carry oil in bulk as cargo, that is, generally laden tankers. Spills from tankers in ballast or bunker spills from ships other than tankers are not covered, nor is it possible to recover costs when preventive measures are so successful that no actual spill occurs. The ship-owner cannot

(contd...)

Table 9.2 (contd...)

	limit liability if the incident occurred as a result of the owner's personal fault.
CLC76	The 1976 CLC protocol provided a new unit of currency or account.
CLC92	Applies compensation limits which were originally established in 1984, for a ship not exceeding 5,000 gross tonnage, liability is limited to three million Special Drawing Rights (SDR) (about US$3.8 million). For a ship 5,000–140,000, liability is limited to 3 million SDR plus 420 SDR (about US$538) for each additional unit of tonnage. For a ship over 140,000 gross tonnage, liability is limited to 59.7 million SDR (about US$ 76.5 million). The 1992 Protocol also widened the scope of the Convention to cover pollution damage caused in the exclusive economic zone, or equivalent area of a State Party. The Protocol covers pollution damage as before but environmental damage compensation is limited to costs incurred for reasonable measures to reinstate the contaminated environment.
FUND71	International Convention on the Establishment of an International Fund for Compensation for Oil Pollution Damage, 1971. It provides additional compensation to the victims of pollution damage in cases where compensation under the 1969 Civil Liability Convention was either inadequate or unobtainable.
FUND76	For similar reasons to the Protocol, this provides for a unit of account, based on the SDR as used by the International Monetary Fund (IMF).
FUND92	The scope of coverage was extended in line with the 1992 CLC Protocol. The 1992 Protocol established a separate, 1992 Oil Pollution Compensation Fund, known as the 1992 Fund, which is managed in London by a Secretariat, as with the 1971 Fund. Two funds (the 1971 Fund and the 1972 Fund) are in operation, given that some members have not yet accepted the 1992 Protocol, which is intended to replace the 1971 regimes.
HNS	International Convention on Liability and Compensation for Damages in Connection with the carriage of HNS by Sea, 1996. In addition to pollution damage, it also covers the risks of fire and explosion. The convention defines damage as including loss of life or personal injury; loss of or damage to property outside the ship; loss or damage by contamination of the environment, the cost of preventive measures and further loss or damage cause by them.
BUNKER	International Convention on Civil Liability for Bunker Oil Pollution Damage, 2001. The Convention was adopted to ensure that adequate, prompt, and effective compensation is available to persons who suffer damage caused by spills of oils, when carried in a ship's bunkers.

Source: http://www.imo.org/Conventions/mainframe.asp?topic_id=260.

geographically, with continental areas, such as Africa, less protected than other areas, such as Europe or Canada. The question asked in this particular research is: do countries that subscribe more stringent conventions suffer less oil spills?

The overall international compensation regime for damage caused by persistent spills of oil from laden tankers was based initially on two IMO conventions: a) the 1969 International Convention on Civil Liability for Oil Spill Damage (1969 CLC), and b) the 1971 International Convention on the Establishment of an International Fund for Compensation for Oil Pollution Damage (1971 Fund Convention). These two conventions were amended in 1992 by two Protocols, which increased the compensation limits and broadened the scope of the original Conventions. The 1969 CLC entered into force in 1975 and laid down the principle of strict liability (that is, liability even when no fault is proven) for tanker owners and creates a system of compulsory liability insurance. However, this strict liability was linked to the tonnage of the tanker causing the pollution (IMO 2006). The 1971 Fund Convention provided for the payment of supplementary funds for those who could not obtain full compensation via the Oil Pollution Compensation Fund, the 1971 IOPC Fund. This 1971 IOPC Fund convention entered into force in 1978. However, although compensation to affected parties was increased, this did not prevent other large oil spills from happening. As it can be seen in Table 9.1, in 1979 there were two major oil spills, the Atlantic Empress in Trinidad and Tobago spilling a total of 276,000 MT, and the Independenta in Turkey, spilling 95,000 MT. The next decade was also characterized by the occurrence of some large oil spills, such as the Castillo de Bellver in 1983, spilling a total of 250,000 MT of oil in South Africa, and the highly publicized Exxon Valdez in 1989 with 40,000 MT.

Following other important oil spills, such as the ABT summer and Haven in 1991, in 1992 a diplomatic conference adopted two protocols amending the 1969 CLC and 1971 Fund Convention. This 1992 Fund entered into force in 1996. As in the case of the original conventions, the tanker owner and the principal and interest (P&I) insurer are liable for payment of compensation under the 1992 CLC and oil receivers in countries that are party to the 1992 Fund Convention. The 1971 Fund Convention was terminated altogether on 24 May 2002. In October 2000, the contracting states to the 1992 CLC and 1992 Fund Convention approved a proposal to increase by about 50 per cent (to about US$ 260 million) the amount of compensation available under the terms of these Conventions. This

Fund, which entered into force on 1st November 2003, will be reinforced by another additional Supplementary Compensation Fund that increases the international regime for compensation of victims of oil pollution from oil tankers. This Supplementary Fund does not replace the existing 1992 Fund, but will make available additional compensation to victims in the states which accede to the Protocol. In total, about US$ 1159 million will be available for compensation for each incident in the states which are members of the Supplementary Fund. This Fund will only cover accidents which occurred after the entry into force of the Protocol on 3 March 2005. Due to the lack of data, this chapter does not analyse the effect of the provision of this recent Supplementary Fund. As Map 9.2 shows, most European countries have ratified this Supplementary Fund. On the other hand, other countries, which have not ratified these IMO international conventions, have their own domestic legislation for compensating those parties affected by oil spills from tankers, such as the Oil Pollution Act in the US.

Although deterrence effects associated with monitoring and liability regimes were studied on several occasions in the economics literature (see for example, Opaluch and Grigalunas 1984; Wayne and Kite-Powell 2005), as well as the level of optimal environmental liability (Jin and Kite-Powell 1999), there is little evidence of whether these international conventions (which carry different levels of compensation based on strict liability of ship owners) have a deterrence effect on oil spill occurrence.

In spite of the fact that oil spills internationally are seriously underreported, due to diverse errors and omissions, (particularly for spills in remote areas and spills of small size), the information presented in Map 1 is relevant in order to understand the dynamics of legislation changes and oil spills. As can be observed, in recent years, the majority of the largest oil spills occurred in European waters. In recent years, there were three large spills in European waters, including the Erika oil spill off the French Coast (1999), the Baltic Carrier (2001) in Denmark, and the Prestige oil spill in Spain (2002), and as previously mentioned, these spills created incentives for regulatory changes in the EU. These recent changes will not be part of the present analysis, given that only a few years have passed by since their adoption.

Presented below is an assessment of whether the international conventions and protocols ratified by IMO country members had any deterrence effect on the occurrence of oil spills. The response to such a question is of vital importance, because if IMO international protocols do not have a deterrence role on reducing oil spills, then additional or substitute measures should be considered by IMO member countries.

II. DATA

The data for our empirical analysis comes from several international databases reporting oil spills. In particular, the information obtained from the following sources is merged: the NOAA historical database of oil spills, the OECD environmental statistics, the CEDRE database, the ETC-Canada database, the CETMAR database, the ITOPF database, and the paper on oil spill costs by Grey (1999). Although international oil spills tend to be underreported, it is hoped that the data are comprehensive enough to show relevant information regarding oil spill characteristics. Our data span nearly a 50-year period and cover 212 oil spills. From all the above databases, all relevant information related to each spill was collected (location, size of spill, time of year, type of oil spill, and so on). In addition, information regarding the international conventions ratified by each IMO country member where the spill took place was obtained from the IMO data set. This information was merged and used in the following analysis.

III. EMPIRICAL MODEL

A logit model was used to estimate the probability that an oil spill (greater than 10,000 MT) was occurring in a given country, while controlling for the fact that different IMO protocols were ratified, as well as the technical improvements that occurred during the period of analysis. Oil spills greater than 10,000 MT were studied in order to contain a subset of observations with less measurement error than other smaller spills that go practically underreported, or in case reported, do not provide much information. Note that because of the nature of our data, the results that follow should be understood as conditional on the fact that an oil spill happens in the first place.

As is well-known, the logit model has the following functional form:

$$(1) \quad P(Y = 1 \mid x) = \frac{\exp(z)}{[1 + \exp(z)]},$$

where the dependent variable denotes the probability that an oil spill greater than 10,000 MT happens. In our case study, the explanatory variables included in the vector z are:

$$(2) \quad z = \beta_0 + \beta_1 AllMarpol_i + \beta_2 CLCFund71_i + \beta_3 CLCFund92_i$$
$$+ \beta_4 Y70s_i + \beta_5 Y80s_i + \beta_6 Y90s_i + \beta_7 Y2000s_i,$$

where the variable *AllMarpol* denotes whether the country has ratified all Marpol Annexes (not linked to liability); and *CLCFund71* is an indicator variable denoting whether the country has signed the 1969 CLC and provided also the additional 1971 Compensation Fund. In the same way, *CLCFund92* indicates whether the country has signed the CLC92 as well as the complementary 1992 Fund. The rest of the included variables $Y70_s$, $Y80_s$, $Y90_s$ and are indicators for each decade.[3] Technology shifts over time may also be responsible for the reduction of oil spills. Means and standard deviations of these explanatory variables are presented in Table 9.3.

Table 9.3   Explanatory Variables used in Analysis

Variable	Obs	Mean	Std. Dev	Min	Max
Allmarpol	212	0.896226	0.305688	0	1
clcfund71	212	0.066038	0.248936	0	1
clcfund92	212	0.641509	0.480692	0	1
y60s	212	0.089623	0.286316	0	1
y70s	212	0.349057	0.4778	0	1
y80s	212	0.207547	0.406511	0	1
y90s	212	0.301887	0.460163	0	1
y2000s	212	0.051887	0.222323	0	1

Summary statistics coming from the spills database indicate that about 40 per cent of the total oil spills occurred in European waters, followed by 26 per cent that occurred in Asia and about 20 per cent that occurred in North America (including U.S., Mexico, and Canada). Overall, the number of oil spills as well as the amount spilled decreased significantly over the last three decades. Thus, almost 35 per cent of oil spills registered in our dataset occurred in the 1970s, while nearly 30.2 per cent occurred in the 1990s. This decrease occurred despite a 46 per cent increase in oil movement worldwide since 1988 (Etkin undated a and b). It should be noted that almost 90 per cent of the observations come from countries which have signed all Marpol agreements and annexes. However, 64.1 per cent

[3]Due to the small number of oil spills occurring during the 1950s, these have been aggregated into the 1960s' indicator.

of all oil spills greater than 10,000 MT have occurred in countries which have ratified the 1992 CLC as well as the additional 1992 Compensation Fund.

The results provided by the logit model (see Table 9.4) indicate that the fact that an IMO country member had ratified the 1969 CLC and the 1971 Fund had no deterrence effect on the occurrence of oil spills greater than 10,000MT (given that an oil spill happened). This may be explained by the fact that although strict liability was imposed, the low liability limit made it possible that compensations to victims were rather small in comparison with the damages that occurred (more emphasis will be added to this point later in the chapter). Therefore, these results show that the IMO has not provided enough incentives for sea pollution control during a long part of its history.

Table 9.4   Logit Results (Dependent Variable Y=1 if Spill>10,000MT occurs, 0 Otherwise)

Spill	Coef.	Std. Err.	Z	P>|z|
Allmarpol	0.029674	0.531754	0.06	0.955
clcfund71	0.272593	0.582773	0.47	0.64
clcfund92	−1.10154	0.342468	−3.22	0.00
Y70s	0.06303	0.550088	0.11	0.909
Y80s	−0.67185	0.58305	−1.15	0.249
Y90s	0.2551	0.561381	0.45	0.65
Y2000s	−1.09198	0.815002	−1.34	0.18
Constant	1.176787	0.675078	1.74	0.081
Log-likelihood	133.91962			

Source:

However, the results also indicate that signature and ratification by IMO member countries of both the 1992 CLC and the 1992 Compensation Fund had a statistically significant deterrence effect on the occurrence of oil spills over 10,000 MT (carrying a coefficient of −3.22 and a p-value of 0.001), given that an oil spill occurred. That is, states which ratify the 1992 CLC and the 1993 Compensation Fund had a lower propensity of having larger oil spills. A higher liability limit and also higher public pressures after recent oil spills may have helped to improve the effectiveness of the most recent IMO international CLCs. Other factors that may also be contributing to the reduction of the size of oil spills are the technical innovations that may be captured by the respective decade indicators. A clear technical improvement is the use of double-hull ships that became mandatory in US waters after the OPA-90. The results show that the indicator variable associated with the decade of 2000 has a negative effect although it is not statistically significant at conventional critical levels (p-value 0.18). These results are somewhat encouraging, providing evidence that states ratifying these international voluntary agreements are less likely to have larger oil spills. To have a more specific assessment about the potential deterrence effect of these international CLC conventions, it would be ideal to have information about the domestic legal setting of each country, as well as the interplay between these international conventions plus the ratification and inclusion of such conventions in domestic law. Unfortunately, such information is difficult to collect, although it is expected that in the near future it would be possible to disentangle the role of the CLCs from the domestic regulations.

CONCLUSIONS AND POLICY IMPLICATIONS

Oil spills generate very serious societal costs and environmental consequences. In order to provide incentives for control and to properly manage the international parties involved in oil transport, the IMO has approved over the years a series of conventions on liability limits and compensation packages to victims. The objective of this study has been to examine the effect of such international conventions and protocols on the deterrence of oil spills. Although the empirical analysis is simple, the obtained results indicate that international conventions on civil liability and their corresponding liability funds did not provide sufficient incentives until recent decades to decrease the probability of oil spills over 10,000 MT occurring internationally. Only in recent years there has been a deterrent effect associated with the application of such conventions on the size of oil spills, given that oil spills still happen. Consequently, the international voluntary conventions for pollution control at sea have produced ineffective outcomes in terms of protection for a long period of time. This result is common to many other international protocols signed to decrease the environmental pollution. However, an interesting aspect is that the increment of the associated financial responsibility of the polluter creates incentives that reduce the probability of spills over 10,000 MT of oil.

Several arguments may help in understanding some of the reasons that are underneath the reduced effectiveness in the early international

IMO CLC protocols. First, there is an inherent difficulty in finding an agreement about responsibilities for liability and compensation of affected parties when the number of negotiating parties is large and diverse. In a recent case, EU countries that have been lately affected by oil spills are more demanding of regulatory changes than the rest of EU members. As was seen after the Erika and Prestige oil spills, France and Spain demanded higher standards for ships passing by EU waters or entering into EU ports. Second, it should not be forgotten that most of the funds provided as compensation by the IMO conventions come from IMO members. Consequently, ship owners play a crucial role in deciding compensation and liability levels. Due to the changes that have occurred in the last 20–30 years in the shipping sector, and in particular, because of the establishment of the open registry system, developing countries have now registered the majority of the shipping vessels around the world. As a consequence, countries such as Panama, Liberia, and Bahamas are the top three IMO contributors to the CLC funds. As is well understood, these countries with fewer economic resources will not make pressure to pass more stringent regulations that would require higher contributions on their side. An additional limitation is that the national transpositions of such international agreements may not be clearly and properly defined, creating confusion in the shipping sector, with respect to procedures to follow in the case of an incident and derived responsibilities. However, an encouraging finding highlighted by the current results shows that more stringent approved conventions have a deterrent effect on larger oil spills. Consequently, in the future, and following the parallelism with this finding, the recent changes approved unilaterally by the EU may also have a positive effect on regulation stringency, consequently reducing the pollution caused by oil spills in European waters.

Nevertheless, and despite the recent regulatory improvements, future studies should investigate whether compensation schemes are currently optimally set. As reflected in Table 9.5, in the past, compensation for damages caused by large oil spills has been rather limited and much delayed. For example, in the Amoco Cadiz oil spill, affected parties received compensation for their damages after waiting for thirteen years, and only about 20 per cent of the claimed damages were compensated. This situation has not much improved in other recent oil spills. For example, in the case of the Eagean Sea that occurred in 1992 off the coast of Galicia in Spain, victims received a compensation equivalent to five per cent of the total claimed damages, after waiting for nine years. In the case of the most recent European oil spill, the Prestige oil spill that occurred in 2002, short term economic costs have been estimated to be € 743.73 million by Loureiro et al. (2006), while the maximum compensation obtainable under the 1992 Fund is approximately € 165.76 million. All these figures are far below the compensation of US$ 1.15 billion paid by Exxon Corporation to compensate affected parties following the Exxon Valdez oil spill. Although a Supplementary Fund entered into force in November 2003, there are still many remaining questions about whether the full costs associated with oil spills will be all covered. Hopefully, future research will deal with these important questions.

Table 9.5   Total Cost Estimates, Compensation Claimed and Paid for six major Oil Spills in Europe

Spilll	Amoco Cadiz	Egean Sea	Braer	Sea Empress	Erika
Date	1–3–78	1–12–92	1–1–93	1–2–96	12–12–99
Oil spilt (TN)	220,000	80,000	86,500	72,000	19,800
Contaminated Coastline (Km)	350	100	40 km2	150–200	400
Duration of Comp-ensation Process	13 years	9 years	8 years	5 years	2 years
Number of Claims	n.a.	4,600	2,270	1,200	5,600
Estimated total cost of spill*	430.6–496.2	n.a.	n.a.	68.1–129.3	526.2–611.0
Compensation Claimed*	469.9	233.1	154.4	56.0	83.2
Compensation Paid *	91.4	11.0	57. 8	34.7	15.

(*) Currency in 2001 £ (million)
Source: Prada and Vazquez, 2004.

References

Etkin, D. S. (a) 'Oil Spill Intelligence Report International Oil Spill Database: Trends in Oil Spill Volumes and Frequency', available at: *http://www.environmental-research.com/publications/pdf/ spill_costs/ paper2.pdf*, accessed on 25 June 2007.

Etkin, D. S. (b) 'Analysis of Oil Spill Trends in the United States and Worldwide', Environmental Research Consulting, available at: *http://*

www.environmental-research.com/publications/pdf/spill_statistics/ paper4.pdf, accessed on 25 June 2007).

IMO (International Marine Organization), 2006, available at *http:// www.imo.org/Conventions*, accessed on 25 June 2007.

Grey, C. J., 1999. 'The Cost of Oil Spills from Tankers: An Analysis of IOPC Fund Incidents'. Paper presented at the International Oil Spill Conference, available at: *www.itopf.com/spilcost.pdf*, accessed on 25 June 2007.

Jin, D.and H. L. Kite-Powell, 'On the Optimal Environmental Limit for Marine Oil Transport' *Transportation Research Part E*, 35, 1999, pp. 77–100.

Loureiro, M. L. A. Ribas, E. López, and E. Ojea, 'Estimated Costs and Admissible Claims linked to the Prestige Oil Spill', *Ecological Economics*, 59 (1), 2006, pp. 48–63.

Opaluch, J.J. and T. A. Grigalunas, 'Controlling Stochastic Pollution Events Through Liability Rules: Some Evidence from OCS Leasing', *The RAND Journal of Economics*, 15(1), 1984, pp. 142–51.

Prada, A. and M.X. Vázquez, Efectos Económicos, Sociais e Ambientais da Marea Negra do 'Prestige', Consello da Cultura Galega (ed), 2004.

Steen, A., M. de Bettencourt, R. Pond, M. Julian, D. Salt, and T. Liebert, 'Global Challenges to Preparenedness and Response Regimes', 2003, Paper available at: *http://www.mms.gov/tarprojects/451/451AA.pdf*, accessed on 25 June 2007).

Wayne K. T., D. Jin and H. Kite-Powell, 'Post OPA-90 Vessel Oil Transfer Spill Prevention: The Effectiveness of Coast Guard Enforcement' *Environmental and Resource Economics*, 30, 2005, pp. 93–114.

Wendel, P., 'Marine Tort Liability', Paper presented for the Seminar on International Comparative Maritime Law, St. Petersburg, 11–18 May 2003.

RELEVANT LINKS AND DATABASES

CEDRE (Centre de documentation de recherche et d'expérimentations sur les pollutions accidentelles des eaux), Database Spills, 2006, available at *http://www.cedre.fr/index_gb.html*, accessed on 25 June 2007.

CETMAR (Centro Tecnológico del Mar) Database, Proyecto Contimar, 'Información sobre los Accidentes de Vertidos de Hidrocarburos en el Mundo', 2006, available at *http://www.cetmar.org/documentacion/mareas_negras_ catastrofes.htm*, accessed on 25 June 2007).

ETC (Environmental Technology Center)-Canada, Database, Environment Canada, 'Tanker Spills Database' 2001, available at *http://www.etccte.ec. gc.ca/databases/TankerSpills/Default.aspx?Path=\Website\river*, accessed on 25 June 2007.

ITOPF (International Tanker Owners Pollution Federation Limited). 'Historical Data. Statistics, 1974–2003', available at *http://www.itopf.com/ stats.html*, accessed on 25 June 2007.

NOAA (National Oceanic and Atmospheric Administration), 'Oil Spill Case Histories, 1967–2001', available at *http://response.restoration.noaa.gov/ book_shelf/26_spilldb.pdf*, accessed on 25 June 2007.

OECD (Organization for Economic Co-operation and Development). 'OECD Environmental Data. Spills from Tankers, 1975–2000', available at *https://www.oecd.org/dataoecd/53/37/2958311.doc*, accessed on 25 June 2007.

Contributors

JENNIFER CLAPP is CIGI Chair in International Governance and Professor, Environment and Resource Studies at the University of Waterloo, Ontario, Canada. Titles of some of her publications include the co-authored book *Paths to a Green World: The Political Economy of the Global Environment* , MIT Press, 2005; and *Toxic Exports: The Transfer of Hazardous Wastes from Rich to Poor Countries*, Cornell University Press, 2001. She is co-editor of the journal *Global Environmental Politics*.

DERICK DE JONGH is Director of the University of South Africa's Centre for Corporate Citizenship. He is on the Editorial Boards of the *Journal of Corporate Citizenship* and the *International Journal of Innovation and Sustainable Development*. His latest co-authored article is 'Corporate Citizenship Education for Responsible Business Leaders' in *Development Southern Africa*, 2006.

NEIL ECCLES is the programme manager for the Noah Chair in Responsible Investment at the University of South Africa's Centre for Corporate Citizenship. His latest co-authored publication is *The State of Responsible Investment in South Africa*, UNEP FI Report, 2007.

RALPH HAMANN is a senior researcher at the Environmental Evaluation Unit, an independent research, training, and consulting unit based at the University of Cape Town. He is also Associate Professor Extraordinary at the Sustainability Institute, Stellenbosch University. His recent articles include 'Can Business Make Contributions to Development? Towards a Research Agenda on Corporate Citizenship and Beyond' ; and 'The JSE Socially Responsible Investment Index and the State of Sustainability Reporting in South Africa', co-authored with D. Sonnenberg, both in *Development Southern Africa*, 2006.

MARIA L. LOUREIRO is a Ramón y Cajal researcher with IDEGA-Universidade de Santiago de Compostela, Spain. Her fields of research interest relate to environmental economics, health economics, and agricultural economics. Her latest co-authored articles are 'Estimated Costs and Admissible Claims Linked to the Prestige Oil Spill' in *Ecological Economics*, 59(1), 2006; and 'Altruistic, Egoistic and Biospheric Values in Willingness to Pay (WTP) for Wildlife', in *Ecological Economics*, 63(4), 2007.

PRABHA PANTH is Professor of Economics at Osmania University in Hyderabad, India. She is author of 'Globalisation and Sustainable Development: Economic and Environmental Conflicts' presented at the *Indian Ecological Economics Society* Conference, Mumbai, 2005 and the article 'Regional Concentration of Polluting Industries— A case study of A.P.', in *Indian Economic Journal*, 2006.

STEFANO POGUTZ is Assistant Professor of Management, "G. Pivato" Department of Management, and Coordinator of the Specialized Master Program on Economics and Environmental Management at Bocconi University, Milan, Italy, where he is also Senior Researcher at the Research Centre on Risk, Occupational Health and Safety, Environmental and Crisis Management (SPACE). His co-authored publications include *Developing Corporate Social Responsibility: A European Perspective,* Edward Elgar, 2006; and 'New Tools to Foster Corporate Socially Responsible Behaviour', in *Journal of Business Ethics,* 53, 2004.

RUNA SARKAR is Assistant Professor of Industrial and Management Engineering at the Indian Institute of Technology in Kanpur, India. Her latest publications include 'Policy Approaches to Induce Corporate Social Responsibility in Public and Private Sector Firms in Developing Countries', in *International Corporate Responsibility,* 2006, and the co-authored article 'Rural Environment', in *India Infrastructure Report 2006,* Oxford University Press, 2006.

RAHUL A. SHASTRI is Director of the Research Centre for International Business, at the CVR College of Engineering in Hyderabad, India and Honorary Joint Director of the National Akademi of Development, India. He was on the Faculty, Department of Economics, Osmania University until 2005. His publications in environmental economics include 'Environmental Awareness and Sustainable Development: Awareness of the Deforesting Effect of Firewood Use in Rural Firewood Users', in *Sustainable Development in India* (Reddy et al. eds), 2005;

and 'India's Foreign Trade and the Depletion of Non-renewable Resources', co-authored with Prabha Panth, in B. Satyanarayana (ed), *Social Sciences and Planning for Sustainable Development*, Himalaya Publishing House, 1998.

PETER UTTING is Deputy Director at the United Nations Research Institute for Social Development (UNRISD), where he also co-ordinates the Markets, Business and Regulation research programme. His publications include the edited volumes *The Greening of Business in Developing Countries: Rhetoric, Reality and Prospects*, Zed Books, 2002; and *Reclaiming Development Agendas: Knowledge, Power and International Policy Making*, Palgrave Macmillan/UNRISD, 2006. His recent articles on CSR include 'Regulating Business for Sustainable Development', in *Organizations and the Sustainability Mosaic: Crafting Long-Term Ecological and Societal Solutions* (Sharma et al. eds), Edward Elgar, 2007; and 'CSR and Equality' in *Third World Quarterly* 28(4), 2007.

ARILD VATN is Professor at the Department of International Environment and Development Studies (Noragric), Norwegian University of Life Sciences. He is also the president of the European Society of Ecological Economics. Titles of recent publications with relevance to institutions and sustainability include *Institutions and the Environment,*, Edward Elgar, 2005; and 'Resource Regimes and Cooperation', in *Land Use Policy*, 24(4), 2007.

Index